Barrier-Free Travel

A Nuts and Bolts Guide for Wheelers and Slow Walkers

Candy B. Harrington
Photographs By Charles Pannell

16

EasyRead Large

Copyright Page from the Original Book

LIBRARY OF CONGRESS CATALOGING-IN-PUBLICATION DATA
. . . .
Harrington, Candy.
    Barrier-free travel : a nuts and bolts guide for wheelers and slow-walkers / Candy
B. Harrington ; Photographs by Charles Pannell. – 3rd ed.
    p. cm.
Includes bibliographical references and index.
ISBN 978–1–932603–83–5
1. People with disabilities–Travel. 2. Barrier-free design. I. Title.
HV3022.H37 2009
910.87—dc22   2009020762

Special discounts on bulk quantities of Demos Medical Publishing books
are available to corporations, professional associations, pharmaceutical companies, health care
organizations, and other qualifying groups. For details, please contact:

Special Sales Department
Demos Medical Publishing
11 W. 42nd Street, 15th Floor
New York, NY 10036
Phone: 800–532–8663 or 212–683–0072
Email: orderdept@demosmedpub.com

Made in the United States of America
09 10 11 12 13   5 4 3 2 1

ReadHowYouWant partners with publishers to provide books for ALL Kinds of Readers. For more information about Becoming A (RHYW) Registered Reader and to find more titles in your preferred format, visit:
www.readhowyouwant.com

TABLE OF CONTENTS

TO *Charles*

Acknowledgments

A project like this doesn't happen in a vacuum, so indeed there are many people to thank. However, in keeping with my own personal tradition, I'll keep it short and sweet and offer a special word of thanks to the following folks.

To Diana for having the vision.

To Connie George for meeting me at the virtual water cooler.

To Bonnie Lewkowicz for again helping me sort out the finer points of accessible travel.

To Noreen Henson for her insight, encouragement, and above all, her level head in stressful times.

To Steve Pisano for creating such a wonderful cover out of Charles' photo.

To Gary Karp, for setting the bar high.

To the hundreds of *Emerging Horizons* readers who shared their experiences, hints and travel resources with me. Keep 'em coming!

And most importantly, to Charles Pannell, for his ongoing support, valuable input, and wonderful photos. And for being the house-husband extraordinaire when my deadline was moved up and my domestic duties fell by the wayside. Yes, I did notice! And thank you for looking the other way when I was on deadline, and my personal hygiene perhaps took a back seat to clean copy. Thanks for not noticing too much!

Preface

A CLEARING IN THE JUNGLE

I can hardly believe it's been eight years since the first edition of *Barrier-Free Travel.* Back then, in September 2001, the title to my preface was "It's a Jungle Out There." And thinking back, it certainly was.

Some folks say that timing is everything, and if that's the case, then I had nothing going for me with the timing of that first edition. It was released a few days prior to the catastrophic events of September 11, a time when travel would soon be the furthest thing from anyone's mind. And Charles and I would be stuck in London for two weeks. Indeed, it was a very dubious beginning for this title.

But despite my less than optimal timing, the book took off. Truth is, people were hungry for the information and resources I presented, and they were ready to travel. As more people got out there, access improved. Some of it was mandated, but some was market driven.

I have to admit that I'm very happy we have access laws and guidelines, but I'm just tickled pink whenever I hear of a small property that makes access upgrades not because they have to, but because they see it as a marketing advantage. That's real progress. And it's something I hear more and more about these days.

Yes, things certainly have changed—for the better—since the first edition of *Barrier-Free Travel.* And that's why I've titled the preface to this third edition, "There's a Clearing in the Jungle."

People often ask me about the changes I've seen in accessible travel; in fact, it's a very popular interview question. My favorite reply is to tell them to just look around the next time they are at an airport and see how many people roll by in wheelchairs. I fly often and I can't recall the last flight I was on that didn't have at least a few wheeler passengers. That wasn't the case 15 years ago when I first started to cover accessible travel.

Certainly the Baby Boomers have added to the mix, and that's a good thing. With more wheelers and slow walkers out there, there's not only more sensitivity to their needs, but also more recognition of this group as a market share.

Although many years ago, someone who tired easily when walking distances might have been hesitant about requesting an airport wheelchair, that's not the case today. And that's a very good thing. The services are there, and you should take advantage of them if you need them. And in the end, what benefits wheelchair users also benefits slow walkers. Things like ramps, curb cuts, and even cart transportation in airports all serve to make our society more accessible. And they are very positive changes.

There have also been huge changes in some access laws since the last edition of this book:

- The Air Carrier Access Act was revised on May 13, 2009.
- Canada's One-Person/One-Fare ruling went into effect January 10, 2009.
- The European Union Passengers with Reduced Mobility regulations covering air travel went into full effect July 26, 2008.

These regulations all make the world more accessible, and the changes are highlighted in this edition of *Barrier-Free Travel.*

Also new to this edition is an expanded ground transportation chapter with contact information for accessible van rental firms around the world. As well, it includes a completely new chapter on accessible shore excursions, which includes contact information for 45 companies that provide accessible shore tours. Both of these inclusions will be equally useful to travel agents.

Of course some things remain the same in this third edition. As I said in the preface of the first edition, "There are, of course, also some things this book won't do. It won't patronize you or give you simplistic advice like 'wear comfortable shoes." That remains true. I've never written about footwear, and I don't intend to start now.

Another thing that remains the same in this edition is that I got a lot of help with it. As the editor *of Emerging Horizons,* I get a lot of feedback—both good and bad—from travelers and I've incorporated many of those tips and resources in this edition. I appreciate all of the feedback and I admire the collective creativity of my readers. Keep those suggestions coming!

Of course one of the biggest changes in the past eight years has been the change in technology. And that's a very good thing. Because although I've thoroughly researched this edition and it was current at the time of writing, I know that over even short periods of time there will be changes. Thanks to technology, I'm able to keep up with those changes on my Barrier-Free Travels Blog (www.BarrierFreeTravels.com), so surf on over for the latest resources, updates and accessible travel news.

In the end, we are still moving forward access-wise. As I write this, the Access Board is preparing to issue final access guidelines for cruise ships and the ADAAG regulations for hotels are being updated. It appears we may soon have real cruise ship regulations and even stricter access standards for hotels.

There *is* a clearing in the jungle. Really. And as time marches on, that clearing will become bigger. Someday soon we will have all the resources, information, and access modifications we need to expand that clearing and make it a truly level playing field. Accessible travel is no longer an impossibility, and someday it will even become commonplace. I look forward to that day, but at the same time I invite you to enjoy the access we already have.

Have a good trip! And let me know how it went!

Candy B. Harrington
horizons@EmergingHorizons.com
Candy's Barrier-Free Travels Blog
www.BarrierFreeTravels.com
Facebook: Candy Harrington

Up, Up, and Away!

AIR TRAVEL

Everyone is flying these days. Indeed, air travel is one of the most popular forms of travel. Unfortunately, for people with disabilities, air travel can also be one of the most problematic areas of travel. Perhaps it's because there are just so many things that can go wrong on any flight. And then again, perhaps it's due to the mountain of misinformation circulating about accessible travel.

I believe it's a combination of both factors; however, I tend to favor the misinformation theory, mostly because of my own experience with this growing phenomenon. So, what's wrong with a little misinformation? Well if you rely on it and accept it as the truth, you may be in for a rude awakening when you take off on your holiday and find out that it's incorrect.

Admittedly, it can be difficult to ferret out the wheat from the chaff, as far as misinformation is concerned. This situation is further complicated by the fact that you can't always determine a person's credibility based on his or her position in the community. Just because someone is a well-respected professional does not mean that he or she is also an expert on accessible travel. The story of Lenny the lawyer comes to mind here.

I had the great misfortune of meeting Lenny, a well-respected corporate lawyer, at a national disability conference a few years ago. I gave a presentation about accessible travel and Lenny was in charge of introducing me. He seemed harmless enough, until he opened his mouth. Lenny knew very little about accessible travel, but he obviously felt the need to include something of substance in his introduction. So he proceeded to tell the audience that Title II of the Americans with Disabilities Act (ADA) entitles all wheelchair users to guaranteed bulkhead seating. Of course nothing could be further from the truth.

He then informed the audience that he always manages to get a bulkhead seat. He elaborated that he merely threatens to file a Title II lawsuit, and *voila* !, the seat is his. Now I'm not arguing that Lenny could definitely be a major pain in the backside; in fact, if I were a reservation agent I would most likely give him the darned seats just to get him off the phone. But that's not the way things usually work in real life.

And, more importantly, Lenny the lawyer did my audience a great disservice by spreading this misinformation. Fortunately, Lenny was not at all interested in hearing my presentation. He left immediately after the introduction, at which point I told the audience of the truth.

Although the Lenny incident is quite memorable, it's far from an isolated case. I've seen many other people spread misinformation—travel agents, rehabilitation professionals, and, yes, even writers. Misinformation is rampant. So what's a traveler to do? Ask for documentation and, if someone can't back up his or her claims with hard facts, then there's a good chance that he or she too is spreading misinformation. It's hard to argue with cold, hard facts. With that in mind, let's talk about the facts of air travel.

AIR CARRIER ACCESS ACT (ACAA)

Contrary to the gospel according to Lenny, the Air Carrier Access Act (ACAA) covers air travel on all U.S.-based airlines. Originally drafted in 1986, the regulations have been amended many times to reflect the changes in technology, equipment, and air travel in general. The most recent version of the ACAA went into effect on May 13, 2008. Although it took many years to update the ACAA, the end result was a full reorganization of the regulations into a more consumer friendly format. Major changes included the extension of the law to non-U.S. air carriers, new regulations for portable oxygen concentrators, revised service-animal regulations, and more details added to the existing regulations.

Generally speaking, the ACAA outlines procedures that airlines must follow regarding to passengers with disabilities. Among other things, the ACAA mandates that people with a disability cannot be denied boarding, solely because of their disability. It also forbids airlines from assessing surcharges for the services mandated by the ACAA.

ACAA JURISDICTION

The ACAA applies to all U.S. airlines and to all commercial flights to and from the United States, including those operated by non-U.S. carriers. In some cases the regulations are slightly different for non-U.S. carriers; and for the purposes of this chapter, we will refer to them as "covered foreign carriers," as the differences are noted.

ACAA Jurisdiction The ACAA also applies to codeshare flights beginning or ending in the United States. A codeshare is a marketing agreement between two airlines, where one airline operates flights under the code of the other airline. It's also important to note that the law does not cover codeshare flights between two non-U.S. cities.

Although many people take the basic non-discrimination rights in the ACAA for granted, it's something that's not guaranteed worldwide. Here are some examples of what can and does happen in places that don't have this kind of legal protection:

- Virgin Blue denied passage to unaccompanied wheelchair users, who happened to be paralympians.
- A woman with cerebral palsy was refused passage on a South African Express flight, because she could not get in and out of her wheelchair without assistance.
- Air Asia prohibited disabled passengers from traveling unaccompanied.
- Tiger Airways, a no-frills Singapore-based carrier, denied passage to a 24year-old wheelchair user, even though she was accompanied by her family.
- Air Sahara denied passage to an unaccompanied passenger with cerebral palsy, on the grounds that he needed an escort or a "fitness to fly" certificate.
- Cebu Pacific denied boarding to an unaccompanied disabled passenger with a "neurological disorder."
- Disabled passengers who wish to fly on Aeroflot must be cleared by the company medical department immediately prior to boarding.

The bottom line is to always err on the side of caution, especially when flying on regional airlines outside the United States, as you may not be protected by the same rights offered under the ACAA. To be fair, however, the United States doesn't stand alone in that respect—both Canada and the European Union have similar air travel regulations protecting disabled passengers. Those are covered in detail in the "Beyond the U.S.A." chapter of this book.

Other than that, watch your step, especially in underdeveloped countries. I've heard more than one story from wheelers who were stranded in the Caribbean because a non-U.S. carrier refused to board them. Their only recourse was to purchase a higher priced, same-day return ticket on a U.S. carrier—a very costly option. Don't let that happen to you.

KNOW YOUR RIGHTS

Before you plan your flight, you should first learn your rights under the ACAA. Once you have an understanding of the regulations, you will also have a good idea of what to expect as far as access in the air is concerned. Education and consumer awareness are the essential first steps to getting the services you need.

To that end, it's always good to go directly to the source and read through the ACAA
in its entirety. You can find the document on
the Department of Transportation Aviation
Consumer Protection website at http://airco
nsumer.ost.dot.gov. In addition to a lot of
helpful tips and consumer information about
air travel, the website also includes various
rules and regulations, including the full text
of the ACAA.

Alternatively you can find the ACAA published in the *Federal Register* at www.gpoac
cess.gov/fr. The final rule was published on
May 13, 2008 (Vol. 73, No. 93; pages
27614–27687).

Several organizations also publish material
about access to air travel, and although some
are good, others leave out a good chunk of
the rules and regulations or contain some
incorrect information. One of the best resources for accurate information on the subject is United Spinal Association. Their useful
publications are available free as PDF down-
loads from their website at www.unitedspina
l.org, or for a nominal charge for a print
version. It wouldn't hurt to carry this information with you when you travel, as it's hard
to argue with something when it's right there
in black and white.

KNOW YOUR AIRCRAFT

Under the ACAA, airlines are required to provide prospective passengers with basic information about the accessibility of their aircraft, facilities, and services. This information includes:

- The location of seats with movable armrests.
- The location of seats not available to passengers with a disability.
- The availability of level-entry boarding.
- The availability of an accessible lavatory.
- Any limitations of storage facilities in the cabin or baggage compartment for assistive devices.
- Details about any services not available to disabled passengers on the flight.

As you might expect, some airlines do a better job of providing this information than others. Some airlines have a lot of information about accessibility on their websites; some even include seat maps that note the accessible seats. Nearly all airline websites have some sort of information for disabled travelers, so it pays to surf a bit before you call the special needs department.

You also need to find out a little something about the aircraft that will be used on your flight. For example, do you know the difference between an EMB-120 and a 777–200? Well, you should if you plan to travel by air. I'm not implying that you should become an aviation expert, but it really helps to know some of the basic differences between different types of airplanes.

In the example given above, the big difference between the two airplanes is their size. The EMB-120 has 30 seats and the 777–200 has 383 seats. This is important, because most of the ACAA regulations regarding aircraft accessibility and boarding are referenced by aircraft size. Here are some important numbers.

The following ACAA equipment rules apply to U.S. airlines for planes ordered after April 5, 1990 or delivered after April 5, 1992 and to covered foreign airlines for planes ordered after May 13, 2009 or placed into service after May 13, 2010. Retrofitting is not required; however, if a covered component is replaced, it must be replaced with an accessible component.

- Planes with 30 or more seats must have moveable armrests on at least half of the aisle seats available to disabled passengers. These seats must be proportionally distributed in all classes of service on aircraft ordered after May 13, 2009 or placed into service after May 13, 2010.
- Wide-body jets (those with two aisles) must have an accessible lavatory.

- Planes with more than 60 seats and an accessible lavatory must have an onboard wheelchair with footrests, movable armrests, occupant restraints, high backrest, handles, and locks. It must be able to fit down the aisle of the aircraft. Aerospatiale/Aeritalia ATR-72 and British Aerospace Advance Turboprop (ATP) aircraft with configurations of 60 to 70 seats are exempt from this requirement.
- Planes with 60 or more seats that do not have an accessible lavatory, must carry an onboard wheelchair upon passenger request (48 hours advance notice is required).
- Planes with more than 100 seats must have priority space to carry at least one folding wheelchair in the cabin.

Boarding assistance is also dependent upon the size of the aircraft. The ACAA mandates that airlines must provide ramp or lift boarding at U.S. airports that lack jetbridges and have more than 10,000 annual enplanements. This applies to all aircraft with 19 or more seats. This part of the rule is effective May 13, 2010 for covered foreign carriers; however, it's not required at foreign airports.

Under no circumstances are airline personnel allowed to hand-carry a passenger (directly pick them up without a chair or other device) on or off any aircraft, even if the passenger consents to this. The only exception to this rule is for the emergency evacuation of the aircraft. Airlines are required to maintain all lift devices, but even in the event of a mechanical breakdown, airline personnel are still not allowed to hand-carry passengers on or off any aircraft.

Additionally, there are a few aircraft that are considered exempt from the boarding assistance requirements of the ACAA. These aircraft are the Fairchild Metro, the Jetstream 31 and 32, the Beech 1900 C and D models, and the Embraer EMB-120. Boarding assistance devices (lifts) are not required for these exempt aircraft or any others that the Department of Transportation (DOT) may deem unsuitable for lift or ramp boarding.

Boarding options can also vary, depending upon the size of the airport. Not all airports have jetbridges to enable level boarding. Additionally even airports that do have jetbridges may not have a level boarding option due to heavy traffic. This is a common occurrence at many large international airports. If all gates are being used, even a large plane will park out on the tarmac, and passengers will board on deplane via boarding stairs. The passengers will then be bussed to the terminal. It's always a good practice to ask what deplaning procedures are available at your destination airport, just so there won't be any surprises.

12

In the end, it pays to inquire about your boarding options, including the weight capacity of the lift. A little advance research can save a lot of time, trouble, and even embarrassment.

BOARDING PROCEDURES

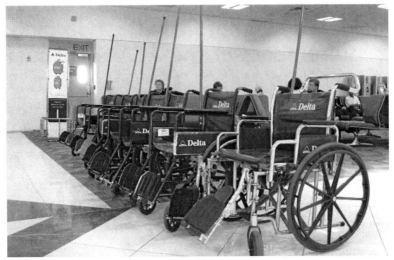

Don't be afraid to ask for wheelchair assistance at the airport, as most airlines have a large fleet of manual wheelchairs.

Generally speaking, boarding a larger aircraft from a level-entry jetbridge is a pretty straightforward procedure. Of course, there are always a few potential trouble spots, so you need to know the standard boarding procedure in order to understand your rights under the ACAA.

First, you have to make it past the reservation agents. To be honest, these front-line employees could use better training on access issues. For example, one wheelchair user reported that a reservation agent informed her that she could fly in her own wheelchair. The agent explained that their recently refurbished planes had removable bulkhead seats with wheelchair tie-downs. Fortunately, the passenger was travel savvy and knew this wasn't true.

The next hurdle you'll likely encounter is at the check-in counter. If you arrive with your own wheelchair or scooter, the ticket agent may insist that you transfer to an airport wheelchair at this time. Here's where you need to be a little assertive and insist that you stay in your own wheelchair or scooter. It's your right under the ACAA to stay in your own wheelchair or scooter all the way to the door of the aircraft.

There are a few exceptions to this rule. One exception is if your wheelchair or scooter has a spillable battery. In that case, you must surrender it to the airline at least one hour prior to the standard check-in time. So if the standard check-in time requirement is two hours prior to the flight, then you must arrive at least three hours prior to the flight.

The other exception is when using your own mobility device is actually prohibited by federal regulations governing transportation security or hazardous materials. As of this writing, there are no specific federal regulations prohibiting the transport of power or manual wheelchairs;

however, it's important to note that this can change, especially in times of high security alerts.

In any case, I strongly suggest you keep your own wheelchair or scooter as long as you can for a variety of reasons.

First, it's best to keep your own equipment with you as long as possible, because in theory, the less time the airlines have it, the less time they have to damage it. Also, as you may know, airport wheelchairs are not exactly what you would call comfortable, and you never know how long you will be stuck in one. It's not uncommon for flights to be delayed or canceled.

Finally, you will loose a lot of your freedom if you give up your equipment. Most airport wheelchairs come with a "wheelchair pusher," even if you can push yourself or if you are traveling with somebody who can push you. Your freedom (or lack of it) depends on the wheelchair pusher, and where he or she is allowed to take you.

Under the ACAA, the wheelchair pusher is required to stop briefly at the entrance to the restroom if requested, but only if the restroom is on the way to the gate, and only if the stop can be accomplished without an unreasonable delay. The wheelchair pusher is not required to provide personal care attendant services (assistance in the bathroom), detour to a different route, or incur an unreasonable delay. Any delay in which the passenger would be late to the gate is considered unreasonable. So, unless you have a lot of time between connections, chances are the wheelchair pusher won't have time to make a restroom stop. And remember, the wheelchair pusher's assistance ends at the entrance to the restroom.

Wheelchair pushers are not required to stop for food or water purchases if there are long lines and there would be an unreasonable delay. Best advice is to take some snack food and water with you. Also, if you connect from another flight, use the lavatory on the airplane before you land, if you are able to access it.

So, by all means, stay in your own wheelchair or scooter as long as possible. Don't fall for the old "it's our procedure" line when the ticket agent tries to get you to transfer to an airport wheelchair. It very well may be their *preferred* procedure, but remember: You do have the right to refuse and you do have a choice.

By the time you make it to the gate, you would assume all of your information (like the fact that you are a wheelchair user) would be entered correctly in the computer. But, that's not the way it works in real life. Don't be alarmed if the gate agent looks down at you with amazement and says something incredibly

Passengers who cannot walk to their seats are transferred to an aisle chair like this model, and then wheeled down the aisle to their seats..

intelligent like, "Are you on this flight?" Don't let comments like that worry you. Things will be sorted out by the time you board the aircraft.

The thing you should remember to do at this point is to tell the gate agent that you would like to preboard the aircraft. This means that you board the aircraft before the rest of the passengers. Preboarding has a lot of advantages. It gives you time to get settled and change your seat if you find out your assigned seat doesn't have a moveable aisle armrest. It also allows you first crack at the overhead storage compartments, and it gives you priority storage for your folding wheelchair The airlines can't force you to preboard, but it's to your advantage to do so.

It should also be noted that the airlines are not required to make a preboarding announcement, so be sure and alert the gate agent that you need to preboard.

When it is time for you to preboard, you will be transferred from your own wheelchair to an aisle chair. This high-backed narrow chair has two or four small wheels, and you are belted in, and rolled down the aisle to your seat. Upon request, you will be assigned a seat with a moveable aisle armrest. This makes transfers a lot easier, as you just flip up the armrest and slide over.

Airline personnel are required to help you transfer to your seat if needed; however, it's always best to tell them exactly how you would like to be transferred. Never assume they know anything, as they deal with a wide variety of passengers.

It's important to note that if an airline employee offers you boarding assistance that seems out of the ordinary, it's time to ask to speak to the Complaints Resolution Official (CRO). For example, in 2003 the DOT responded to numerous customer complaints against Kansas-based Ryan International. Among other things, one complaint alleged that a passenger was actually strapped to a wooden office chair with clothing belts and carried off the plane! After an extensive investigation, the airline was fined $400,000 but was granted a $355,000 credit for the purchase of wheelchairs and ACAA training equipment.

It should also be noted that if you travel with your own wheelchair, always ask to have it delivered to the gate. This is called "gate-checking" in airline language. Never assume that just because you drop off your wheelchair at the gate, that it will be returned to you there. Always specify that you need it delivered to your arrival and connecting gates.

Now, if you just need a wheelchair for distance, the airlines will supply you with an airport wheelchair. Although advance notice is recommended, you can still get an airline wheelchair on a walk-up basis at most any ticket counter. I highly recommend an airline wheelchair for anyone who has trouble doing distances. Not only will you be fast tracked through security at most airports, but it also alleviates standing in long lines. Some airports are huge, and an airport wheelchair will allow you to arrive at your destination refreshed instead of exhausted.

Airline employees (or their contractors) are also required to assist passengers who cannot carry their own luggage, and to provide connection assistance by wheelchair or motorized cart.

And finally, let's talk about tipping. Is it appropriate to tip a skycap for wheelchair assistance? Some people claim you shouldn't tip for this service because under the law it's illegal to charge for a disability-related service. True, it is illegal to charge for wheelchair assistance, but a tip certainly isn't a mandatory charge. A tip is a way to show your appreciation for good service.

Granted, tipping is a personal matter, but it is customary to tip skycaps. That said, the appropriate tip for regular wheelchair assistance is $5, more if the skycap provides luggage assistance. Again, tipping is a personal choice, but it's always nice to reward good service.

FULL DISCLOSURE?

So how much personal medical information are you required to disclose to airline personnel? According to the ACAA, you are required to tell the airlines when you will be traveling with canister oxygen, stretcher, incubator, portable oxygen concentrator, CPAP machine, or ventilator, or if you are traveling with a group of 10 or more disabled people. Other than that, disclosure is at your own discretion: sometimes, however, sometimes it's actually in your best interest to share a few personal details with the gate agent.

Take the saga of the following wheelchair users who encountered problems while trying to board their flight at Heathrow. Even though they made all the proper arrangements and informed the ticket agent they would need assistance boarding, the lead flight attendant refused to board them because "they would not be able to use the toilet unassisted."

When the gate agent relayed this information to the passengers, they assured him they would not need to use the toilet for the entire flight. Now mind you, they did not tell the gate agent *why* they would not need to use the toilet (they both wore catheters), so the discussion went on, and the flight attendant stood his ground. As general boarding commenced the problem was still not resolved.

Finally, after about 25 minutes of arguing, one passenger mentioned that they were both wearing catheters. As soon as the "c"-word was mentioned, the gate agent grabbed his handbook and noted that there was an exception for catheters. He quickly informed the flight attendant of this new development. In the end, the flight attendant backed down and the passengers were allowed to board; however, they were somewhat of a spectacle as they missed their pre-boarding opportunity.

Could this whole fiasco have been avoided? In retrospect, if they had mentioned the catheter issue in the beginning, it's quite likely the whole situation would never have escalated. The passengers would have been allowed to preboard and it would have saved everyone a whole lot of frustration.

So how much information is too much to disclose? Generally speaking, I say evaluate the situation and trust your instincts. Even though covered airlines cannot deny wheelers boarding these days, you never know when problems will arise. Remember, it's likely that most people don't have a clue about your disability, especially if they haven't been exposed to it before. If sharing a few personal details will help clarify the situation and get you quickly on your way, then I say go for it. If not, then button your lip. In the end, it's *your* call.

SEATING

Seating is another source of great confusion. Who is entitled to what type of a seat, and how do you actually get it? First off, let me debunk a popular myth. Wheelchair users are not always guaranteed seating in bulkhead areas. Some airlines will seat you there, some will not; but it is not a right given carte blanche to all wheelchair users under the ACAA.

Seating was first addressed in the 1998 amendment to the ACAA, and further clarified in the 2009 revision of the law. Regarding bulkhead seating, this amendment requires air carriers to designate an adequate number of bulkhead seats as priority seating for individuals with a disability. These seats are required to be available to people who travel with a service animal or to people who have a fused (immovable) leg. Carriers can also assign bulkhead seats upon advance request to anybody with a disability who self-identifies as a person who needs this particular seating accommodation, providing those seats are not already assigned to other passengers.

Air carriers are not required to bump other passengers from bulkhead seats to accommodate passengers who do not meet the ACAA definition of disabled. In other words, only those passengers who have a service animal or a fused (immovable) leg qualify for priority bulkhead seating under the ACAA.

So, if you are a wheelchair user (and you don't have a fused leg), you will be given a bulkhead seat only if one is available at the time of your request. Most airlines block a few bulkhead seats as they are required to refrain from assigning them to anyone who does not meet the "disability criteria" until 24 hours prior to the flight. Still, because of the definition of the criteria, it does not mean that all wheelers will get bulkhead seats.

The best advice is to make your travel arrangements as early as possible. Additionally, some airlines give priority bulkhead seating to all passengers who have a disability. Call all the airlines in advance to find out their individual policies on this matter, and then do business with the ones that will give you the seating accommodations you need.

This seating provision applies to flights on U.S. air carriers worldwide, and on foreign carrier flights traveling to or from the United States. Additionally, these carriers cannot force a disabled person to sit in a window seat, or exclude them from any other seats except to comply with Federal Aviation Administration (FAA) regulations. An adjoining seat for a companion who is required to assist a disabled passenger is also mandated under the law.

Additionally, airlines are not required to provide more than one seat per ticket to any passenger, including those with a disability or additional medical equipment.

Moveable aisle armrests are another story though. The ACAA requires airlines to designate an adequate number of seats with moveable aisle armrests as priority seats for individuals with disabilities. These seats are required to be available to passengers who use an aisle chair to board the aircraft and who cannot readily transfer over a fixed armrest. Because there are a higher percentage of these seats, they are usually easier to get.

Still, sometimes there can be confusion during boarding, as some airline employees don't readily know the locations of these seats. It's usually not much of a problem, as the cabin crew will reassign you to another seat that has a moveable armrest, even if they have to try to flip up every armrest on the airplane to find it. Another point to keep in mind is that bulkhead seats usually do not have moveable aisle armrests, as the tray tables are installed in the armrests.

Passengers are not required to give advance notice for special seating accommodations; however the airlines are only required to make their best effort to accommodate passengers who do not give at least 24 hours notice. They are not required to displace another passenger with less than 24 hours notice. Best bet is to let the airline know exactly what you need, as far in advance as you can.

And, of course, these seating provisions only apply to airlines that provide advance seating assignments. Airlines that have open seating must let disabled passengers board first, so they can select their seats before the general boarding announcement is given.

Another source of seating confusion (and frustration) are the highly prized exit row seats. The criteria for exit row seating is pretty well established. You must be able to operate the emergency door (which weighs 70 pounds), be able to understand and follow directions in English, be over 15 years old, and be able to assist crew members in case of an emergency.

That "be able to assist crew members in case of an emergency" qualification is somewhat open to interpretation by the airlines, but they are given this latitude under FAA regulations. Generally speaking, most airlines don't consider wheelchair users "able to assist in an emergency situation." The airlines are well within their rights to determine this as it's not an area covered under the ACAA. In fact it's an area exempt from the ACAA because it has to do with a safety issue. Safety issues are covered under FAA regulations. Final discretion in all safety matters is left up to the crew, and ultimately the captain.

Most wheelchair users, or anybody who requires a wheelchair assist, won't intentionally be seated in an emergency exit row: sometimes it happens, however, and it does, the cabin crew will simply reseat passengers who are inappropriately assigned to exit row seats.

The bigger problem with exit row seats is that some airlines insist that the center aisle of the bulkhead exit rows are also exit rows. I have known people who received their priority seating in bulkhead, only to be told by the cabin crew that they would not be able to sit there because it was an exit row. I find this reasoning somewhat absurd because the same airlines routinely seat families (with kids under 15) in this row. Still, some employees have it in their minds that this is an exit row. So, if you find yourself in this situation, ask to have the CRO resolve the matter. It is the quickest solution to this unfortunate situation.

And finally, a word about upgrades. Years ago, when fewer people traveled, wheelchair users were routinely upgraded to first class; however, today those upgrades are few and far between, partly because more people are traveling, and partly because the airlines are now giving those upgrades to their highest echelon frequent flyers. I shudder whenever I read a travelogue that even mentions a wheeler's first class upgrade. It's a great perk when it happens, but stories like that tend to create false expectations.

Don't count on getting an upgrade. If you absolutely need that extra room, then buy a business class or first class ticket. There is no provision in the ACAA (or anywhere) that requires carriers to upgrade people with disabilities to first class. But, by all means, go ahead and ask for an upgrade at the gate, but don't be disappointed if you don't get it. My friend John has perhaps the best (or at least the most creative) upgrade technique around. John tries to "look as large as possible." Sometimes it works, but most of the time John ends up in coach with the rest of us.

SAFETY ASSISTANTS

Under the ACAA, U.S. airlines cannot discriminate against a passenger solely because of a disability; however, they *can* require some passengers to travel with a safety assistant. Which passengers? Well, according to the ACAA, they are "passengers who have a disability so severe that they can't physically assist with their own emergency evacuation." In other words, being able to just call out for help is not adequate; you must be able to physically assist with your own emergency evacuation.

Although passengers are primarily responsible for determining if they meet the above criteria, airline personnel can override that decision if they believe there is a compelling safety issue. It should be noted that airline personnel are not mandated to find a required safety assistant. If they don't, however, if they don't, the passenger can select his or her own safety assistant, and that person can travel for free. This part of the law has often been misinterpreted to mean that all attendants travel for free. That is not the case. In practice, most airlines just ask another passenger or a deadheading crew member to serve as a safety assistant, and the selection process is never even placed in the passenger's hands.

Unfortunately it doesn't always work out that way. In fact, in 2007 a disabled U.S. Airways passenger was informed by a gate agent that he could not fly alone, because of safety issues. The passenger asked his mom, who brought him to the airport, if she could accompany him. U.S. Airways was willing to let her travel for free, but because of the short notice she was unable to accompany her son. Ultimately the passenger was denied boarding. Since the airline was not required to find a safety assistant, and the passenger was unable to provide one, it was all very legal. Unfortunately it never occurred to the passenger that he could ask another passenger to serve as his safety assistant. It would have been a win-win situation for everyone, as the passenger would have been able to board the flight and the safety assistant would have gotten a free trip. So the moral of the story is, if this ever happens to you, just ask another passenger if they will serve as your safety assistant. With free airfare for the taker, you'll probably have a long line of eager volunteers.

If there are no available seats for an airline required safety assistant, the airline must compensate the passenger for denied boarding, as mandated by the DOT.

Under no circumstances can the airlines require a disabled passenger to travel with an attendant to assist with personal care. Additionally, a concern that a passenger may not be able to provide for his or her own personal care during the flight is not a basis for denied boarding.

A personal care attendant should not be confused with a safety assistant. The former is responsible for assisting the passenger during the flight, while the latter is only required to provide assistance in the event of an emergency evacuation. A safety assistant is not required to provide any type of personal service to the passenger. They just sit next to the passenger and in the event of a water landing, well, you know the drill. In short, a safety assistant won't help you eat or use the toilet, but he will help you get off the plane if it crashes.

Additionally, airline employees are not required to provide personal care assistance to passengers. They are required to provide help opening food packages, assistance with the onboard wheelchair and help with stowing or retrieving mobility aids. They are not required to provide assistance with eating or in the restroom. If you require this type of assistance, you need to travel with someone who can assist you, or else opt to forego those services during the flight.

These safety assistant rules apply to all flights on U.S. airlines and on foreign carrier flights to and from the United States.

WHEN NATURE CALLS

What do you do when nature calls at 30,000 feet? That's a question I hear over and over again, as it's a major concern for first-time flyers. There are actually many solutions to the toilet problem, but they all take some sort of advance preparation. I also must stress here that everyone is different, and what works for one person may not necessarily work for the next. Sometimes it takes a bit of fine tuning and adjustment to find a method that works best for you. With personal experience you will be able to do this, but for now let me just outline your options.

One option is to travel on an aircraft with an accessible lavatory. For U.S. airlines, all post-1992 wide body aircraft must have at least one accessible lavatory. For foreign carriers arriving or departing the United States, this rule applies to all aircraft ordered after May 13, 2009 or placed into service after May 13, 2010. Retrofitting is never required; however, if a lavatory on a wide body aircraft is replaced, it must be replaced with an accessible model.

All planes with an accessible lavatory must also carry an onboard wheelchair. Although this is the standard procedure, it's always best to request an onboard wheelchair when you make your reservations.

Be forewarned, though; in most cases the accessible aircraft lavatories are not the same models you'll find on the ground. According to the guidelines, an accessible aircraft lavatory must permit a disabled passenger to enter and use all of the lavatory facilities while seated in the onboard wheelchair. It must include a door lock, accessible call button, and grab bars; however, there are no specifications about the height or placement of the grab bars or the toilet.

Space is at a premium and in most cases you won't find a five-foot turning radius in onboard accessible lavatories. The roomiest accessible lavatories are found on the newer wide body jets. Although most airlines can't provide the exact dimensions of their onboard accessible lavatories, you can get a good idea of their size by looking at the aircraft diagrams on www.seatguru.com. Although measurements aren't included on this website, you can tell from the diagram if the accessible lavatories are substantially larger than the standard models.

Looking to the future, the new Boeing Dreamliner promises to have some very accessible facilities, including a 56-inch by 57-inch convertible lavatory with a movable center wall; so that two separate lavatories can be converted to one large, wheelchair-accessible facility. Other access improvements include an additional toilet flush button on the sink cabinet and a fold-down assist bar to aid independent transfers.

Most accessible aircraft lavatories are considerably smaller than those on the ground. This lavatory aboard an Air Canada Airbus 319 is classified as "accessible."

For now, if you can use the onboard wheelchair and transfer independently, the onboard lavatory is a doable option. The flight attendants will help you use the onboard wheelchair, but their assistance ends once you reach the lavatory door.

Some travelers totally write off the onboard lavatory, and wear a catheter instead. This is usually easier for men than women, as men can use a condom catheter while women have to use an internal catheter. If you don't normally use a catheter, the downside (for women) is that you have to arrange for some-body to remove the catheter when you get to your destination.

And, of course, if you are on a long flight, you also need to find a discreet way to empty your leg bag. I consider this a learned skill, as I have heard from many people who manage this feat, under the cover of a blanket. Of course you should practice this procedure before you leave home (with the blanket). Fortunately most long haul flights have several movies, so the cabin is dark for a majority of the time, and darkness works in your favor.

I've also been told to make absolutely sure that your transfer container is leak proof, and that it has a very secure lid. I have heard about some unfortunate accidents, where the lid came off the container while it was safely stowed in a duffel bag. This can be very embarrassing, and quite difficult to explain to customs officials.

Of course, some people prefer a more personalized solution to the bathroom dilemma. By this I mean many people experiment with diets, vitamins, and limit their fluid intake. And in fact, many people swear by their personal preflight regime; however, I hesitate to recommend anything specifically, as it's such a personal choice. And, as I said earlier, what works for one person may not work for the next.

I do recommend that you don't schedule things down to the last minute though. Flights are often late or delayed, and sometimes it takes a long time to deplane. Finally, if you do cut it a bit close, it never hurts to wear a diaper for extra protection. I know it seems a rather insulting suggestion, but the extra protection may come in handy. And if you plan to go the diaper route, consider wearing two for extra protection, as leakage is a common problem.

GETTING OFF THE AIRPLANE

You would think that getting off the plane would be a piece of cake, but here's another area where problems can develop. To nip things in the bud, remember to remind the flight attendant that you need your wheelchair brought to the gate when you land. This should be done about 30 minutes before landing, well before the flight attendants are busy scurrying through the cabin making last minute prelanding preparations.

One good method is to make friends with a particular flight attendant. Introduce yourself to that flight attendant and learn his or her name. Address the flight attendant by name during the flight. Then when you are ready to land, remind that flight attendant about your wheelchair. When you call flight attendants by name, it puts more of a personal responsibility on them to follow through with your request. They realize you know their names, and if something goes wrong, they know they will be held personally responsible.

Now, if you need an aisle chair to disembark, you must wait until the rest of the passengers deplane. At that point the aisle chair will be brought to you, and you will be wheeled to the aircraft door where your own wheelchair will be waiting for you. That's how it's supposed to work, but in practice sometimes it doesn't go that smoothly.

I've received countless reports from people who have waited an inordinate amount of time on an empty airplane. They waited for somebody to bring them an aisle chair, or for their own wheelchair to be brought up from the baggage compartment. Sometimes the baggage handlers get confused and send the wheelchair to the baggage area, even though it has a gate tag.

In response to the glut of complaints, the DOT strengthened the ACAA in 2008, and added a provision stating that the prompt deplaning of disabled passengers is required. They further defined prompt as meaning immediately after the other passengers have deplaned. This applies to all flights on U.S. carriers as well as foreign carrier flights arriving or departing the US.

Still, delays do occur, so don't plan your connections too tightly, and do hold the airline responsible if you miss your flight. Additionally, take nonstop direct flights whenever possible.

I've heard a few creative solutions to the deplaning problem but the best suggestion comes from my friend Dan. He takes his cell phone with him, calls the airline from his seat, and asks to speak to the CRO whenever there is a delay in deplaning. Although he shouldn't have to do that, at least it gets the job done. Never leave home without your cell phone.

SECURITY ISSUES

In the wake of the September 11th tragedies, the Transportation Security Administration (TSA) was created to enforce security at U.S. airports. Previously security was handled by contracted workers, and the procedures varied greatly from airport to airport. The creation of a centralized agency offers some consistency; however, it's important to note that procedures can change at any time due to a heightened security threat.

Initially the biggest security concern for wheelchair users was the elimination of curbside check-in. Fortunately this ban has been lifted, but it may be reinstated if the security threat rises. In the absence of curbside check-in, airline employees are available to assist disable passengers. The best bet is to check with your airline for their current procedures

Another area of concern is the prohibition of non-ticketed passengers beyond security checkpoints. Again, accommodations have been made for disabled passengers who travel with an aide, attendant, or companion. In such cases, the attendant should present photo identification at the check-in counter to receive a security checkpoint pass.

Another issue involves gate checking assistive devices. In times of heightened security, this procedure may be temporarily discontinued. Remember, as a federal agency the TSA is not subject to ACAA regulations. The good news is that the agency has developed a set of standardized guidelines for dealing with disabled passengers. Although these can change depending on the security outlook, they are listed on the TSA website at www.tsa.gov .

All passengers now face higher security measures and longer lines at airports; however, wheelchair users can expect even closer scrutiny at all security checkpoints. Wheelchair users and people who wear prosthetic devices are usually screened with a hand-held metal detector and patted down. Private screenings are available upon request.

Wheelchair users should remember to stow their wheelchair repair tools in their checked baggage to avoid having them confiscated at security checkpoints. Assistive devices, such as canes and walkers, are permitted onboard the aircraft after they are inspected. Syringes are also permitted with medical documentation. Manual wheelchairs are still allowed to be stowed aboard the aircraft, provided they fall under the provisions of the ACAA.

Here are some additional security screening tips for wheelers and slow walkers:

- If you can't walk or go through the metal detector, tell the TSA agent. You will be hand-wanded and given a pat-down search.
- If you tire easily or can't stand for long periods of time, request a chair during the screening process.

- Keep in mind that you are not required to transfer from your wheelchair or scooter for any portion of the security screening process.
- You are not required to remove your shoes if your disability prevents you from doing so. You will, however, be subject to a pat-down search and your shoes will be swabbed and tested for gunpowder residue.

In the end, patience is really the keyword; however if you feel your needs as a passenger with a disability are not being adequately addressed, ask to speak to a supervisor or call the TSA Office of Civil Rights at (877) 336–4872.

It's also important to note that the TSA only has jurisdiction in U.S. airports. Passengers at foreign airports may be subject to security screening measures required by that country.

CRO

I've already mentioned the CRO a few times in this chapter, so by now you should know this is the person you need to contact if you reach an impasse with frontline personnel. The CRO is a problem solver, and is specifically educated on traveler's rights and airline responsibilities under the ACAA. All U.S. airlines are required to have a CRO on duty while the airport is open, so if you encounter a problem at any stage of the game—from reservations to deplaning—this is the person to contact. Foreign carriers are required to have a CRO available at each airport serving flights that begin or end in the U.S. Alternatively, the CRO can be available by phone.

The CRO has the authority to overrule the decision of any other personnel, including third-party contractors. They even have jurisdiction over the airline websites. The only exclusion to their jurisdiction is the pilot on an aircraft who makes a decision based on safety issues.

Of course, as I pointed out earlier, it really helps to know your rights when talking to the CRO. In other words, don't misquote the law and demand bulkhead seating or a first-class upgrade. The CRO will help you resolve access problems, and ultimately get you the services you need and are entitled to under the law. But knowing the law is the first and all important step in advocating for yourself. On the other hand, if airline personnel want you to transfer to an airline wheelchair at check-in, this is a good time to contact the CRO. The law is on your side, and the CRO will help to enforce it.

The DOT operates a toll-free aviation consumer disability hotline at (866) 266-1368. Travelers are invited to call this hotline to obtain information and assistance if they should experience disability-related   air service problems.

As far as air travel goes, the best survival tactic is to try and prevent problems before they happen. Of course, there are a lot of unknown variables that factor into the accessibility equation, but you're ahead of the game if you confirm and reconfirm all your travel arrangements. I know this is a time-consuming process, and many people think it's an unfair burden to put on travelers with disabilities, but in reality it's the best way to head off potential disasters and help things go smoothly.

If you want to make a political statement, then go ahead and leave things to chance. If you actually want to take a vacation, remember to confirm and reconfirm all your travel arrangements. You can never be too careful, especially where access is concerned.

On a Wing and a Prayer

PROTECTING YOUR EQUIPMENT

Getting to your holiday destination with a minimum of muss and fuss can sometimes be a challenge. Getting your wheelchair or scooter to that same destination—in one piece—can be an even greater chore. No matter how hard travel is on people, it can be even harder on assistive devices. Generally speaking, passengers aren't stripped of their clothing and thrown into the cargo bin, a fate many wheelchairs and scooters must routinely endure.

Unfortunately, equipment damage is still a top-ranked problem for wheelers, but don't throw in the towel yet, as it's still possible to get your equipment to your final destination relatively unscathed. Of course, as with all aspects of travel, it takes a bit of planning and preparation. Although the whole process may seem rather daunting at first, after a few trips you'll have it down to a science and then you'll be ready for just about anything.

Before we get into the nuts and bolts here (literally!), I must share an anecdote with you. This unfortunate travel tale comes from a reader named Dan. It's about his first air travel experience as a wheeler, and it definitely gets my vote as the ultimate in wheelchair damage stories.

Dan uses a power wheelchair with gel cell batteries, and even though he could have gate checked his wheelchair, he relented at check-in and transferred to an airport wheelchair. His plane was then delayed due to weather, and he ended up spending an extra hour in the uncomfortable airport wheelchair. But Dan saw past the pain, as he was really looking forward to his vacation. He remained optimistic.

To his delight, when boarding time came things went like clockwork. Dan was boarded first. He had no problems with the aisle chair and his reserved seat had a moveable armrest. Things couldn't have gone any better. Dan sat back and stared out the window while the other passengers boarded. He was in a semi dream state when he noticed an unusual object out on the tarmac.

Upon closer examination, it appeared to be his wheelchair. Just as he was about to call the flight attendant, he noticed another object on the tarmac approaching the wheelchair—a 747 backing up out of the gate. He sat there speechless as he watched the jumbo jet crush his wheelchair. Ultimately he canceled his trip. On the positive side, this incident happened while he was at home rather than while he was on the road.

Fortunately Dan's experience is not the norm, but it does illustrate the importance of staying in your own wheelchair as long as possible. In Dan's case the cargo handlers forgot to move Dan's wheelchair off the tarmac when his flight was delayed. In theory, if Dan had stayed in his own wheelchair up to the aircraft door, it would have been taken directly to the cargo bin instead of sitting on the tarmac. Today Dan always turns down the airport wheelchair, no matter how hard the check-in agent tries to convince him otherwise.

Dan's story pretty much represents the worst case scenario. (The only thing I can ever imagine being worse is actually being in your wheelchair when a 747 backs over it.)[1] So when you encounter equipment damage problems, think about Dan. You'll be able to take some comfort in the fact that, no matter how bad things are, at least a jumbo jet didn't roll over your wheelchair.

CANES, CRUTCHES, AND WALKERS

The best way to protect your assistive device from damage (short of staying home) is to keep it out of the cargo bin. The good news is, in many cases, it may be stored onboard. Under the Air Carrier Access Act (ACAA), airlines must permit canes, crutches, and walkers in the cabin, provided they can be stowed in the designated storage areas, in the overhead compartments, or under the seats. Additionally, assistive devices (and other medical supplies) do not count toward the carry-on baggage limit.

Assistive devices must be stowed for takeoff and landing; in most cases, canes and crutches can be placed in the overhead bins. You should make it a point to retrieve your cane right after takeoff, as you will need it to move about the cabin. Additionally, if there were an emergency, it would be important to have it with you. If you have problems retrieving your assistive device, just ask a flight attendant for assistance.

Alternatively, you might consider traveling with a lightweight folding cane that can fit in the seatback pocket. That way you know it will always be within your reach.

Walkers can usually be carried in the passenger compartment, but again it depends on their size. Under the ACAA, the priority storage area for assistive devices must be at least 13 inches by 36 inches by 42 inches, so if your walker can fit in that space, there's a good chance it can be carried onboard. Be aware that other assistive devices may also need to be stored there, and that this space is only required on aircraft with 100 or more seats. Walkers may also be stowed in overhead bins, if they can fit. Frankly, walkers don't fare very well in the cargo bin, so it's a good idea to invest in a folding model that will fit the onboard storage space. It's also a good idea to check the seat maps on www.seatguru.com to see if your aircraft has an onboard closet, as many folding walkers can fit in that space.

Although you're not likely to stow a support harness during the flight, it's worth noting that some people have had problems bringing them onboard. The most recent incident involved 15-year-old Avery Ottenbreit, who was refused a return flight to Regina on Canada's WestJet. The issue at hand was Avery's butterfly harness, which she wears for torso support. WestJet flight attendants had problems with the harness because they claimed it would prevent her from assuming the "brace" position in case of an emergency landing. Ultimately she was taken off the plane.

It should be noted that this incident took place aboard a Canadian airline. In the United States, you can't take aboard any type of a harness that straps to the seat, unless it's approved by the Federal Aviation Administration (FAA). At this time only one model makes the cut, and it can only be used on children over one year old who weigh between 22 and 40 pounds. But medical harnesses or casts aren't specifically prohibited. Still, the incident is worth noting, especially if you plan to travel on WestJet.

MANUAL WHEELCHAIRS

Manual wheelchairs can also be stored in the cabin on many aircraft. Under the ACAA, aircraft with more that 100 seats must also contain a priority storage space for one adult collapsible wheelchair. This space must measure at least 13 inches by 36 inches by 42 inches. It cannot be in the overhead compartments or in the underseat spaces routinely used for passenger carry-ons.

If your wheelchair has quick release wheels, the wheels can be removed and stored in the overhead bins if the assembled wheelchair won't fit in the priority storage space. If the wheel removal requires the use of any tools, the wheels are not permitted to be removed, and the wheelchair will need to be placed in the cargo bin if it won't fit in the priority storage space.

This rule applies to U.S. carriers for new aircraft ordered after April 5, 1990, or delivered after April 5, 1992. It also applies to foreign carriers on flights beginning or ending in the United States on aircraft ordered after May 13, 2009, or delivered after May 13, 2010

Remember to take advantage of the pre-boarding privilege, as your assistive device only gets priority space in the designated storage area if you preboard the aircraft. In fact, under the ACAA, if crew members have their gear stored in the priority storage space, they are required to move it. Same goes for other passengers. Again, this only applies if you preboard, so never pass on the opportunity.

Additionally, remember that the priority storage space can only accommodate one wheelchair, so if happen to be on a flight with another wheeler, one wheelchair will end up in the cargo bin. It never hurts to be first in line to preboard.

Although priority storage space is mandated under the ACAA, the Department of Transportation (DOT) has granted some exemptions, and allows some airlines to strap the wheelchairs to empty seats. This is usually done because of the configuration of the aircraft; although rare, you may see it done. Under the ACAA, U.S. airlines may not use the seat strapping method on aircraft ordered after May 13, 2009, or delivered after May 13, 2011.

As you can see, it's very important to learn the rules of the ACAA as they apply to onboard wheelchair storage. Don't be afraid to speak up when you feel your rights have been violated. Front-line employees don't always know or understand the rules under the ACAA, so sometimes you have to go up a few levels in order to get results.

Of course if you can't keep your wheelchair out of the cargo bin, it's a good idea to travel with an older wheelchair (if you have one). Some people travel with an old backup wheelchair. Another good solution is to rent a wheelchair or scooter at your destination. Obviously this option only works for people who use a wheelchair or scooter for distance, but it is something to consider.

POWER WHEELCHAIRS AND SCOOTERS

Most power wheelchairs and scooters must be carried in the baggage compartment, except for some small lightweight folding models. Again, this depends on the aircraft size and the availability of onboard storage space. The bet is to purchase a model that will fit in the priority storage space. The down side to this is that many of the compact travel scooters have plastic parts and they don't fare too well in the baggage compartment.

Full-sized scooters and power wheelchairs routinely go into the cargo bin, but the rules and regulations differ depending on the battery type of the assistive device. Those that have non-spillable (gel cell) batteries do not need to have the batteries removed and packaged separately. Furthermore, the ACAA prohibits airlines from disconnecting the cables and wrapping the terminals on non-spillable batteries, unless the FAA or the Pipeline and Hazardous Materials Administration (PHMSA) or foreign government safety regulations require them to do so. Currently no U.S. regulations require this, so these batteries should not be disconnected.

On the other hand, if your wheelchair has a spillable battery, in most cases the entire battery is removed and packed in a protective container. The one exception is if the wheelchair can be loaded, stored, secured, and unloaded in an upright position. This is usually dependant on the aircraft type, as some chairs have to be tilted or turned in order to fit through the cargo door. It's best to just assume your battery will be removed.

If you travel with an assistive device with spillable batteries you are required to give the airline 48-hours notice and check in one hour prior to the standard check-in time. This means you'll have to use an airport wheelchair for at least two hours, perhaps longer. You might want to consider changing to non-spillable batteries if they are compatible with your wheelchair. This simple change will save you a lot of time and trouble.

It's also important to remember that the airlines will not transport damaged or leaking batteries, so make sure your equipment is in good repair before you head to the airport. Additionally, the airlines will remove and package any battery that is inadequately secured to a wheelchair or scooter. And finally, lithium batteries may not be permitted under the hazardous materials rules. It depends on the lithium content of the battery, so check with the airline before you book your flight.

You will be asked about the specifics of your batteries when you check in for your flight. If you have non-spillable batteries, ensure they are clearly marked so they won't be inadvertently removed. If you don't have any labeling on your batteries, check with a local medical supply house as they usually carry labels that are appropriate.

You should also learn how to reconnect your batteries. Although your assistive device is supposed to be returned to you with the batteries reconnected, sometimes this just doesn't happen. Knowing how to reconnect your batteries will save you time and frustration. Even if you are physically unable to reconnect them yourself, you can always direct someone else to do this. In the end, it may save your wheelchair or scooter from further damage.

EXCESS BAGGAGE OR ASSISTIVE DEVICE?

With the airlines tightening their belts these days, most carriers now charge extra for just about everything, including checked baggage. So if your wheelchair or scooter has to be carried in the cargo bin, can the airlines charge you for it?

Well, although the ACAA doesn't specifically prohibit charging passengers for the transport of assistive devices, it does prohibit them charging passengers for accommodations required under the rule. And since the ACAA states that the airlines must accept wheelchairs and other assistive devices, the airlines are not allowed to charge for this required accommodation. Nor can they charge for wheelchair assistance at the airport or for the use of the aisle chair.

And if they ever start to charge for carry-on bags, they can't charge for assistive devices stowed in the cabin either.

But what about things like medical supplies, commode chairs, or even shower chairs? Under the ACAA, an assistive device is defined as any piece of equipment that assists a passenger with a disability to cope with the effects of his or her disability. These devices are intended to assist a passenger to maneuver or perform functions of daily life and may include medical devices and medications. So under that definition, it seems that medical supplies, commode chairs, and shower chairs qualify as assistive devices, and thus are required to be transported free of charge.

On the other hand, items like handcycles or adaptive skiing equipment may be classified as recreational equipment instead of assistive devices and subject to baggage charges.

But like everything else, check with your airline in advance just so there are no misunderstandings or surprises at the check-in counter.

And again, this applies to all flights on U.S. air carriers, and flights beginning or ending in the United States on non-U.S. air carriers.

Ironically, Jet2, a budget British carrier, considers prosthetic devices baggage, but will transport wheelchairs free of charge. Although the European Union Passengers with Reduced Mobility (EU PRM) regulations requires EU-based airlines to carry up to two pieces of mobility equipment free of charge, the regulations don't define the term "mobility equipment." Ultimately that determination is left to the airlines, so be aware that you may find some inconsistency throughout Europe. What may be considered an assistive device in the United States may be considered excess baggage across the Big Pond.

SOME DISASSEMBLY REQUIRED?

Many wheelchairs can be transported in the cargo bin without being disassembled, but that of course also depends on the aircraft type. Here's where knowing the dimensions of the aircraft, especially the width of the cargo door, comes in handy. For example let's compare two aircraft: the EMB 145 which has 50 seats and the ATR 42-500 which has 46 seats.

Although both aircraft have approximately the same passenger capacity, the dimensions of their cargo doors vary drastically. The EMB 145 has a 39-inch cargo door while the ATR 42-500 has a 54-inch cargo door. So the EMB 145 might not be the ideal choice for a large wheelchair.

Even if your only choice was the EMB 145, it would help to know in advance that your wheelchair was going to be disassembled for transport. This knowledge also gives you the flexibility to shop around and perhaps find a larger aircraft. Sometimes this is the best bet, even if you have to drive to another gateway city.

PROTECTION

One of the best things you can do to protect your assistive device is to attach clear assembly and disassembly instructions to your wheelchair or scooter. In fact, the ACAA requires the airlines to allow passengers to submit these instructions and mandates that they follow them to the greatest extent possible.

Instructions should be written clearly and simply in both English and Spanish. If possible, also use numbered illustrations or simple drawings to illustrate the assembly and disassembly procedures. Laminate the instructions and attach them securely to your assistive device. Clear assembly and disassembly instructions will help protect your assistive device. Many people leave these instructions attached to their wheelchair or scooter all the time: it saves preparation time when it's readying for travel.

Remove any loose or protruding parts from your wheelchair or scooter. This includes items like mirrors, cushions, and leg rests. Put them in a duffel bag and carry them on the aircraft. Do not check them! Wheelchair parts fall under the category of assistive devices and are not counted as carry-on luggage.

Remember, something may be piled on top of your wheelchair in the cargo bin. If your wheelchair or scooter becomes a projectile object, loose or protruding parts may break upon impact. Additionally, remember to let a bit of air out of your tires and to carry on all gel cushions. Most cargo bins are not pressurized. It's also a good idea to carry a compact bicycle pump with you so you can reinflate your tires when you reach your destination.

You will also need to protect your joystick if it's not possible to easily remove it. A plastic cup and packing tape works well for this purpose.

It's equally important to protect your controller. Says one frequent traveler, "I discovered that the very sturdy cardboard tubes that carpets are rolled on makes a great controller protective device. I scrounged an empty tube (some places call them cores) from the carpet store, then used a hacksaw to cut off the right length to slide over my controller. It works great."

Says another traveler, "My controller unplugs easily so I just take it off (along with the entire armrest), stuff it in a duffel bag and carry it on with me."

And one veteran road warrior swears by his tried and true method. "I carry a spare joystick and controller when I travel," he says. "This is easy to do with an Invacare chair because all of the parts swap out. I stick some Velcro to the bottom of the spare controller. If I break down I just peel and stick my spare controller to the top of the battery box, disconnect the wires from the busted one and connect them to my backup. I do the same thing with my joystick."

Many people come up with creative ways to protect their wheelchairs during transit. My friend Karen devised the following cheap and easy technique. "I travel fairly often and use an electric wheelchair," she says. "I carry on all removable parts and wrap the entire base of the chair with plastic cling wrap. This helps prevent scratches and dings. It also encapsulates the wires so nothing gets unplugged." I like Karen's method. It's simple, and the only out-of-pocket expense is for a roll or two of plastic cling wrap.

Says frequent-flyer Mike, "I've found that bubble wrap (which you can buy at an office supply store) works well in protecting my wheelchair from damage. I just take some to the airport with me and then before I turn my wheelchair over to the airline I pad the areas most likely to sustain damage. I also take some tape with me so I can secure the bubble wrap. So far, it works pretty good."

Other travelers go a bit further (and spend a bit more money) in their quest to limit wheelchair damage. In fact, Gloria even went so far as to build her own transport crate. "I was tired of the airlines damaging my son's wheelchair, so I had a crate building company build a protective container for transport," she says. "They built a crate that has four locking caster wheels, handles and a side door with a moveable ramp. All the major airlines have accepted the crate so far, although I do have to make advance arrangements for it. Now the crate comes back beat up but the wheelchair remains undamaged."

Gloria is on the right track; in fact, there is even a company that sells protective containers for wheelchair air transport. The Haseltine Corporation manufactures and sells such protective containers, which are constructed out of rigid molded plastic. There are two models of the Haseltine Flyer, one for folding manual wheelchairs and another for power wheelchairs and scooters.

Model 504-A is designed for folding wheelchairs and consists of a polyethylene container with foam padding and internal straps to hold accessories in place. It is also available with wheels. The larger 504-C model is designed for rigid motorized chairs and scooters.

The Haseltine Flyers are priced from $368 to $689, depending on the model.

The Haseltine Corporation manufacturers a variety of protective containers for wheelchair air transport. Pictured here is Model 504 – A for folding wheelchairs.

The downside is that you have to arrange for storage of the container at your destination. Contact your airline in advance for more information on this matter. The Haseltine containers have been tested by several airlines, but thus far no airline has purchased any. On the other hand, travelers are starting to realize the advantages of the Haseltine Flyer and so far they are the primary market. We can only hope that the airlines will one day follow suit.

And finally, remember to take a tool kit of basic tools with you when you travel. It's best to take the bare minimum required to prepare your wheelchair for transport in your carry-on luggage, as others may be confiscated from you at the security checkpoint. Pack a more extensive tool kit in your checked baggage, even duplicating the tools you carry through security. That way, if they get confiscated, you will at least be able to assemble your wheelchair at the other end.

Additionally, a tool kit will enable you to make quick repairs on the road, which will save you time and money. Your tool kit should include items such as a small screwdriver with interchangeable bits, a crescent wrench, a couple of Allen wrenches, a small roll of electrical tape, a few lengths of electrical wire, an assortment of electrical connectors, and a variety of nuts, bolts and washers. Your own tool kit will of course depend on your particular equipment. Additionally, if you use a scooter, don't forget to pack a spare key in your emergency tool kit. You never know when you will need it.

WAITING FOR YOUR WHEELCHAIR

Under the ACAA, the airlines are required to return assistive devices carried in the cargo bin as close as possible to the aircraft door. In airline language this is known as gate checking your wheelchair or scooter. You drop it at your departure gate and pick it up at your arrival gate.

Although the airlines are required to gate check some power wheelchairs and scooters upon request, there is one huge exception to the rule. That exception is whenever it is prohibited by federal regulations governing transportation security. So conceivably in times of high security threat, gate checking assistive deices could be temporarily curtailed. It's not a huge issue, but it's something to keep in mind should the security threat rise.

The ACAA also calls for the timely return of gate-checked assistive devices. In fact, the regulations specify that assistive devices get priority over all other baggage. The airlines must make sure that they are the first items to be retrieved from the baggage compartment to ensure their timely return. This means your wheelchair should be waiting at the gate for you when you disembark.

But that's not always the way it works. I receive a fair number of complaints from travelers who experienced long delays waiting for their gate checked wheelchairs or scooters. In most cases, these people traveled with heavy power wheelchairs. The problem seemed be a product of poor airport design, as the facilities in question didn't have an elevator near the gate. In some cases, rope winches were used to get assistive devices up to the gate area, but such machinery couldn't accommodate heavy power wheelchairs. So airline employees had to take the heavier items all the way out the baggage claim area to use that elevator, and then bring them back out to the gate. As you can imagine, this took a fair amount of time.

Is it right? No. Does it happen? Yes. Just be prepared for the possibility. And if you want to see it happen less, then write a letter of complaint to the DOT. And while you're at it, write a letter to the airline, too, and don't forget to ask for some sort of compensation for your inconvenience.

WHEN PROTECTION ISN'TENOUGH

Sometimes no matter how hard you try, the inevitable happens, and your wheelchair is damaged in transit. Unfortunately it does happen, so you do need to be prepared for it. The first thing you should do is learn what the ACAA says about airline liability for damage to assistive devices.

Under the ACAA, U.S. airlines are responsible for all repairs to damaged devices; however, if the devices are lost or damaged beyond repair, the airlines are only responsible for the original purchase price. For example, if you paid $3,000 for your wheelchair 10 years ago, but it would cost $5,500 to replace it today, you can only expect to recover the original purchase price ($3,000) if your wheelchair is damaged beyond repair. You are responsible for the additional $2,500 it would cost to replace your wheelchair.

Travelers are cautioned to know both the purchase price and the replacement cost of their assistive devices, and to be aware of the difference between these two figures. If the difference is substantial, you may want to carry additional insurance with a high deductible to cover this gap.

Airlines are also required to pay for consequential damages such as wheelchair rentals and unrefundable tickets, tours, or deposits.

The ACAA liability limits only apply to flights within the United States on U.S. airlines. The liability limits on international flights are covered under the Warsaw Convention. They are set at $9.07/lb for checked baggage and $400 for carry-on baggage. Obviously those limits are woefully inadequate for many high-end power wheelchairs and scooters, so it pays to know the value of your equipment before you fly and make sure you have adequate insurance coverage to cover your assistive devices.

It's also important to remember to report any damage to your wheelchair or scooter immediately, ideally before you leave the airport. Admittedly some internal damage is hard to detect immediately, but it is important to report it as soon as you become aware of it. Even though you may be in the middle of a holiday, you need to take the time to file a claim with the airline if you expect to recover your damages. The airline may deny a claim if they feel it is not filed in a timely manner. Additionally, under the ACAA, airlines are not required to respond to complaints that are more than 45 days old.

Again this seems like a very simple task, but it amazes me how many people don't understand the importance of timeliness in such matters. For example, one lady I talked to at a health fair last year told me about some damage done to her scooter on a recent airline flight. When I inquired as to her definition of recent, she matter-of-factly replied, "About eight months ago. Should I file a claim?" Unfortunately this is not an isolated incident. If you had an automobile accident and you waited eight months to report the damage, do you think your insurance company would pay the claim? Most likely they wouldn't. And neither will the airlines. Report all damage (no matter how small it seems) immediately. You can always amend your claim later, if you should find more damage.

Unfortunately, every now and then a wheelchair or scooter is permanently lost. How long do you have to wait before your missing wheelchair is officially declared lost? Carlton Duke waited seven months while United Airlines strung him along—that's way too long.

There are no federal standards that mandate when missing baggage becomes lost forever; however, most airlines consider it permanently lost after it's been missing for 10 days. So I'd say that's a good guideline for assistive devices as well. After that time, tell the airline you'd like your claim settled, and don't let them string you along. And if necessary, speak to a Complaints Resolution Official (CRO).

Finally, no matter how bad things seem (even if your wheelchair is returned to you in pieces), don't panic. I know this is easier said than done, but I would like to illustrate the importance of this point with a story about my friend John. John is a pretty well-seasoned traveler, but every now and then life throws him a few curves.

On a recent trip to the Bahamas, John's wheelchair was returned to him literally in pieces. John relates his humbling experience, "First they brought out the frame, then they kept bringing out smaller and smaller pieces," he says. "I didn't even know my wheelchair had that many pieces. Actually I didn't care about the wheelchair, as I travel with my old backup klunker; but I didn't want to ruin my long-anticipated holiday. I just blew a fuse and started cussing and screaming. I was quite a sight right there in the middle of the airport."

The embarrassing thing was that the baggage handler had my wheelchair back together in about two minutes. Apparently this was standard procedure. I wheeled out with my tail tucked between my legs. On the positive side, I didn't even think about renting a car there. I figured if they could assemble my wheelchair that quickly, they could do wonders stripping a car."

And remember, under the ACAA, the airlines must reassemble all assistive devices and return them to the passenger in the condition that they received them. So if they give you your wheelchair in pieces, or with a disconnected battery, don't let them off the hook. After all, it's their responsibility to reassemble things.

LOANERS

Although your tool kit will allow you to make quick repairs on the road, if your wheelchair is badly damaged you will have to relinquish it while it is being repaired. In the interim you will need an appropriate loaner. But what is an appropriate loaner? That depends on who you ask, as some airline personnel have an interesting definition of "appropriate." It's not that they are trying to pull a fast one: it's just that they really don't understand the difference between your Quickie and their E&J airport wheelchair.

So here's where a little patience comes in. Again, this is easier said than done, especially if you are tired and cranky. In order to advocate for yourself and get what you define as an appropriate loaner wheelchair, you need to calmly explain the facts of life to the airline personnel assigned to help you. You may even have to do this more than once, as you'll probably have to talk to a supervisor or another clerk. No matter how frustrating this is, it's the only way to get a wheelchair that adequately suits your needs.

If you have a highly specialized chair, you might even do some advance research and find an appropriate rental outlet at your destination (just in case). Whatever happens, keep your temper and remember that the airlines are responsible for providing you with an appropriate loaner chair. In other words, if their E&J won't suit your needs, the airline has to foot the bill for an appropriate rental. Keep talking until they get it right.

Finally, if you don't get satisfaction from talking with front-line personnel, ask to speak to the CRO. The CRO will help you get the services you are entitled to, including an appropriate loaner chair.

SHIP, DON'T SCHLEP

If you're tired of schlepping luggage around airports, then consider shipping it to and from your destination. A number of luggage forwarding companies offer this service for a premium price, but if you plan ahead and deal directly with the shipper, you can rack up a substantial savings. In this case the shipper is FedEx, and although they don't advertise a specific luggage shipping service, you can use FedEx Ground to get your suitcase to and from your destination.

Frequent traveler Carroll Driscoll recently used this service to get her suitcase from New Mexico to Connecticut. Says Carroll, "It took four business days and the cost was about $45. As a wheelchair-traveler I usually tip about $10 for a person to push me from the plane to the baggage carousel and retrieve my luggage for me. So, for a little extra money, I don't have to worry about it being lost."

FedEx recommends that luggage be packed inside a cardboard box or a medium FedEx bag, as their airbill pouches do not stick well to fabric. Each piece must weigh under 70 pounds and must not exceed 109 inches in length and 165 inches in length plus girth. FedEx will pick it up at your house if you have a FedEx account, otherwise you need to drop it off at their office. The five-day ground service is the most economical, with a 40-pound suitcase being shipped from California to New York costing $36 for delivery to a business, and $44 for delivery to a residence.

Other Air Travel Issues

BEYOND WHEELCHAIRS

> *"I use therapeutic oxygen. Is it possible for me to travel by air?"*

> *"I need to remain in a reclining position. What are my options for air travel?"*

> *"I use a ventilator and want to travel by air. Is this possible?*
> *What advance arrangements do I need to make?"*
> *"I've never traveled by air with my service animal.*
> *What can I expect? What are my rights?"*
> *"Where can I find an attendant to travel with me?"*

People approach me with questions like these all the time. Admittedly there are no pat answers to these questions; in fact, the answers are usually dependent upon the individual circumstances of the traveler. These topics all fall into what I call the "beyond wheelchairs" category of air travel. In some instances, such as stretcher travel, special medical clearance is required. In other instances, such as travel with a service animal, travelers merely need to learn the rules and regulations so they know what to expect. In all instances, in-depth research is usually required. So let's take a look at some of these special cases.

THERAPEUTIC OXYGEN

Travel with therapeutic oxygen (liquid or compressed gas) is not specifically covered under the Air Carrier Access Act (ACAA); in other words, U.S. airlines are not required to provide therapeutic oxygen services to their passengers. Each airline sets its own policy regarding therapeutic oxygen services, and some airlines don't provide it at all. This exclusion is well within their legal rights, as travel with therapeutic oxygen is considered a safety issue, and as such it is regulated by the Federal Aviation Administration (FAA).

The Department of Transportation (DOT) is currently reviewing their position on therapeutic oxygen, so the regulations could change to require U.S. airlines to provide this service. For now, however, as the airlines are allowed to set their own policies, your only choice is to deal with an airline that provides the therapeutic oxygen services you need. Before you decide which airline to use, call around and ask them about their specific policies and procedures regarding therapeutic oxygen. Procedures and charges vary widely among carriers and can change at any time. Please note that many non-U.S. carriers also accept passengers who use therapeutic oxygen.

Under the ACAA, if an airline chooses to provide therapeutic oxygen services, they usually require 72-hours advance notice for international flights and 48-hours advance notice for domestic flights. They may also require therapeutic oxygen passengers to check in one hour earlier than other passengers.

Although different airlines have different procedures regarding therapeutic oxygen, they all prohibit passengers from using their own equipment onboard. Passengers must use airline-supplied oxygen. There is a charge for this service, and it usually runs between $50 and $150 per flight leg on most U.S. air carriers; however, it may be substantially higher for international routes. A flight leg is defined as the time between one takeoff and one landing, so try and book a non-stop, direct flight whenever possible.

Most insurance policies do not cover in-flight oxygen, so check in advance with your insurance carrier. Even if your insurance carrier does cover in-flight oxygen, the airlines require payment in advance and they won't accept an insurance assignment. You will have to pay the cost up front and seek reimbursement from your insurance company.

All U.S. airlines require a doctor's statement for passengers to travel with therapeutic oxygen. Some airlines require the doctor to fill out specific forms, while others simply ask for a prescription.

When making your travel arrangements, be sure and ask what kind of oxygen equipment is provided. Some airlines provide flow meters that can be adjusted from 2 to 8 liters, while others have flow meters with a low (2 liter) and a high (4 liter) setting.

Ask the airline if you need to bring your own mask or cannula. Some airlines provide them and others don't. It's also a good idea to take some empty tanks with you, so you can have them refilled at your destination.

Airlines will allow you to carry empty tanks, but you must check them with your baggage. You cannot carry them onboard the aircraft with you.

It's extremely important to confirm and re-confirm all airline oxygen arrangements. This letter from a traveler explains what can happen if you don't.

"My husband has emphysema and needs to have oxygen on hand at all times," she writes. "We made arrangements with our travel agent to fly on Air France from Washington, D.C. to Paris. I told the travel agent that my husband would need his own supply of oxygen onboard, and she informed me my husband's doctor would have to contact the Air France physician. This was done.

"When we boarded the plane there was no oxygen at our seat," she continues. "When I questioned the flight attendant, he asked to see my ticket. Several minutes later he informed me that our travel agent failed to follow up and order the oxygen after it was cleared by the Air France physician. We had to reschedule our trip because of this mistake.

"In retrospect I should have followed up with my travel agent," she adds. "I thought it was a bit strange that we were not charged extra for our oxygen, but I just figured somebody forgot to enter the charge."

So be forewarned, if an extra charge for oxygen does not appear on your credit card statement, there is a good chance the oxygen hasn't actually been ordered. It never hurts to follow up, and in many cases it can even save a trip.

You will also need to make arrangements for oxygen services at your destination. Check with the airport to make sure they allow oxygen use in the terminal. Then check with your local oxygen supplier to see if they are affiliated with a national chain that can provide service to you at your destination. You will have to have the oxygen delivered to the airport, as you cannot use the in-flight oxygen in the terminal. Alternatively, you can have a friend or relative meet you at the airport with your oxygen supplies. If you go this route, they will have to make advance arrangements with the airline to get a security checkpoint pass.

The price for airport delivery of oxygen varies; however, since it's a labor-intensive service, it's cheaper during regular business hours. You will pay a premium price for this service on weekends and in the evenings, so try and time your arrival accordingly.

In any case, it never hurts to call more than one supplier to get a competitive price. Many oxygen suppliers will not accept an insurance assignment

OTHER AIR TRAVEL ISSUES for oxygen delivered to the airport, so be prepared to pay cash. You will also have to arrange for airport oxygen at your connecting airport if you cannot arrange a direct flight.

Finding an oxygen provider outside of the United States may be a little more difficult. Oxygen prescriptions written by U.S. doctors are not valid outside of the United States. Check with a foreign oxygen supplier to see if you need a prescription. If you do, sometimes the best bet is to work with a U.S. provider that has contracts with foreign oxygen providers. Your local oxygen supplier should be able to give you some good resources.

A good resource for therapeutic oxygen users is *Breathin' Easy,* a handy guide to oxygen suppliers around the world. Updated monthly, it also includes helpful tips for traveling by air, sea or land with therapeutic oxygen. The *Breathin' Easy* website (www.breathineasy .com) features a list of therapeutic oxygen policies for airlines around the world, which includes advance notice requirements, charges, and flow rates. Airlines that do not permit therapeutic oxygen are also listed. Additionally, you can search their online database to locate an oxygen supplier for your next trip.

PORTABLE OXYGEN CONCENTRATORS (POCs)

Although airlines are not required to provide in-flight therapeutic oxygen, they are required to let passengers bring FAA-approved POCs onboard and to operate them during all phases of air travel. This applies to all U.S. airlines operating flights on aircraft with 19 or more seats. It also applies to foreign carriers operating flights to or from the United States on aircraft with 19 or more seats. In order to be considered an approved POC, the device must bear a label stating that it meets the FAA requirements for medical portable electronic devices. The law also applies to ventilators, respirators, and CPAP machines.

It's the passenger's responsibility to make sure the POC unit is in good working order and free of grease and oil. Additionally, passengers must travel with an adequate supply of batteries in their carry-on luggage to ensure uninterrupted operation of the POC. All batteries must either have recessed terminals or be packaged so that the terminals do not come in contact with metal objects.

Passengers must also give the airlines 48-hours advance notice and check in one hour prior to the general boarding requirements if they intend to travel with a POC, ventilator, or CPAP machine. Check with the airline for their exact procedures and documentation requirements, and follow them to the letter.

VENTILATORS

Although FAA approved ventilators are allowed on covered U.S. and foreign flights, the availability of onboard electricity is also dependent on the aircraft type. Check with your carrier directly to see what flights have onboard power. Always carry a backup battery and charger with you because even if onboard power is available, it can be dependent on the operational needs of the aircraft. Additionally, onboard electrical power is subject to power surges during hookup and disconnection from ground power.

If you can't find a carrier that is able to provide onboard power for your ventilator, you might want to consider traveling under battery power. This option obviously depends on your equipment and on the length of your flight. It's not a possibility for everyone, but it may be worth your consideration.

If you do travel under battery power, take a backup battery and a charger with you on-board the aircraft. That way if you run low on battery power (and happen to be on the ground), you can have somebody get off the plane and recharge one battery for you. This method is especially useful if there is a delay in deplaning. Above all, know the limitations of your equipment and don't plan things too tightly. Always allow for delays when making your calculations.

Make sure your equipment has gel cell batteries and that they are clearly marked. Wet cell (spillable) batteries are not allowed onboard the aircraft. Your equipment must fit under the seat in front of you. If your equip-ment does not fit in this area, you may strap it to an adjoining seat, but you will have to purchase the adjoining seat if you go this route.

While in the terminal, keep your ventilator plugged into a wall receptacle until the last possible moment, so your battery will have a 100 percent charge when you board the aircraft. Also take along a 25 to 50 foot extension cord and an adapter to convert a three-pronged plug into a two-pronged plug. The control panels at the end of most jetbridges have an AC plug, so keep this in mind for emergency situations. Keep an eye open for these AC plugs when you board the plane, just in case there is a lengthy delay in boarding.

Speaking of delays, what do you do if you experience a long delay on the tarmac? Well, firstly, if you give yourself some extra time, you won't have this problem under usual circumstances. But then there are always unusual circumstances, which are either weather or traffic related. So, what do you do if you end up sitting on the tarmac for an hour, or more? Experienced ventusers say the best thing to do is to calmly explain the situation to the flight attendant. You need to stress that it is a matter of life and death, not merely a comfort issue. As silly as this sounds, some people just don't understand the concept of a ventilator. Be patient; and if your efforts fail, ask to speak to the Complaints Resolution Official (CRO) by radio.

Although it's not travel specific, a good resource for vent users is the International Ventilator Users Network (IVUN). An affiliate of Post-Polio Health International, IVUN is a worldwide network of ventilator users and health professionals experienced in and committed to home care and long-term mechanical ventilation. IVUN publishes *Ventilator Assisted Living,* a quarterly newsletter, offering articles on family adjustments, equipment, techniques, medical topics, ethical issues, travel, and resources.

STRETCHERS

Although most people consider stretcher travel a medical necessity rather than a vacation option, it may be the solution if you are not able to sit upright or if you require additional head and neck support. To be clear here, I'm not talking about travel by a private air ambulance, but stretcher travel on a commercial air carrier. Many people don't even know this option is available, and although it's more costly than standard airfare, it's still much cheaper than an air ambulance.

Before you decide to travel by stretcher on a commercial airline, you should first rule out the possibility of first class travel. Although seat comfort varies from carrier to carrier, a first class seat might do the trick. The drawback to a first class seat is that it may not offer enough head and neck support while in the upright position. If it's possible for a travel companion to give you the needed support during takeoff and landing, you can spend the bulk of the flight reclined, in which case, a first class seat will work for you.

Air New Zealand offers a special torso harness to provide additional support while seated, but this must be requested when the flight is booked. Check with your airline to see if they offer this type of equipment. Alternatively you might want to devise your own support device. I've seen some very creative efforts, but most center around a neck pillow and chest straps. Be forewarned, though; if it's too big and mechanical looking, the airlines may disallow it for safety reasons. Think subtle when designing your support system.

If you decide to go the stretcher route, call around to see what airlines offer this service. Some airlines offer only stretcher service on certain routes or aircraft. Under the ACAA, airlines can require a medical certificate for stretcher travel. Stretcher passengers are also required to give at least 48-hours advance notice and check in one hour earlier than other passengers.

Pricing for stretcher travel is dependent upon both the aircraft and the destination. The airlines are allowed to charge extra for this service, as a stretcher takes up many seat spaces. Some airlines charge up to nine times the cost of an unrestricted coach fare for stretcher travel, so it's not an economical option. Additionally, stretcher passengers must also pay for ambulance service to and from the airport, which can significantly add to the cost.

SERVICE ANIMALS

By now, I'm sure you've heard the tale about the two ladies who boarded a US Airways flight with their 350-pound pig in tow. They claimed porky was a service animal, and US Airways employees bought their story and allowed the pig to ride in the first class cabin. Although much confusion surrounds the exact events that transpired during the flight, everybody agrees that the pig defecated on the jetbridge.

So, was the pig a service animal as defined under the ACAA? No, it wasn't. And not because it was a pig, or because it reportedly took four people to wheel it aboard the aircraft. It's not considered a service animal because it did not behave appropriately onboard the aircraft. What is "appropriate behavior"? Well, what it isn't is (as one passenger reported) "running loose through the aircraft, and squealing loudly."

In response to this much-publicized incident, the DOT clarified the regulations about non-standard service animals when the ACAA was revised in 2008. According to that document, airlines are not required to accept unusual or exotic service animals such as miniature horses, pigs, or monkeys if they determine that they are too large or heavy to be safely carried in the cabin, or if they would pose a direct threat to the safety of other passengers. It should also be noted that airlines are never required to accept snakes, other reptiles, ferrets, rodents, or spiders as service animals. Foreign air carriers are only required to accept dogs as service animals, and that only applies to flights to and from the United States.

Under the ACAA, U.S. airlines must allow service animals to accompany any qualified person with a disability onboard the aircraft. This rule only applies to service animals while they are traveling with a person with a disability. For example, if a non-disabled animal trainer needed to transport a service animal by air, the service animal would be subject to the airline's general regulations regarding the carriage of animals. In other words, the service animal would not necessarily have the right to accompany the trainer in the cabin.

Although no advance notice is needed for passengers traveling with a service animal, it is required for those passengers traveling on flights that are expected to last more than eight hours. Additionally, on flights over eight hours, airlines can require documentation that the animal will not need to relieve itself on the flight, or that it can relieve itself in a way that will not create a health or sanitation issue.

Under the ACAA, U.S. air carriers are also required to carry an emotional support or psychiatric service animal if the passenger presents the required documentation. This includes a letter from a mental health professional stating that the passenger has a mental health-related disability. The letter must state that the emotional support animal must accompany the passenger in order to ensure the passenger's mental health or to physically assist the passenger. The letter must be less than one year old and be on letterhead from a mental health professional who is currently treating the passenger. Additionally, 48-hours advance notice is required in order to travel with an emotional support animal. Foreign airlines are not required to carry emotional support animals.

Assuming that a qualified service animal is traveling with a person with a disability, the service animal is allowed to accompany that individual everywhere on the aircraft. People who travel with a service animal are entitled to bulkhead seating if they desire; however, they are not required to sit in the bulkhead section. They may choose a non-bulkhead seat if they prefer. The service animal must not obstruct the aisle or any other area required by FAA safety rules to remain unobstructed. If the service animal cannot be accommodated at the original seat, the airline must allow the passenger to move to another seat where the animal can be accommodated.

Most of the time, service animals have no problems traveling on commercial air carriers. The exception might be on some smaller aircraft where there may not be enough room for the animal to sit at the owner's feet without protruding out into the aisle. If a small aircraft is your only choice, ask for the seating dimensions (before you make your reservations). You can then determine if there is enough room for your service animal to sit at your feet without obstructing an area that must remain clear for emergency evacuation purposes.

Of course it is the owner's responsibility to ensure that their animal acts appropriately while on the aircraft. This is usually not much of a problem, as service animals are trained to act appropriately in public situations. If the service animal exhibits inappropriate behavior such as growling, barking, or running up and down the aisle, the airlines are not required to treat it as a service animal.

Airline personnel are trained to try and mitigate the effects of such behavior. For example, if a service animal barks, they might first suggest a muzzle to try and solve the problem. If mitigation doesn't work, they do have the right to require that the service animal travel in the cargo bin. Generally speaking, however, a properly trained service animal should have no problems traveling on a commercial air carrier.

One subject that comes up a lot when talking about service animals and air travel is damage fees. Are they legal? The ACAA prohibits special charges such as deposits or surcharges for accommodations made for passengers with a disability. However, an airline can charge a passenger with a disability for damage done by a service animal, as long as it's the policy of the airline to charge non-disabled passengers for the same type of damage.

For example, if the airline regularly charges non-disabled passengers for cleaning and repair to damaged seats, they can also charge a person traveling with a service animal for similar damages. Again, a properly trained service animal should have no problems, but it's always a good idea to know your rights.

Of course bathroom facilities are always a matter of concern, and the obvious question is how do you handle this situation while you are en route with your service animal? Under the ACAA, the airline is responsible for working with the airport to provide a relief area for service animals. Foreign carriers are only required to provide this area in terminal facilities for flights to or from the United States.

Another issue of concern to people who travel with a service animal is the whole security screening process. What is the best way to train or prepare your service animal for the wanding procedure at the security check-point? One traveler suggests this method.

"I familiarized Oscar (my service dog) with the screening procedure by using a cordless telephone as a practice wand," she says. "After he was comfortable with it, I got a friend to do it. Then I got several strangers to go through the same procedure until Oscar was totally desensitized to it. When it finally came time for us to go to through airport security, we didn't have any problems at all. Oscar was so used to the procedure, he didn't even bat an eye. He's an old pro at it now."

And finally, be sure to inquire in advance about any restrictions or special procedures for importing animals at your destination. Some countries impose strict quarantines on incoming animals, and most of these quarantines do not exclude service animals.

As of December 11, 2002, the United Kingdom lifted quarantine restrictions on animals that follow the regulations contained in the PETS Travel Scheme. These regulations apply to dogs and cats arriving from specific countries, including the mainland United States and Canada. Under the PETS Travel Scheme, animals must be microchipped, tested and vaccinated for rabies, treated for ticks and tapeworms, have a veterinary certificate, and arrive on an approved air, rail, or sea route in order to bypass the quarantine.

Originally the PETS Travel Scheme also specified that all animals must travel in a sealed crate in the cargo section of the aircraft. In April, 2004, that regulation was amended to allow service animals to accompany their owners in the aircraft cabin, if the individual air carriers chose to modify their practices and procedures regarding service animal transport.

For more information about approved procedures and routes for service animals visit www.defra.gov.uk/animalh/quarantine/index.htm or call the PETS Travel Scheme Help line at +44 870-241-1710.

The United States is not free from restrictions either. Although Hawaii lifted their strict quarantine in 1998 (actually it's a settlement to a lawsuit), Hawaii-bound service animals still face some entry restrictions. The terms of the settlement apply to appropriately trained service dogs entering Hawaii at Honolulu International Airport on Oahu. This is the only port of entry for these animals, so service animals on cruise ships are not covered. The settlement allows these animals to enter Hawaii without quarantine, provided that they adhere to a required program of vaccinations, exams, titers, and microchip identification. For more information on Hawaii's specific procedures for service animals, contact the Animal Quarantine Station in Hawaii at (808)-483-7151 or rabiesfree@hawaii.gov.

The Pets Welcome Database (www.petswelcome.com/milkbone/quarmap.html) is another helpful resource for service animal travel. Even though this on-line database is geared toward traveling with pets, some of the information may also be useful to people with service animals. This worldwide database includes information about a number of animal quarantines, embargoes, restrictions, and policies.

It's important to note that some countries have restrictions on pets but not on working dogs, and the Pets Welcome Database only applies to pets so it's best to use this database only as a general guide. Contact the consulate of your destination country for the most accurate and updated information regarding service animal quarantines and policies.

The National Federation of the Blind also has a good worldwide database of regulations and laws about service animals at www.nfb-na gdu.org/laws/laws.html.

ATTENDANTS

What if you need some assistance with your personal care, transfers, medications, or other activities? Can you still travel? Well the answer is a qualified yes. Generally speaking, if you need help with any of these activities at home, you will also need assistance on the road. It's also important to realize that you may need more assistance when you travel, as you will be outside your familiar environment.

But where can you find someone to help you? The obvious choice is to take your regular personal care attendant (PCA) with you, but that's not always possible. Many PCAs have multiple clients and often can't really afford a week of travel. Additionally you'll have to foot the bill for their travel expenses, and that can add up quickly. Still, I know some people who go this route and it works out very nicely for them. There's something to be said for having a PCA who is trained and familiar with your routine.

Another option is to ask a friend or family member to go with you. Although you'll still have to pay for their travel expenses, they probably won't accept a salary. The downside is that you may not be comfortable with a friend or family member doing your personal care.

If you just require assistance in the morning and the evening, it may be more economical to find care at your destination. Contact a medial staffing agency in your destination city to see if they can meet your needs. It should be noted that some state laws require only RNs to perform certain tasks when hired through an agency, so it may be an expensive proposition. If you do hire someone at your destination, be sure you have a backup plan, in case they are a no-show.

Alternatively, contact the local Center for Independent Living and colleges in the area for private referrals. The former is a good option for getting a personal recommendation while the latter may be a good avenue for finding a nursing student interested in a temporary job. You might also try placing an ad in your local newspaper.

Remember, if you do hire someone to travel with you, it's best to try and spend a the day together first, just to make you are compatible. Although someone may do a good job attending to your needs, a personality conflict could ruin the whole trip.

Some tour operators can also provide attendants, but expect to pay extra for this service. In most cases, they provide RNs even for basic care. If you go this route, make sure the attendants are licensed and insured. There are also a handful of travel companion services around; however, exercise caution when dealing with these companies, as many are not licensed or insured. It's a real tough market and they tend to close up shop quickly, so be very wary when dealing with them. You don't want to end up stranded if they shut their doors.

As far as sleeping arrangements, if you'd prefer your own room, consider booking a suite instead of two adjoining rooms. Many one-bedroom suites include a fold-out sofa bed in the living area, and they are usually cheaper than two separate rooms. It's a good way to retain your privacy and save money at the same time.

One traveler came up with a creative PCA solution for her cruise. She posted a note on a cruise message board and asked if anyone on her sailing wanted to share her PCA. She found two other passengers who needed assistance and they were able to split the expense three ways.

Last but not least, consider staying at a barrier-free resort that is able to provide attendant services. They are few and far between, but places like Freedom Shores (**951-801-2716;** www.isla-aguada.com) not only provide accessible facilities and airport transportation, for an extra charge they can also arrange for a local PCA. It's a truly all-inclusive vacation choice.

Getting Around on the Ground

SEAMLESS TRAVEL

Accessible ground transportation is an important components of any trip because without it, you can literally fall flat on your face. You can also be stuck at the airport, trapped at your hotel, or segregated and separated from the rest of your party. The availability of accessible ground transportation can literally make or break a trip. It's also one of the major components of "seamless travel".

Seamless travel is defined as "travel without any gaps in accessible services or facilities." Quite simply it means you can get from the airport, train, or bus station to your accessible accommodations. And it means that once you get there, you won't have to sit in your hotel room because the tourist attractions or public facilities are not accessible. If you're talking about cruises, seamless travel means that cruise ships, as well as shore excursions and transfers, should all be accessible. Obviously we have a long way to go in making seamless travel a reality; I believe, however, it's a very reachable goal.

Until seamless travel becomes a reality, it pays to thoroughly investigate your accessible ground transportation options before you leave home. This will not only save you a lot of time and trouble, but in some cases it will also save you money.

AIRPORT TRANSPORTATION

Since many people travel by air, finding accessible airport transportation is a top priority. Your options vary depending on your destination and, in most cases, even on your arrival time. There is some advance research you can do, but it's not a foolproof system. The best advice I can give you is to do your research, know your options, and make advance arrangements whenever possible; however, be prepared for unexpected delays.

If you are staying at a hotel, find out if they offer courtesy airport transportation. Under the Americans with Disabilities Act (ADA), hotels that offer courtesy transportation must also provide accessible transportation free of charge. The catch is that most front desk personnel don't know this fact, so you have to know your rights and learn how to advocate for yourself. I shudder to think how many people are charged for this service because they don't know that it must be provided free of charge.

In fact that's exactly what (almost) happened to my friend Dana.

When Dana first made her hotel reservation she inquired about airport transfers. The clerk told her that they did have a courtesy shuttle but it wasn't accessible. Before Dana had a chance to express her disappointment, the clerk chimed in and said he could make arrangements for her with a local accessible transportation company. Dana was relieved that somebody else could take care of the details. The clerk called her back later and told her that everything had been arranged and even gave her a confirmation number. He also told Dana that it would cost $25.

This seemed fine to Dana until I told her that legally the hotel could not charge her for this service. She immediately called the manager and registered a complaint. The manager apologized profusely, and told her that of course there would be no charge for her airport transfers.

Remember, if a property offers free airport transfers, they must also provide accessible airport transfers at no charge. Additionally, they cannot charge guests for this service, even if they have to contract it out. Don't let hotels off the hook on this issue; if you run into problems (like Dana did), ask to speak to the manager. Management is usually well educated on ADA matters.

Many cab companies now have at least some accessible vehicles in their fleet. If you are staying at a hotel you may be able to glean a little information about the local cab companies from the desk clerk. Call the companies directly and ask if they operate any accessible vehicles. If not, ask if they know of any local companies that do have accessible vehicles.

Be sure and specify your needs when talking to a cab company. Some cab companies operate ramp-equipped vans, while others consider a cab with a large trunk an accessible vehicle. If you can travel with a folding wheelchair, it greatly increases your accessible ground transportation options. If this is the case, you can use a standard taxi as long as your wheelchair fits in the trunk. It's also a good idea to carry a transfer board with you.

You may be able to make advance arrangements for an accessible cab. This policy varies, and most companies only accept reservations 24 to 48 hours in advance.

If a cab won't suit your needs, find out if there are any airport transportation companies that serve the area. Some of these companies also have accessible vehicles but the service varies from company to company. The good news about airport transportation companies is that you can always book them in advance; the bad news is that sometimes they show up without the accessible vehicle.

Many large cities now have accessible taxis. Pictured here is a ramp-equipped accessible taxi in San Francisco.

My friend John travels with his Hoyer lift and uses airport transportation companies frequently. John reports that there seems to be no consistency in service, as even national companies are locally managed. Sometimes John has a great experience and sometimes it's the pits. The best strategy is to call and reconfirm your reservation at least 24 hours in advance and, of course, remind the company that you need an accessible vehicle.

Super Shuttle is usually a good airport transportation option if it is available in your city. Granted, there were some access problems with this company in the 1990s; however, as the result of a 2002 ADA settlement, Super Shuttle added more accessible vehicles to their fleet. Today you can even make reservations for accessible transportation on their website at www.supershuttle.com. It's important to note that all accessible services require at least 24 hours advance notice.

Of course accessible airport transportation is far from flawless. For example, take Paula and Mike's recent experience at Miami International Airport (MIA). Paula and Mike planned ahead and made reservations with a shuttle company for accessible airport transfers. Upon arrival at MIA, Paula called the company as instructed. She was told a vehicle was on the way. Two hours later Paula and Mike were still waiting.

The problem? Well, it seems the shuttle driver had never driven the accessible vehicle, so he wasn't aware of the extra clearance required for the high-top van. Somehow he managed to wedge the vehicle under a pedestrian overcrossing at MIA. He did manage to extricate the van, but in the interim he also attracted the attention of the police, security guards, and a good number of curious onlookers. Suffice it to say that in this day and age of heightened security, the police took a while to sort out the matter. And, of course, the shuttle company had no other accessible vehicles to dispatch. Three hours after they touched down at MIA, Paula and Mike finally made it to their hotel.

So, what's a traveler to do? Plan ahead and be aware of the weakest link. Always have a back-up plan when accessible transportation is involved. Ask yourself, "What will I do if the transportation is late, or doesn't show up at all?" Never schedule tight connections when accessible ground transportation is involved.

Public transportation is another option, although I tend to shy away from buses. There's nothing worse than riding on a crowded bus after a long plane trip. Plus, buses are at the mercy of traffic, and if you hit it at the wrong time of day, a 15-minute trip can easily turn into a 45-minute ordeal. Find out if there is a local rail or metro station at the airport and whether it stops close to your hotel. Contact the public transportation authority to find out if it is accessible.

Many airports have great metro service. However, If you arrive late at night, I'd stick to private transportation. It's never a good idea to wander around a large city, suitcase in tow, after dark.

One of the big drawbacks of metro systems is that most of the stations are located underground. Access is usually by elevator; however, most elevators are routinely down for maintenance at one time or another. Many transit systems have a hotline you can call for an updated status report on the working (or non-working) elevators. It's a good idea to get this number in advance and then call just before you hop on the metro. It could save you a lot of time and trouble. It's nice to know if the elevators at your destination station are operational before you get on the train.

Finding accessible airport transportation is sometimes just a matter of whittling down your options. Contact the local Convention and Visitors Bureau (CVB) and find out what airport transportation options exist. Then inquire directly with the individual providers to find out if they offer any accessible transportation. Most CVBs don't know a lot about accessibility, but they can usually provide you with a long list of transportation providers.

No matter what type of transportation you choose, it's a good idea to take a cell phone with you when you travel. It comes in handy when you're curbside, waiting for that long-delayed hotel shuttle. It sure beats trekking back to the terminal in search of a phone. Shop around and find a cellular plan that allows you to make long distance calls at no extra charge, and one that doesn't add roaming charges for calls made out of your home area.

PUBLIC TRANSPORTATION

Most people require some form of transportation once they get to their destination, although many travelers rely on public transportation. When choosing your hotel, try and find one that is close to many of the attractions you wish to see. Additionally, remember to pick one that is close to bus and metro stops, as utilizing public transportation will save you money. Of course, you will have to do some pre-trip research to find out what types of accessible public transportation are available.

One of the best resources for accessible transportation is the Project Action Accessible Transportation Database. Created by the Easter Seals Society, this on-line database lists accessible transportation providers throughout the United States, including taxis, buses, hotel shuttles, and airport transportation. There is no charge to access it, and it can be found at www.projectaction.org.

Another great resource is the local Center for Independent Living (CIL). These nationwide centers go by a variety of names, including Independent Living Center (ILC), Resources for Independent Living (RIL), and Independent Living Resources (ILR). The one thing they all have in common is that they provide resources, advocacy, and support for people with disabilities who want to live independently.

The focus of each CIL differs, and some are better than others. Still, accessible public transportation is a big issue for people with disabilities, so many CILs have information on this subject. Many people working in the CILs rely on accessible public transportation themselves, so you may get some helpful first-hand information. Again, it depends on the CIL and in some cases even the contact person, but it can be a valuable resource. I encourage travelers to contact the CIL in their destination city whenever possible.

Lift-equipped trolley cars, like this one in St. Petersburg, are now available in many U.S. cities.

TIRR publishes the most accurate CIL directory through their Independent Living Research Utilization (ILRU) program. They also have an excellent on-line CIL database at www.bcm.ed u/ilru. There is a small charge for the print directory but it's primarily designed for organizations doing bulk mailings. For personal use, the free website database is the best choice.

RENTAL CARS

Admittedly, public transportation is not for everyone. Some people just like the convenience of driving their own vehicle. People that want this convenience can either take their personal vehicle on a road trip or rent a vehicle at their destination. Either way, it's best to investigate the availability and pricing of parking at your destination before you make this decision. In many cities, parking is expensive and pretty much non-existent.

And although most cities in the U.S. honor parking placards from other states, New York City is the exception to this rule. Parking regulations in the Big Apple are pretty confusing, but in most cases you need to have a New York City parking placard in order to take advantage of accessible street parking options. In some cases (off-street lots, for example) out-of-state placards are acceptable; however I've also received numerous complaints from readers who have been towed from those spaces. Generally speaking, in New York City, it's best to leave the placard at home, and leave the driving to someone else.

Most rental car agencies offer a variety of adaptive equipment for rental cars. Depending on the location, 24 to 48 hours notice is required for the installation of hand controls and spinner knobs. Since there are a wide variety of manufacturers of adaptive equipment, there can be a bit of confusion when it comes to getting the proper equipment installed.

A good tip is to take a picture of the adaptive equipment you need, and then fax, mail, or e-mail a photo to the rental car agency. They will then know exactly what you need, and they can give the photo to their mechanic to ensure that the proper device is installed. It's always a good idea to deal directly with the local franchise to make sure that your adaptive equipment request is treated appropriately.

Even a simple request like "hand controls" can cause some confusion. Such was the case with my friend Patty who had driven her own hand control-equipped van for many years. Patty is a bilateral above the knee amputee and she uses either a manual or power wheelchair when she travels. Since she was traveling with her 13-year-old son, she thought it would be a good idea to take her manual wheelchair and rent a sports utility vehicle (SUV) with hand controls. She figured that she could drive the vehicle, while her son could fold up her wheelchair and stow it in the back. Well, in theory it was a great idea, but in practice it didn't work out very well.

When Patty arrived at the rental facility she could not get into the SUV because the hand controls protruded out near the bottom. Her own hand controls protrude out at the top, allowing her easy access. She ended up having to rent a much more expensive van because. In retrospect, she thinks she could have avoided this situation by asking the rental car company to send her a photo of the hand controls, as she clearly knows what styles work for her. She also says that renting the SUV wasn't really a good idea, as there wasn't enough space for her on the driver's side.

There are some limits on what types of services and equipment rental car agencies are required to offer. Title III of the ADA states that rental car companies must remove barriers that prevent people with disabilities from using rental cars whenever doing so is readily achievable. This covers most adaptive equipment like hand controls, and in most cases spinner knobs.

Rental car agencies have long held that some types of mounting hardware used to attach spinner knobs can cause damage to steering wheels. According to the Department of Justice (DOJ), rental car agencies are not required to install spinner knobs if they damage the vehicle. It all boils down to the type of vehicle and mounting hardware, so if you need a spinner knob on a specific vehicle model, make sure and state this at the time you make your reservation. Theoretically, this should give the rental agency time to make alternate arrangements.

Of course the biggest complaint about most rental car agencies is that they do not rent accessible vans at all. Under the ADA, rental car companies are not required to retrofit vehicles by installing hydraulic or other lifts. Moreover, companies who are in the business of renting vehicles are not required to purchase or lease lift-equipped vehicles.

A few car agencies have affiliate agreements with accessible van rental companies, which allow them to provide accessible vans to their customers. The drawback is that these vans are expensive, with the average rental rate topping $100 per day. It never hurts to ask, but remember that rental car agencies are not required to provide accessible vans.

Getting to your rental car from the airport can sometimes be a challenge as well. Although airport locations are required to have accessible shuttle buses, in reality sometimes this just doesn't happen. It's best to inquire directly with the rental location about the availability of accessible shuttles when you make your reservation. Some rental locations are located in the terminal and do not require a shuttle, which is an added bonus for all customers. If, for whatever reason, the rental company cannot provide an accessible shuttle, ask if your rental vehicle can be delivered to you at the terminal.

On the plus side, some companies have even added extra services for their disabled customers. For example, Avis Rent A Car offers customers the option of also renting a lightweight, folding scooter, a power or manual wheelchair, or a heavy-duty scooter with their car rental. This service is available at all Avis locations across the United States.

Some people want to skip the fuss and muss at the rental car counter and take their own hand controls with them when they travel. I have to say that although this method does appear to streamline the process, there are some definite drawbacks. First off, many car rental companies will not let you install your own hand controls. Furthermore, if you have an accident with self-installed hand controls, you won't be covered under most insurance policies.

Even so, some people claim that this is the greatest thing since sliced bread. I can't really endorse this method because it leaves you open for liability in case of an accident, but, if you are going to try it, do remember the following story.

My friend Bob always takes his hand controls with him when he travels. In fact, he's really quite smug about it, bragging all the time about how much money he saves and how he always has the equipment he needs—that is, until his recent trip to London. It seems that Bob forgot that people drive on the "other side of the road" in England. Suffice it to say that his U.S.-hand controls would not work on the British cars. He ended up renting a very expensive accessible van. Bob's not quite so smug any more. Watch out for the same thing in Australia and New Zealand.

Now, a few words about rental vehicles in Europe. Although practices vary from country to country, with a little research you can find a car rental company that will install hand controls for you. It's usually easier to find a car with hand controls than an accessible van. The most updated resource on adapted rental cars in Europe can be found at www.users.act com.co.il/~swfm. It's a private website and includes a lot of Europe resources.

Additionally, don't forget to pack your parking placard if your travel plans include renting a car in Europe. In 1997, the ECMT passed Resolution No. 97/4 on Reciprocal

Recognition of Parking Badges for Persons with Mobility Handicaps. As of January 1, 1999, travelers from associate countries, including the United States and Canada, are also included in this resolution. The resolution requires permit holders to "display a document that shows the international symbol for persons with disabilities, as well as the name of the holder of the document," in order to receive reciprocal parking privileges in ECMT countries.

ADAPTED VANS

Of course another option is to rent a accessible van. For many people this is the only vehicle that meets their needs, while for others it seems a wasted expense. Basically it's just a matter of personal preference and need. However, it's good to know that there are many companies that specialize in renting accessible vans throughout the world.

In the United States, the two major accessible van rental companies are Wheelchair Getaways (www.wheelchairgetaways.com) and Accessible Rental Vans of America (www.accessiblevans.com). Although each franchise is independently owned and operated, they do benefit from a national network.

There are also a number of local companies, and even some smaller franchise operations that span two or three states. Since these tend to change hands more often than the national operations, I've not listed them here. However, I maintain an updated database of them on the Emerging Horizons resource page at www.EmergingHorizons.com.

It should also be noted that some van conversion outlets also offer rental vehicles. Although they don't readily advertise this service, many locations offer a good selection of accessible rental vans at very reasonable prices.

Outside of the United States, it's more difficult to find adapted rental vans, but they are available. Again, some outlets come and go, but here are the URLs of some of the more prominent outlets.

Canada

Freedom Rentals
www.wheelchairvanrentals.com

Jean Legare
www.locationlegare.com

Australia and New Zealand

Disability Hire Vehicles
www.disabilityhire.com.au

Flashcab Rentals
www.flashcabrentals.com.au

Wheel Chair Tours Australia
www.wheeltours.com.au

Wheelaway Van Rentals
www.wheelaway.com.au

Galaxy Autos
www.galaxyautos.co.nz

Europe

Wheelchair Travel (UK)
www.wheelchair-travel.co.uk

Libertrans (France)
www.libertans.com

Ptitcar (France)
www.ptitcar.com/

Lobbes (Netherlands)
www.lobbes.com

Paravan (Germany)
www.Paravan.com

Wheeling Around the Algarve (Portugal)

www.player.pt

Mieauto (Switzerland)
www.mietauto.ch

PARATRANSIT

Although paratransit services are available in many communities across the United States, it's not exactly the ideal option for most travelers. This door-to-door accessible transportation service is used by disabled residents who cannot access their local public transportation systems.

Generally speaking, paratransit fares are comparable to bus fares and the service operates the same hours as public transportation. So what's the big drawback for travelers? Advance reservations are required for all paratransit services and priority is usually given to local residents who need transportation to medical appointments. Sometimes you need to make reservations as far as a week in advance, and delays and cancellations are commonplace. It's not unusual for local residents to wait one or two hours for scheduled pickups, and leisure riders (including those visiting the city) can experience even longer delays. Additionally, most paratransit companies will not provide airport transportation.

So, although some people recommend paratransit as an economical choice for traveling wheelers, it's not really a viable option unless you plan to spend several months at your holiday destination. In that case, check with the paratransit authority well in advance to see what you need to do to get paratransit certification at your destination. Some paratransit authorities have reciprocal arrangements with those in other cities, while others require that you submit a lengthy application. Additionally, some paratransit services plainly state that they cannot provide services to visitors.

TOUR VEHICLES

Although technically not ground transportation, many people use city tours for at least a brief overview of their destination. There are many types of city tours available, and access varies among the different options.

The good news is that as of October, 2002, many bus type tours (those that operate in over-the-road buses) are required to offer an accessible option. Of course there are exceptions to this rule, but according to Department of Transportation regulations, tour operators who use over-the-road buses are required to provide accessible (lift-equipped) transportation upon 48 hours advance notice. Additionally, they cannot charge more for their accessible services.

Of course just because a tour operator owns an accessible vehicle, doesn't necessarily mean they can actually provide accessible transportation. While visiting a Missouri tourist attraction, I flagged down a bus and asked the driver if they had an accessible tour. "Well," he replied, "we used to have accessible tours, but Joe was the only driver trained to operate the accessible bus. After Joe quit, they just parked the bus."

On the other hand, it's nice to know that accessible sightseeing options are expanding. Many cities, including San Diego, St. Petersburg, and Cleveland offer lift-equipped trolley tours. Other cities like San Francisco operate vintage streetcars (the F-Line), but have raised platforms for wheelchair boarding. And some cities like Baltimore even offer lift-equipped city tours in amphibious DUKW vehicles.

Some tour operators are pretty imaginative about making their tours accessible. For example, one innovative Baltimore tour operator does not have any accessible tour vehicles, so she offers wheelchair users the option of using their own vehicles for the tour. Of course this option won't work for everyone, but it's an excellent example of a small business working to make their services more accessible. Don't be afraid to ask about accessible options. You never know what the answer will be.

WHAT ABOUT SEGWAYS?

Although Segway scooters are not technically considered assistive devices, many people with disabilities use them in place of wheelchairs. In fact, some people hold that they are easier to use than wheelchairs, and that they offer more dignity because they put the user at eye level. Obviously, Segways are not an option for everyone but they are gaining popularity with people who can stand but just can't do distances.

And so the debate continues. If you use a Segway as an assistive device, can you take it on public transportation, tours, and inside tourist attractions? Currently the answer is a big maybe. Since there are no regulations designating Segways as assistive devices, you are at the mercy of the local transportation authority, tour operator, or business owner. So, if you use a Segway, it's best to call in advance to see what the rules are, just so there won't be any surprises when you arrive.

Currently the DOJ is considering expanding the definition of "wheelchair" to also include Segways in the new Americans with Disabilities Act Accessibility Guidelines (ADAAG). If this happens, Segways will most likely be permitted every place that other assistive devices are allowed to go. Initial response to this issue indicated a strong support for the change; however, opponents argued that Segways travel too fast and can be a danger to pedestrians, so they should be prohibited in many public places. Suffice it to say that this remains a very controversial issue. Although there is no timeline for the release of the final ADAAG, it's expected that the new version will address the Segway issue. It will probably take many years, however, to sort out the logistics and to issue clear and concise Segway regulations.

For now, it's best to keep in mind that some states have passed laws prohibiting the operation of Segways on sidewalks, bicycle paths, and roads; other states have minimum age requirements or mandatory helmet laws. Additionally, some theme parks like Walt Disney World and Sea World Orlando prohibit them entirely, even if they are used by disabled guests. So again, it's best to research the law and call ahead to find out about any restrictions.

On the other hand, Segway tours are available in many major cities, including Atlanta, Chicago, and Washington, D.C. These narrated tours, which are offered by City Segway Tours (www.citysegwaytours.com), hit the major tourist attractions and allow plenty of time for photo stops. Think of it as a walking tour on a Segway. You need to be able to stand and hang on to the handlebars with both hands in order to use a Segway, but it may be an option for many slow walkers. This tour option is also available in many foreign cities including Paris, Berlin, and Vienna.

RECREATIONAL VEHICLES (RVs)

Although most people don't really consider RVs ground transportation, some people use them for both transportation and lodging. Many RVers consider this lifestyle to be especially conducive to people with disabilities because you don't have to worry about accessible hotels, restaurants, or restrooms. Still, it's not an entirely worry-free existence.

RVers have to worry about accessible campgrounds and facilities, and, of course, they have to choose an RV that meets their needs. Since it's a major expense, many experts advise renting an RV before you purchase one. Unfortunately, accessible rental RVs are hard to find. Because rentals of RVs were so inconsistent, many dealers sold off the accessible vehicles.

Today, the best resource for finding an accessible rental RV is the Handicapped Travel Club (www.handicappedtravelclub.com). The club has over 250 members with the goal to encourage people with disabilities to join the RVing crowd. Many members have converted their own rigs, while others have purchased custom-made rigs. Some members rent out their rigs when not in use, and most members are happy to share resources and information with newbies. Membership is just $8 a year; it's a good investment if you think you might like RVing.

The Handicapped Travel Club has also compiled a database of accessible RV parks (also called campgrounds) across America on their website. The parks are evaluated by members and they are listed by state. Each listing contains a short description along with access details. This database is continually updated, and new parks are added as members visit them and complete access surveys.

ROAD TRIPS

Of course the best way to ensure accessible transportation at your destination is to take your own vehicle with you. Still, there are a few things to consider before you hit the road.

First and foremost, make sure you have emergency road service before you leave home.

Although most towing companies will tow adapted vehicles, very few tow trucks are wheelchair accessible. To avoid being stranded on the highway after your car is towed, check out specialty services such as ADA Nationwide Roadside Assistance, (www.americandriversalli ance.com), that can provide lift-equipped transportation to the garage.

And then there's the restroom issue. Chances are if you take a road trip, you'll have to stop at least once along the way. But where? For the best accessible restrooms, look for newer fast-food restaurants. Most fast food restaurants are consistent in their restroom design, so when you find a restroom that has the access features you need, stick with that fast food chain.

But what if you need an unisex or family restroom? These are harder to find, so it's important to know the law regarding having someone of the opposite sex assist you in a public restroom.

Title III of the ADA prohibits discrimination against individuals with disabilities by places of public accommodation, including restaurants and hotels. The ADA requires public accommo-dations to make "reasonable modifications" to their policies, practices, and procedures so that everyone can enjoy the goods and services they offer. Designating restrooms for separate use by men and women is a policy or practice subject to this "reasonable modification" requirement.

So basically an establishment can't prohibit patrons from having an attendant of the opposite sex assist them in their restroom facilities, but they can ask that patrons wait until the restroom is vacant to protect the privacy of their other patrons. In practice I suggest first checking to see if the restroom is even usable before going through the trouble of waiting or talking to the other patrons. Although this all seems kind of cumbersome, it's nice to know it's an option if you can't locate a family restroom.

It should also be noted that gas stations with mini-marts have the best shot at having a family restroom. It's not foolproof, but if you need gas anyway, it's worth investigating.

Last but not least, Most Flying J truck stops (www.flyingj.com) have accessible shower rooms, complete with roll-in shower, roll-under sink, and toilet with grab bars. There is a charge for using the shower room; however, it's a good emergency alternative if you can't access the shower at your hotel. They also have nice accessible restrooms, which *are* free.

We Will Ride

BUS TRAVEL

Although many people tend to discount over-the-road (OTR) bus transportation as a viable leisure travel option, in reality it's one of the only transportation links to many rural U.S. towns. Indeed, it's also a very economical and (sometimes) flexible way to travel. Additionally, it's a great way to see the country while leaving the driving to somebody else. Today, buses are much more accessible than they were 10 years ago; however, because we still haven't achieved 100 percent accessibility, advance planning is necessary for any bus trip.

THE LAW

Like any other form of travel, it's essential to learn the access rules and regulations about OTR buses so you know what to expect along the way. First, an OTR bus is defined as a bus that has an elevated passenger deck over a baggage compartment. The rule further categorizes OTR bus travel into fixed route service and demand responsive service. A fixed route OTR bus runs along a prescribed route according to a fixed schedule, while a demand responsive OTR bus is one that operates on a charter or tour basis.

Access to all OTR buses was officially mandated in the Americans with Disabilities Act (ADA), however it took an additional seven years to sort out the access regulations. Finally on September 28, 1998, the Access Board published the Americans with Disabilities Act Access Guidelines (ADAAG) for OTR buses.

Under the rule, it's considered discriminatory for any OTR bus company to deny transportation to a person with a disability. Furthermore, it requires all OTR bus companies to provide service in an accessible bus upon 48-hours advance notice. An accessible bus is further defined as one that includes a lift, wheelchair locations, tie-downs, and seat belts. In short, passengers must not be hand-carried on board, and they must be allowed to either stay in their own wheelchair or to transfer to a coach seat.

And although the term wheelchair accessible is often used, the lift is not only meant for wheelchair access. It can also apply to scooters, depending on their size. Although the ADAAG does not mention scooters specifically, it uses the term "common wheelchairs and mobility aids," which applies to most scooters. Under that definition, the mobility aid must not exceed 30 inches in width and 48 inches in length, and must not weigh more than 600 pounds when occupied. So if your scooter falls under those specifications, then you must also be accommodated on an accessible OTR bus with 48 hours notice.

Unfortunately the new rule stopped short of requiring accessible lavatories on board OTR buses; however, it does require OTR bus companies to provide boarding assistance to passengers with disabilities at rest stops. Adequate time must also be allocated for disabled passengers to use the restroom facilities. This rule applies at all stops that are at least 15 minutes long. So if you need to use the facilities at a rest stop, be sure to inform the driver.

One of the best provisions in the OTR ADAAG addresses the future. Large OTR fixed route bus companies (those that have gross annual transportation revenues equal to or exceeding $8.1 million) must make 100 percent of their fleets accessible by 2012. Although there's no timeline for full accessibility for smaller OTR fixed-route bus companies, they are required to provide accessible service with 48-hours notices until their fleets are fully accessible. In the interim, these smaller fixed-route OTR bus companies may alternatively provide equivalent service, such as transportation in an accessible van, if it is not possible to accommodate passengers on a lift-equipped bus. Large, fixed-route OTR bus companies and companies that operate demand responsive OTR bus services are not allowed to provide equivalent service. They must accommodate passengers on lift-equipped buses whenever adequate notice is given.

COMPENSATION FOR DENIEDBOARDING

The OTR ADAAG was very controversial when it was first released; in fact, it was opposed by many folks in the bus industry. To that end, the American Bus Association sought legal intervention to overturn the OTR ADAAG after it went into effect. The case was originally heard in Washington, D.C. District Court (*American Bus Association, Inc. v. Rodney E. Slater*), and was later appealed in Federal Appeals Court. The initial decision upheld the rule in its entirety, but on November 14, 2000, the appellate court ruled to delete Section 37.199 of the rule.

The deleted section required monetary compensation ($300 to $700 per occurrence) for the denial of accessible services on OTR buses. On March 8, 2001, the Department of Transportation amended the final OTR ADAAG to reflect this change. It should be noted that this change does not affect accessibility requirements for OTR buses, nor does it prevent people from seeking judicial remedies under the ADA.

So what does this mean to consumers? In simple terms, it means that if you are denied boarding because of the unavailability of an accessible bus, the bus company is only legally required to refund your fare. Customers are not entitled to any other expenses or damages resulting from the denied boarding. You can, of course, file a complaint with the Department of Justice; however, that won't result in any personal compensation. For example, there's no further recourse available to this reader's daughter.

"My daughter and her boyfriend purchased tickets to travel home to visit us on Greyhound last Christmas. She uses a wheelchair and informed Greyhound two weeks in advance that she needed a lift-equipped bus. When the time came to board, a lift-equipped bus was not available and she was not able to make the trip. Her Christmas was ruined. She lives on a fixed income and it took her quite some time to save the money for this trip. Surely Greyhound can be held financially liable for her disappointment, can't they?"

Unfortunately, the answer is no. That's the part of the OTR ADAAG that was repealed. The bus company is only required to refund the unused ticket. That's it. Under the law, they are not required to provide any other monetary compensation for denied boarding.

GREYHOUND

Greyhound is the major large fixed route OTR provider in the United States, and although it's been a rocky road over the years, access has greatly improved on this line. Today, they have a dedicated Customers with Disabilities Travel Assistance Line (800–752-4841) where passengers may call for information about accessible services and to reserve an accessible bus.

Reservations must be made at least 48 hours in advance for lift-equipped buses; however, Greyhound will make every reasonable effort to accommodate passengers who do not make advance arrangements. In other words, they will do whatever they can if you just show up, but if you want a guaranteed seat you must call 48 hours ahead, especially around holidays and during peak travel periods.

Greyhound also provides a 50 percent discount to personal care attendants (PCAs) traveling with a disabled passenger. Under this voluntary program, you must provide the name of your PCA when you make your reservation, and this must be done at least 24 hours in advance (48 hours if you require a lift-equipped bus). The PCA must be at least 12 years old and capable of providing assistance to the passenger. Additionally, the PCA must travel the entire trip with the passenger. PCAs are not required as a condition of travel; however, Greyhound employees cannot provide personal assistance to passengers.

Although passengers can travel safely in their own wheelchairs, it's a good idea to also know the liability limitations for damage to assistive devices carried as baggage. Greyhound's liability for damage to anything carried in the baggage compartment is only $250 per item. This includes wheelchairs and other assistive devices.

This pittance won't go very far if there is any substantial damage to your assistive device, so be sure you have adequate insurance coverage. Check your existing insurance policies first to see if you are covered, then ask your insurance agent about low-cost options for additional coverage. In the long run, it's better to be safe than sorry.

Additionally, the maximum dimensions of any item carried in the baggage compartment is 33 inches x 33 inches x 48 inches, and the maximum weight is 200 pounds. Assistive devices that exceed these limits will not be accepted.

On the plus side, Greyhound's service to disabled passengers has greatly improved over the years. Gone are the days of hand-carrying (and dropping) wheelchair users aboard. And although lapses in accessible services do occur, more lift-equipped buses are available today than they were 10 years ago. And with the entire fleet required to be accessible by 2012, the access outlook for the future is excellent.

SMALL BUS COMPANIES

Of course Greyhound is not the only player in town when it comes to fixed route intercity bus service. In fact, there are a lot of small regional operators who only serve one or two states, or just a region within a state. Still, they're all required to provide accessible services, given 48 hours notice.

Although many small OTR fixed-route bus companies have lift-equipped buses, under the law they are also permitted to provide equivalent transportation in another accessible vehicle if a lift-equipped bus is not available. It's important to note, though, that even though this equivalent accommodation is allowed until their fleets are fully accessible, hand-carrying passengers aboard is never considered appropriate, or even legal. Whether dealing with a large or small bus system, you still have the right to stay in your own wheelchair for the entire trip.

On the plus side, many smaller bus companies provide excellent service. Two worth noting—Megabus and BoltBus—even manage to provide low cost fares to and from major cities in accessible vehicles.

Megabus features low cost fares from Chicago and New York to a number of Midwest and Northeast cities including Cleveland, Indianapolis, Milwaukee, Philadelphia, Baltimore, and Boston. And believe it or not, fares can be had for as little as $1 (plus a 50-cents reservation fee). Sounds too good to be true? Well it isn't, but the key is booking early. To keep their fares down, Megabus doesn't own any terminals and picks up passengers at public bus stops. Additionally, most tickets (except those for passengers who require an accessible bus) are booked on-line. All this lowers operating costs so Megabus is able to offer some very affordable rates.

Megabus does a good job at accommodating slow walkers and wheelchair users, too. Wheelchair users who are able to climb up the bus steps and sit in a regular passenger seat can make their reservations at megabus.com ; those that require a lift-equipped bus must call Megabus (877–462-6342) at least 48 hours in advance to request accessible services. For the best fares, try and book at least 40 days in advance. The $1 fares are available on every route, but once the bus starts to fill up, the fares also increase.

And if you're looking for affordable and accessible express transportation between New York City and Washington, D.C., Boston, or Philadelphia, then look no further than BoltBus. Like Megabus, BoltBus doesn't maintain any terminals or ticket offices and their ticket prices are based on the number of seats available.

All BoltBus vehicles are lift-equipped, and wheelchair passengers simply need to check the "wheelchair-user" box in the special needs section when booking on-line. Reservations for accessible services must be made at least 48 hours in advance. For more information on stop locations, fare prices, and schedules, visit www.boltbus.com.

CHARTER AND TOUR COMPANIES

The OTR ADAAG also applies to charter and tour companies, sometimes referred to as demand responsive OTR bus services. This is great news as it really opens up travel opportunities for wheelchair users and slow walkers. As of October, 2002, all tour operators are required to provide lift-equipped buses upon 48-hours notice on all tours operated in OTR buses.

It's important to note that tour company reservation deadlines still apply. For example, if a tour company requires 30-days advance reservations, then accessible reservations must also be made 30 days in advance.

Additionally, tour operators are not required to displace other passengers in order to accommodate a disabled passenger. For example, if a tour operator only had one seat left on the bus, the operator wouldn't be required to accommodate a wheelchair user who couldn't transfer, as one wheelchair takes up the space of six seats. Since only one seat was open, the tour operator would not be required to displace five other passengers in order to create enough space for the wheelchair user.

By the same token, if a slow walker who only required lift access wanted to book space on the same tour, the tour operator would be required to provide a lift-equipped bus, provided 48-hours notice was given. In this case, the slow walker would only take up one seat.

In the end, the key to getting the service you need is booking early—in most cases, well ahead of the 48-hour minimum time required by the law. Remember, many popular tours fill up fast, so book as early as possible for the best availability.

It should also be noted that charter and tour operators are not permitted to make equivalent access arrangements for wheelchair users. In other words, they cannot provide accessible transportation in a separate van. The rationale behind this decision is that on tours and charters, being part of the group is essential to the total tour experience, so everyone must be accommodated in the same vehicle. Additionally, under the ADA, services must be provided in the most integrated environment. In this case "most integrated" means on the same bus. So, the bottom line is, if a reservation is made in a timely manner, the tour operator must provide a lift-equipped bus. Substitutes are not allowed.

This part of the OTR ADAAG applies to all tours operated in OTR buses—from one-day gambling excursions to week-long package tours. In the long run, it will make tours and travel more accessible. In the short run, people with disabilities will most likely have to become skilled at self-advocacy in order to get the accessible services required under the law. In the end, the most effective plan of action is to learn the law, and then speak up for your rights.

All Aboard

TRAIN TRAVEL

Train travel is much more than just a mode of transportation. Throughout time, "riding the rails" has been portrayed as an exciting and romantic way to travel. Whether you choose the Orient Express or the Northeast Express, there are many advantages to train travel. It's a great way to enjoy the countryside in relative comfort, and if you travel on a rail pass, it's also very economical. As with everything else, train accessibility varies throughout the world. With that in mind, let's take a look at some of the major rail systems throughout the world, and see how they stack up access-wise.

UNITED STATES

Amtrak (800–872-7245; www.amtrak.com), the U.S. passenger rail carrier, operates routes throughout the country and into a few portions of Canada. Access varies depending on the route and the train, but all Amtrak trains have at least one accessible coach car. Amtrak passengers can either travel in their own wheelchair or opt to transfer to a coach seat.

Boarding options vary depending on the train and the station, but all Amtrak stations offer at least one accessible boarding option. Some stations have raised platforms and wheelchair users can roll right on to the train. Be careful at stations with raised platforms; often there is a substantial gap between the train and the platform. Many stations have bridge plates that can be put down to eliminate this problem, so be sure and ask about this option.

There are many boarding options for stations without raised platforms. Some trains have onboard wheelchair ramps or wheelchair lifts, and most stations also have manual lifts. So, even if there is a mechanical failure of the onboard lift, the manual lift at the station can be used in an emergency. At some stations, manual lifts are the only option for boarding wheelchair users.

All wheelchair spaces, seats, and even some special cars are supposedly for the exclusive use of people with disabilities and their travel companions. In reality, Amtrak employees selectively enforce this priority seating policy. I've seen conductors tell able-bodied passengers they had to move because the seats were reserved for people with disabilities, but I've also seen employees treat wheelchair spaces as overflow baggage storage compartments. Again, it depends on the employee, the train, and the route.

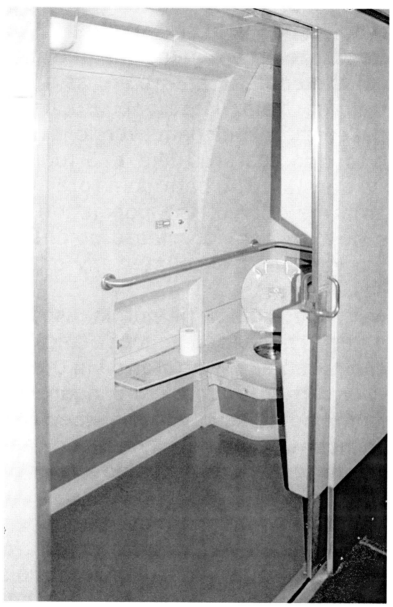

Accessible bathrooms vary from train to train. Here's one on Amtrak's Northeast Direct train.

Many trains have accessible bathrooms, but the configuration varies depending on the train. Be sure to inquire about bathroom accessibility when you make your reservation. Don't be afraid to ask for the dimensions and measurements of the onboard bathroom, as size varies from train to train. Most onboard bathrooms are smaller than their land versions, so don't expect to find features like a 5-foot turning radius in the stall. The bathrooms are accessible to a large majority of the population, but it's always best to ask for measurements in advance so you won't encounter any unexpected surprises.

Power wheelchairs (if not in use) can be carried as checked baggage and manual wheelchairs can either be stowed in the passenger car, or carried as checked baggage. Amtrak can accommodate scooters and wheelchairs up to 30 inches wide by 48 inches long, and with a maximum passenger-occupied weight of 600 pounds.

Advance reservations must be made for all wheelchair seats, even on unreserved trains. A 15 percent discount is available to disabled passengers, but the reservation must be made by phone or in person. The discount is not available with on-line booking. You must also provide written documentation of your disability in order to receive the discount.

Wheelchair access is also available on Amtrak Thruway buses.

Amtrak offers two types of accessible sleeping accommodations: the Superliner and the Viewliner accessible bedrooms. The Superliner accessible bedroom has two berths and accessible bathroom, and it takes up the entire width of the car. The accessible bathroom has a privacy curtain, grab bars, and a 5-foot turning radius. The whole compartment measures 9-feet 5-inches by 6-feet 6-inches.

The Viewliner accessible bedroom can accommodate three passengers, but it's more comfortable with only two passengers. It measures 7-feet 1-inch by 6-feet 8-inches and features two berths, sofa, and accessible bathroom.

There is one accessible bedroom in each sleeping car, and the availability and type depends on the route. Advance reservations are a must, as these accessible bedrooms go fast. Under a 1998 Department of Justice (DOJ) settlement, only passengers with a mobility disability can reserve an accessible bedroom up until 14 days prior to the departure date from the train's city of origin.

Amtrak employees will assist you in a variety of ways during your journey, including the delivery of your food to your seat or bedroom. Amtrak employees will also assist you with reasonable food preparation tasks, such as opening packages and cutting meat. On some long-distance routes, wheelchair users may opt to transfer to and from the lounge cars at appropriate stops and assistance is available upon request. Additionally, onboard staff will help you board and leave the train, and assist you in reaching the accessible bathroom.

Passengers may carry therapeutic oxygen on Amtrak trains, however there are a few restrictions. Oxygen tanks and associated equipment must not exceed 50 pounds per tank for a two-tank system, or 20 pounds per tank for a six-tank system. One passenger can carry a maximum of two 50-pound tanks or six 20-pound tanks. If your oxygen equipment requires the use of onboard power, you must carry at least a four-hour backup supply of oxygen that does not require the use of onboard power.

For safety reasons, oxygen tanks are not permitted in any cars that have a smoking area, however you can keep them in the enclosed area of a private sleeping room. In this case, you must keep the door closed and refrain from smoking for the duration of the trip. Amtrak requires at least 12-hours advance notice if you intend to travel with therapeutic oxygen.

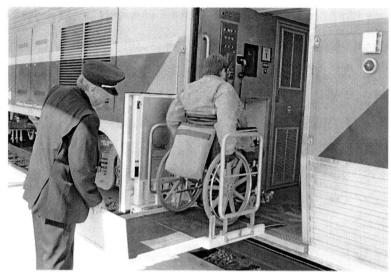

Some trains, like this one on Amtrak's Capitol Corridor route, feature onboard lifts for wheelchair boarding.

Although it's not disability specific, John Pitt's *USA by Rail* presents a good overview of U.S. rail routes. This handy resource, which published by Bradt Travel Guides, lists and describes rail routes throughout America. It's an excellent travel planning tool for any rail trip.

CANADA

With the exception of a few Amtrak routes, rail service in Canada is operated by VIA Rail (888–842-7245; www.viarail.ca), the Canadian national rail carrier. The good news is, all VIA trains are accessible to wheelchair users, but access varies depending on the type of rail car.

Most VIA Rail stations do not have raised boarding platforms, so wheelchair users are boarded either with the use of a station lift or with the help of VIA Rail personnel. On some routes, passengers must provide their own boarding assistance. Contact VIA Rail in advance to find out if boarding assistance is available on a particular route.

VIA Rail uses a Washington Chair to board wheelchair users who cannot stay in their own wheelchairs. This narrow chair has no arms and small wheels and is very similar to the aisle chairs used on airplanes. Wheelers are transferred to the Washington Chair for boarding, and then transferred to their seat. Once on board the train, wheelchair users must use the Washington Chair to move about the train or to use the bathroom. VIA Rail personnel are available to assist passengers with the Washington Chair en route.

The most accessible VIA Rail passenger coaches are the LRC first class coaches. Each first class coach has wheelchair tie-downs and an accessible bathroom. The accessible bathroom has grab bars and a sliding door with an entry width of 35 inches.

Some standard coach cars also come equipped with tie-downs and an accessible bathroom. The major difference between these two types of coach cars is the door width between the cars. On the LRC cars the width is 28.5 inches, while on the standard coach cars it is only 26.5 inches. The standard VIA Rail coach cars come equipped with reduce-a-width tools, which are used to help manual wheelchairs fit through the smaller doorways.

VIA Rail's Renaissance rail cars, which were refurbished and added to the fleet in 2000, feature doorway widths of 27.5 inches. In the 1990s, these cars were used in Europe on the overnight trains between France and England, so even though access features have been added, they are the least accessible cars in the VIA Rail fleet.

In fact, many disability organizations openly opposed the purchase of such inaccessible cars, and the Council of Canadians with a Disability brought the access shortcomings to the attention of the Canadian Transportation Agency (CTA). To that end, the CTA ruled that VIA Rail had to make access modifications to 39 of their Renaissance cars. These modifications included widening the doors and adding wheelchair tie-downs to the accessible suites, modifying the economy washrooms, installing companion seats for the economy class wheelchair tie-down spaces, and adding more moveable armrests to the economy class cars.

Still, because of the age of the cars, some folks claim that these access improvements didn't go far enough. VIA Rail is working to resolve the issue, but it's important to be aware that these rail cars may not work for everyone.

The cars are used on the overnight train between Montreal and Toronto, on all trains between Montreal and Quebec City, and on certain trains between Montreal and Ottawa and Montreal and Halifax.

Folding manual wheelchairs can be stored in VIA Rail coach cars. VIA Rail also accepts wheelchairs as checked baggage, as long as the owner travels by rail in at least one direction. In most cases, power wheelchairs and scooters cannot exceed 150 pounds, be wider than 32 inches, or longer or higher than 72 inches. In some cases VIA Rail will accept power wheelchairs and scooters weighing up to 250 pounds if a lift is available for loading and unloading.

On transcontinental trains, passengers who cannot access the dining car or snack counters may have their meals served in their compartment. Be sure to inform a VIA Rail employee if you require this service.

Passengers who use therapeutic oxygen are allowed to bring their own equipment aboard, but they must give VIA Rail 48-hours advance notice. Passengers can carry one oxygen canister in the passenger car, but it must not exceed 36 inches in length and 6 inches in diameter.

All other canisters must be carried in the baggage compartment. VIA Rail can provide voltage regulators on certain trains, but passengers are required to provide adequate battery backup for their equipment.

Passengers must give VIA Rail 48-hours advance notice if they use a mobility device or need any accessible services. Passengers who cannot attend to their own personal care (eating, personal hygiene, or medical care) can bring along an attendant for free. Proper documentation is required to take advantage of this benefit. Contact VIA Rail directly for details.

UNITED KINGDOM

BritRail, the national rail network of the United Kingdom, is made up of over two dozen regional rail carriers. These regional carriers provide rail service to Scotland, Wales, and England. To compliment this regional service, high-speed Eurostar trains travel under the English Channel to connect the United Kingdom with continental Europe. Under the provisions of the Disability Discrimination Act of 1995, all of these regional rail companies are required to provide service to passengers with disabilities. Of course, access varies from do-able to excellent, depending on the route you choose.

The first step in planning a BritRail trip is to determine where your journey will begin. Although this sounds like simplistic advice, it's really quite useful as the rail company that services your departure station is responsible for access arrangements throughout your entire rail journey. This applies even if you travel on several other regional rail companies throughout your trip.

To find out what rail company serves your departure station, visit the National Rail Enquiries website at www.nationalrail.co.uk. Just type in the station name or location and hit the search button. Not only does the database contain regional rail contact information, it also lists station accessibility details. Alternatively, you can call National Rail Enquiries at +44 20 7278 5240, for this information. Once you have the regional rail information, contact the rail company directly to make access arrangements for your entire trip.

Although some websites claim that you can make access arrangements directly with BritRail, this method doesn't really work in practice, as one wheelchair user explains.

"When I called BritRail here in the United States, none of the agents could answer my questions regarding access, or make the appropriate arrangements for me. In fact they hadn't the foggiest idea of what to do with me, or even where to begin. Unfortunately I got similar results on all my inquires directly to BritRail in the United Kingdom. I got the best results when I dealt directly with the regional rail companies."

BritRail's primary function is to sell rail passes to overseas travelers. These rail passes are good for unlimited train travel over a specific period of time, and they can be a great bargain if you plan to do a lot of train travel. So, plan your route, check out the access, and then calculate your fares. If a rail pass proves to be bargain, then buy it directly from BritRail before you leave home. But don't rely on BritRail for access information, as you will literally be left waiting at the station.

Although access varies from one regional rail company to the next, there are some general guidelines that hold true throughout the system. Generally you will find the best access in the manned stations in the larger cities. Access to the rural stations varies widely, and in some cases wheelchair users even have to be carried up steps. Accessible ground transportation is also more difficult to find in the smaller rural stations.

Remember to ask a lot of questions regarding station access when you make your reservations. The best method is to ask the employee to describe the station access, rather than to just ask if it is accessible. Even if they say the station is accessible, it's always good to follow up with, "How many steps are there?" You'll be surprised at how many times the answer will be something like, "Only two."

The maximum width for wheelchairs on BritRail trains is 26 inches and the maximum length is 47 inches. None of the regional rail companies officially allow scooters, however some lines look the other way when small, lightweight travel scooters are concerned. Be forewarned that you will have to maneuver in some very tight quarters, though. It's best to ask about the prohibition of scooters before you make your reservation, as some regional rail companies are more adamant than others about the "no scooter" rule.

You should confirm your reservation and access arrangements at least 24 hours in advance, and even further ahead in peak travel seasons. And always allow plenty of time for connections.

Eurostar (+44-1233-617-575; www.eurostar.co.uk) service from the United Kingdom to continental Europe is a great deal, as wheelchair users get to ride in first class while paying coach fares. There are designated seating areas for wheelchair users (and their companions) in Eurostar Leisure Select and Business Premier trains. Wheelchair users are allowed to stay in their own chairs in these seating areas. It should be noted that the boarding gangway is 29.5-inches wide, and the accessible toilets have doorways which are 27.5inches wide. Scooters may be carried in the baggage compartment, but they cannot exceed 39 inches in width.

It's great to travel on the Eurostar, as you can be in Paris in just under three hours. Says wheelchair user Mark of his Eurostar experience, "It was a smashing three-hour trip, and even though I didn't get the free meal, I could access the toilet. It's a great deal for wheelers."

EUROPE

European rail travel has long been touted as a very economical way to see the continent. Economy aside, it can also be a very accessible. I do stress "can be," as advance planning is essential. You will, however, be well rewarded for your research efforts, because with proper planning you can choose the most accessible Eurail routes, and avoid taking those not-so-accessible trans-European commuter flights. Additionally, you can save money by purchasing a Eurail pass before you leave home.

Like BritRail, the Eurail network is made up of many regional carriers. These regional carriers are usually country specific, but some long distance trains cross borders. Also included in the Eurail network are some regional ferry and bus routes that connect the train network. So when planning your Eurail vacation, make certain you investigate access on all modes of transportation along your route.

As you can imagine, access varies throughout Europe; however, regional carriers in Finland, France, Germany, Italy, the Netherlands, Spain, Sweden, and Switzerland all officially offer some type of access. Even in those countries, the access varies depending on the route. Remember, your rail travels need not be limited to those countries, as some long-distance trains cross borders.

The best bet is to contact the regional carrier directly. Although there are several outlets that sell rail passes in the United States, these offices have very little knowledge of the true accessibility of the trains. You will need to contact the regional carrier directly to find out the access details.

For example, even though it is possible to travel by rail in Italy, in most cases power wheelchairs can only be carried in baggage cars. So although most rail pass outlets can tell you that Italian trains provide "disabled access," most are unaware of specific access details. Contact rail pass offices for information on rail passes, and contact the regional carriers for detailed access information. It's also important to specify what type of access you require and what type of an assistive device you use when making your inquiry, as some trains can only accommodate manual wheelchairs.

Rail passes are very economical, but it's important to note that there are many different types. Most passes are valid for unlimited travel within a certain time frame. Some passes cover only one country, some cover a combination of countries, and some cover the entire network. Plan your route before you purchase a rail pass, as the economy of a rail pass is directly dependent on your needs.

Although not all trains are officially accessible, some are do-able. It really depends on your ability and attitude. Jack spent several weeks riding the rails in Europe. Jack is in his mid twenties, uses a manual wheelchair, loves to travel, and is in pretty good physical shape. He traveled throughout Europe with his friend Tim. Although he had a great time, he readily admits there were a few "incidents." Here's his recollection of one of the more memorable glitches of his trip.

Rocky Mountaineer Railtours uses this station lift for
wheelchair boarding in Vancouver.

"I had a great time in Europe, although some of the trains I took didn't exactly have roll-on access," recalls Jack. "At several stations, Tim had to pick me up and carry me on the train, and then go back and get my wheelchair. This worked OK, except for one time in Germany when the train left the station before Tim had a chance to load my wheelchair. At the time, I was hysterical. We both just kept shouting *rollstuhl,* which is the German word for wheelchair. I thought I'd never see my Quickie again. It all worked out OK, and eventually I was reunited with my wheelchair, but it was a very stressful situation."

But don't let Jack's *rollstuhl* experience dissuade you from train travel in Europe. Some trains have excellent facilities, and with a little advance planning an accessible journey is indeed possible. Most rail pass offices should be able to give you contact information for the regional rail carriers, where you will get the most updated access information. You can also find this information on the official Eurail website at www.eurail.com.

AUSTRALIA

Rail Australia (+61 8 8213 4592; www.rail australia. com.au) provides support to the international market for the major tourist orientated passenger rail operators in Australia.

These include Queensland Rail, which operates passenger rail service in Queensland; CountryLink, which is based in New South Wales; and the Great Southern Railway, which is based in South Australia.

Access varies depending on the route. Not all trains have wheelchair spaces, so wheelchair users may have to use a boarding chair and then transfer to their seat. The best station access is generally found at the larger city terminals, however, even the Alice Springs station now has a lift.

The XP trains operated by CountryLink are some of the more accessible trains in the country. They operate on the Sydney to Brisbane, Sydney to Melbourne, and Sydney to Dubbo routes. One car per train has a wheelchair space, lock-down straps, and an accessible toilet. These features allow wheelchair users to remain in their own wheelchairs for the duration of the trip. Wheelchairs and scooters must be no wider than 27.5 inches in order to be able to be carried on CountryLink trains.

The other regional rail companies have some accessible trains, but again access varies by route and rail car configuration. Contact Rail Australia for the contact information for the regional rail providers, then contact the rail providers directly for specific access information.

RAIL TOURS

Rail tours are another train travel option but, to be honest, many of them are not accessible. Most of these tours are operated by private tour companies and many are operated in historic rail cars. The latter makes access difficult; however, the historic Grand Canyon Railway (800–843-8724; www.thetrain. com) is the exception to that rule.

With daily departures from Williams, the Grand Canyon Railway offers passengers a look back at the Old West on a 2.5-hour trip through the high desert and pine forests to the South Rim of the Grand Canyon. The vintage rail cars are pulled by a steam engine during the summer and a diesel locomotive the rest of the year.

The historic Grand Canyon Railway offers lift access on
their first-class cars.

The first class and coach cars are the most accessible, as they can be boarded by a portable lift and they all feature wheelchair tie-downs, nearby companion seats, and an accessible restroom. The parlor car and the observation dome can also be accessed by a portable lift; however, they are more appropriate for slow walkers, as there are no wheelchair tie-downs in the parlor car and the observation dome has seven steps to the top.

This historic train trip can be taken as a day excursion—traveling round trip in the same day—or as a package tour with overnight lodging at the Grand Canyon and Williams included. Accessible rooms with roll-in showers are available on both ends, and the folks at Grand Canyon Railway are great at accommodating disabled guests.

The folks at Rocky Mountaineer Railtours (800 665–7245; rockymountaineer.com) are also very good at accommodating disabled passengers. This multi-day, all-daylight train excursion through the Canadian, Rockies includes all onboard meals, ground transportation and lodging.

Due to the availability of accessible services along the Vancouver to Calgary Kicking Horse Route, Rocky Mountaineer Railtours is able to work with local suppliers to create a very accessible travel experience. That includes accessible hotel rooms with roll-in showers and ramp-equipped transportation to and from the stations.

Boarding the Gold Leaf dome cars is via platform lift and onboard access is reasonably good. There is a spiral staircase to the upper level with handrails on both sides. Alternatively, a small elevator is available for wheelchair users. The elevator measures 2 feet 10 inches by 4 feet, so in order to use it you must transfer to an aisle chair.

The doorways and aisles are too narrow for wheelchairs, so you must transfer to your assigned seat for the rail journey. The Gold Leaf seats do not have flip up armrests but there is plenty of legroom, so you can just pull the aisle chair up in front of the seat. Wheelchair users are seated close to the elevator, and an onboard aisle chair is available for use during the trip.

The bathrooms are located downstairs. The accessible bathroom has a large double-door entry and grab bars near the toilet. There is not enough room for a lateral transfer to the toilet, but it is larger than the standard bathroom.

The Gold Leaf cars work for many people; however, you must inform Rocky Mountaineer Railtours about your specific access needs when you make your reservations. All access needs are flagged in the manifest, and most requests require advance preparations. It's one of the few accessible rail tours around, and it's a great way to see the scenic Canadian Rockies.

Finding the Right Room

THE RIGHT ROOM

If I've heard it once, I've heard it a thousand times, "I reserved an accessible room and when I got there, I couldn't even get into the bathroom!" Of course there are many variations on that theme, but it all boils down to the same issue—appropriate access. What is appropriate access? The answer varies from person to person because what's adequate for one person, may not necessarily meet the needs of another. That's what makes finding the right hotel room such a challenge; not only are people's needs different, but so are access standards.

WHAT IS ACCESSIBLE?

How can you tell if a property has accessible rooms? Well, the first thing you must do is define the word accessible. That's a tall order. Truth be told, the experts have been trying to do that for years. The bottom line is, there's no one uniform definition of accessible. Granted, we do have the Americans with Disabilities Act Accessibility Guidelines (ADAAG) for lodging; however, the access requirements vary, depending on when the property was constructed.

Properties constructed after January 26, 1992, are subject to the new construction standards in the ADAAG. Under these criteria, new properties are required to have a minimum number of accessible rooms, which ranges from 2 percent to 4 percent of the total number of rooms depending on the property's size. The ADAAG also specifically defines the required access features, however the inclusion of some features is also dependent upon property's size.

Properties constructed before January 26, 1992, are subject to different guidelines. The Americans with Disabilities Act (ADA) states that these existing facilities are required to remove architectural barriers when it is readily achievable. "Readily achievable" is further defined as being easy to accomplish without much difficulty or expense. On the other hand, if the property undergoes a major renovation, the new construction ADAAG applies.

In the end, what might be readily achievable for a large hotel chain would not necessarily be readily achievable for a small owner-operated motel. So, two properties literally next door to one another could, in fact, have ADA compliant rooms with completely different access features.

Additionally, some cities and states have local access codes; where two laws conflict, the more stringent of the two applies. Sometimes it's the ADA, sometimes not. Throw historical buildings into the mix—which may or may not be subject to access standards—and you can see why sometimes it takes an attorney to decide exactly how the ADA applies to public accommodations.

If you take only one thing away from this chapter, make it this: Never just ask for an accessible room because there isn't a universal standard for accessible rooms, even within the United States. The terms "accessible" or "ADA compliant" are meaningless, unless you understand how the property defines them, and to do that you have to ask a lot of questions.

ASK THE RIGHT QUESTIONS

Roll-in showers are not included in all accessible rooms, so if you need one, be sure and ask for it. Don't just ask for an accessible room!

Not only do you need to ask the right questions as far as access is concerned, you also have to address those questions to the right people. Always call the property directly, rather than calling the central reservation number. Sometimes access improvements at a local property are not yet entered in the central reservation database. On-site employees can usually give you more detailed access information, as they are more familiar with the property. In fact, many new employee training programs include a tour of the rooms and public areas.

Unfortunately, you will still run across reservation clerks who assume that their accessible rooms are a one-size-fits-all solution for every traveler. The results are disastrous, and many novice travelers end up in ADA-compliant rooms that just didn't meet their needs.

To avoid that fate, it's important to ask the reservation agent to describe the access features of the room. Try to refrain from asking "yes" or "no" questions. For example, instead of asking if there is a roll-in shower in the bathroom, ask the agent to describe the bathroom. Additionally, be especially careful about asking "yes" or "no" questions in the Orient, as many customer service employees consider it rude to answer a question (any question) with a "no." If there is a particular access feature that is important to you (such as an open-frame bed), make sure you specifically inquire about that feature. Never assume anything.

It's also very important to understand that a roll-in shower is not a standard feature in every accessible room. An accessible room can also have a tub/shower combination with grab bars. If you need a roll-in shower, you need to specifically request one instead of just asking for an accessible room. Sometimes a roll-in shower is also called a wheel-in shower or a no-hob shower. Terminology varies around the world.

And if you need a roll-in shower, you should remember that the magic number is 50. Properties that have 50 or fewer rooms are not required to have any guest rooms with a roll-in shower; so if that's an absolute necessity for you, stick to the larger properties.

Of course, even when you ask all the right questions, you can still be in for some surprises. I remember one time I called a hotel and asked if they had any accessible rooms with roll-in showers. Not a hard question, right? Well, apparently the reservation agent was new, or just didn't understand the question or was having a really bad day. After talking with me for about 10 minutes she put me on hold and vowed to find an answer to my perplexing inquiry. After another five minutes she came back on the line and breathlessly replied, "We have kits that we can put in the shower so that deaf people can use the shower." Then she shouted, "Are you deaf?"

Which brings me to my next point. Trust your instincts. If you think you are talking with a flake, you probably are. Hang up and start over.

If, on the other hand, the reservation clerk seems competent but is just having problems describing the room, ask if they have ever been in the room. If the reply is no, then ask to speak to somebody who has been in the room. If the reservation agent doesn't know who you should talk with, ask to speak to somebody in housekeeping. Nobody knows the rooms better than the housekeeping staff who have to clean them each and every day!

Don't be afraid to ask for specific measurements. If door width is a concern, ask for the measurement. Don't forget about the door width of the interior (bathroom) doors, too. Some readers have reported having success in asking for floor plans when specific measurements were a concern. On the other hand, some properties either don't have this information readily available or just don't want to share it. It never hurts to ask, but don't be disappointed if floor plans are not available.

Sometimes you need to employ a little creativity when making your lodging arrangements. For example, if you need some specific equipment in your room, and the reservation agent doesn't seem to understand the difference between a shower chair and a pool chair, then try communicating your needs with a photograph.

Snap a photo of your assistive device and e-mail it to the property. If you don't have a camera, then look through an on-line medical supply catalogue or search the internet to find a photo of the type of equipment you require. Then e-mail the photo to the hotel to illustrate your needs. Spin Life (www.spin life.com) has a wide selection of assistive devices, so it's a good place to look for photos.

Finally, always request a written confirmation notice that includes the specifics of your reserved accessible room. Bring this confirmation notice with you when you check into the hotel. Additionally, I always ask for the name of the reservation agent; in fact I even ask them to spell it, for emphasis. Sometimes when people know you have their name, they tend to do a better job, as they are more accountable. It's not a 100 percent guarantee, but it takes so little time, and the benefits far outweigh the effort.

BLOCK THAT ROOM

Have you ever arrived at a hotel, reservation in hand, only to discover that your accessible room had been given to another guest? Well, you're not alone. More and more travelers are learning that a reservation by itself doesn't necessarily guarantee an accessible room upon arrival. Furthermore, the ADAAG doesn't require properties to block accessible rooms for their disabled guests.

But that may change in the future, as the U.S. Access Board included that very provision in the preliminary version of the revised lodging ADAAG. Although there's no telling if it will be included in the final version, it's promising that it was mentioned in the draft. There's no timeline for the completion of the ADAAG, but from past experience it may take several years to be implemented. The preliminary draft was released in 2008. The American Hotel and Lodging Association formally opposes the new provision, as they claim it would impose a significant cost on many properties. The decision could go either way, so it's definitely something to watch.

For now, the only way to determine if a property can block an accessible room is to ask, but be careful how you phrase your query. Many people mistakenly ask if the property will guarantee the room. This is the wrong terminology; in hotel-speak "guarantee" means to secure with a credit card deposit. In other words, your room rate and reservation will be guaranteed with your credit card. This locks in your rate, and ensures that a room (any room) will be there for you, even if you arrive late. It does not ensure that your room will be accessible. Instead, you need to ask them to block the accessible room for you. In hotel terminology, "block" means to reserve a specific room for a specific guest.

It should also be noted that some chains do better than others with blocking accessible rooms.

- Microtel CEO Mike Levin claims their company will block accessible rooms upon reservation. Although there is no written policy on this matter, in practice Microtel seems to follow through on Levin's promise.
- Under the terms of a 1996 Department of Justice (DOJ) settlement, all Marriott Courtyard properties are required to block their accessible rooms.
- All BASS Properties (Holiday Inn, Crowne Plaza, and Staybridge Suites) are required to block their accessible rooms under the terms of a 1998 DOJ settlement.

Unfortunately it takes extra time to locate properties that block accessible rooms, so shop around and give your business (and your money) to those that do. Remember, even the most accessible room in the world is useless unless it's actually available when you arrive.

GROUND FLOOR ROOMS

It's always a good idea to request a room on the ground floor. This is done as a safety precaution, because if the electricity goes out, the elevators will not be operable. The same holds true if there is a fire. If you can't get a room on the ground floor, ask for one on the lowest available floor. And although you don't want to be paranoid, it's always good to know what to do in the event of an emergency.

If an emergency alarm sounds, remain in your room unless you are specifically told to evacuate. The security staff keeps a record of all guests who require emergency evacuation assistance. If you don't have a visible physical disability yet require emergency evacuation assistance, inform the desk clerk of this at check in and your name will then be added to the list.

If evacuation is necessary, you will notified by intercom or telephone. The security staff should know within three to five minutes after the alarm sounds if evacuation is imminent. If immediate evacuation is necessary, security personnel should be at your room within 60 to 90 seconds to provide assistance. If you do not hear from the hotel staff, then call the front desk to inquire about the situation and to remind them you may need assistance.

If you smell smoke, place wet towels beneath the door and stay in your room as long as you feel safe. If you leave the room, stay low to the ground, beneath the layer of smoke, and head for the area of emergency refuge (usually the stairwell). Although the stairwell might not seem like it offers much protection, it is pressurized and can withstand intense heat. Emergency rescue personnel are also trained to look for people in the area of emergency refuge.

Additionally, it's a good idea to carry a pocket-sized flashlight with you. I keep one in my suitcase at all times. You don't want to be left in the dark in the event of an emergency.

BEDS

Hotel beds are a huge source of confusion, mostly because they aren't covered under the ADA and no ADAAG regulations exist for them. Legally there's no such thing as an accessible bed, and to add to the problem, there's really no consistency from one property to the next. In the end, you just have to find the bed that works best for you. So it pays to know what to look for, and where problems may arise.

One of the biggest points of contention about hotel beds centers around bed height. With no regulations, everyone has their own definition of ideal bed height. Wheelchair users tend to prefer lower beds, while slow walkers or those who have problems standing prefer higher models.

The current trend in the industry seems to be with using the higher pillow top models, which usually measure 28 inches high and sometimes even more. If bed height is an issue for you, be sure and ask about it when you make your reservation. Chances are that if the hotel advertises luxurious or specialty bedding, their beds are going to be on the high side. Additionally, properties that have a Victorian ambiance can have extremely high beds, sometimes with a step stool beside them. I've seen some of these beds top 36 inches, which is even too high for some slow walkers. So call around until you find a property with a bed height that's right for you, because outside of having the box spring removed, it's hard to fix a bed that's too high.

Another bed issue centers around open-frame versus platform beds. Some people need open-frame beds so they can use a Hoyer type lift. In actually, however most hotels have platform beds. Again, there are no federal regulations that cover this issue, but Florida and New Jersey have state laws that require properties to have adequate clearance under beds so that lift-type devices can be used.

But if you are in the other 48 states, you'll have a hard time finding open-frame beds. Still you need to inquire about their availability when you make your reservation. That said, the reservation agent will probably give you the wrong answer at least 50 percent of the time.

So what do you do when you arrive and discover the hotel only has platform beds when you need an open-frame bed? The first step would of course be to call the front desk and see if they have any rooms with open-frame beds. If not, then explain your problem and ask if they can send up somebody from the engineering staff to remedy your problem.

Some people come up with their own do-it-yourself solutions. "We can't use platform beds because we need to use a lift when traveling," says one traveler. "When we have been unable to get a room without an open-frame bed we placed wood blocks made from 6 inch squares of lumber at the four corners of the bed. They raised the bed enough to use the lift. Of course, they are heavy, so not very practical except for driving trips."

It should also be noted that most hotels do not provide Hoyer type or track lifts. The one exception are a few Las Vegas hotels. The best option is to arrange to rent one at your destination. Most medical supply houses will pick up and deliver them to your hotel if you make advance arrangements.

Alternatively you can purchase a portable travel lift. The Take-Along Lift (877-667-6515; www.takealonglifts.com) is an ideal choice, as it only weighs about 50 pounds and is easy to wheel through an airport.

Another hotel bed issue involves roll-away beds and cots. "Cots or rollaway beds are often much too low for a transfer back into the wheelchair," say savvy traveler Sharon Myers. "I found a simple solution by asking the hotel engineer to bring another mattress and place it on top of the cot or roll-away bed. It brings the level up and makes for a much easier transfer."

If you need a hospital bed, you must make arrangements with a medical supply company to have one delivered to your hotel room. Some travelers have even found a creative solution to this problem.

Says frequent-traveler Ann, "I need to sleep with my head elevated, but I've often found it difficult and expensive to get a hospital bed delivered to my hotel room. My solution is to contact a furniture rental company and rent a recliner. It's usually a lot cheaper (and easier) than renting a hospital bed. However, I always remember to first ask the hotel if they have a recliner they can put in my room. Sometimes they do, and then I get it for free. Of course this won't work for everybody, but I'm very comfortable sleeping in a recliner."

Finally, there is the issue of bed firmness. "The first thing we worry about when staying at a hotel is the bed," says Robert. "Most of the time it's as hard as a rock. This means my wife would have to turn me three or four times a night to prevent skin problems. Since that's not much of a vacation for her, we tried an Aero Bed on our last trip. We purchased one for under $100 and placed it on top of the hotel bed. Then she transferred me onto the bed and we inflated it with the electric pump. Whenever my wife woke up during the night she just let some air out of the bed. We were able to get through the night with only one turn and sometimes none at all, and I didn't develop any skin problems."

TOILETS

Toilets are another source of confusion as far as access goes. Although there are access standards for toilets, some of the regulations allow for a range of installations, hence the confusion.

Let's start with toilet height. Different people prefer different toilet heights; however, under the ADAAG, the top of the toilet seat must be between 17 and 19 inches high. Although it's just a two-inch range, some people think that 17-inch high toilets are too low, while others feel that 19-inch toilets are too high. Again, it depends on your disability and your needs.

Although there's nothing that can be done to lower a toilet, a raised toilet seat can be added to make it higher. Some hotels will install a raised toilet seat upon request. Raised toilet seats are not legally required, but some properties keep them on hand as an added amenity. Ask about this option when you make your reservation. If you absolutely need a higher toilet, then consider traveling with your own raised toilet seat. If, on the other hand, you get to your room and find a raised toilet seat installed, call the front desk to have it removed if it's too high for you.

Toilet grab-bar placement is another source of confusion. The ADAAG requires one grab bar on a side wall and another on the back wall; however, the regulations allow for the grab bars to be installed on either side wall. If you need a grab bar on a specific side, be sure to ask about this when you make your reservation. In practice, most reservations for specific sided grab bars are not flagged or blocked, so you'll probably have to change rooms. It's just important to know that this is an option. Your chances of finding something that meets your needs are better at large hotels, as there's just more to choose from. At small properties and B&Bs, it's very important to research grab bar placement before you make your reservation, as changing rooms may not be an option.

SHOWER CHAIRS

There is also a lot of confusion about hotel shower chairs or benches. It would be nice if there were some sort of standardization of this equipment from one property to the next, but that's just not the way it works. I've seen everything from plastic pool chairs to padded shower chairs—and lots of stuff in between.

If you need a shower chair, it's best to find out what specific type of shower chair the hotel has. When you make your reservation ask if they have a shower bench or a shower chair, if it has arms, and if it is padded. You might also want to find out the make and model of the shower chair. Most likely someone will have to call you back with that information, but it could save you a bathroom accident in the long run.

Of course, it's always a good idea to be prepared just in case an unsafe or inadequate chair is provided. "When I'm faced with roll-in shower that doesn't have a suitable bench or even a bench at all, I solve the problem with a lightweight plastic poncho," says Sharon Myers. "After transferring onto the bed, I cover my chair with the poncho, transfer back into my wheelchair and roll inside the shower and proceed with taking a shower as usual. Sometimes, I've even placed the shower curtain beneath me and it works fine."

Many roll-in shower enclosures have built-in shower benches, but the fixed height can be a problem for some wheelchair users. One frequent traveler offers this suggestion. "If the bench is too low, I usually fold up three to five bath towels and set them on the bench. This usually raises the level enough for an easy transfer. It's very important to remember to wet the towels before you transfer, as wet towels won't slip but dry ones can be a real safety hazard."

Additionally, if you need a roll-in shower chair or a commode chair, you are probably going to have to provide that yourself, as it is beyond the scope of the equipment that most properties provide. There are a number of portable shower chairs on the market, but Nuprodx (415–472-1699; www.nuprodx.com) makes one that can be converted to a roll-in shower chair or commode chair. It breaks down for transport and although it's made out of lightweight aircraft aluminum, it's very sturdy and a good choice if you plan to travel a lot.

POOLS

Finding a property with a truly accessible pool can also be a challenge. Although pool accessibility is mandated under the law, it's dependent on the size of the pool and when it was built. The ADAAG concerning pools took effect on October 3, 2002, so the rules apply to pools constructed after that date.

Large pools (those with over 300 linear feet of pool wall) must have at least two accessible means of entry to the pool. The primary means of entry must be either a sloped entry into the pool or pool lift. The secondary means of entry can be a sloped entry, pool lift, transfer wall, transfer system, or accessible pool stairs. Pools that have less than 300 linear feet of pool wall are only required to provide one accessible means of entry, however it must be either a sloped entry or a pool lift.

Look to the newer properties for the most accessible pools. However, be very careful how you phrase your access inquiry. Many reservation clerks assume that pool access means access to the pool area, not necessarily to the water itself. In most cases, it's best to simply ask if they have a pool lift. Additionally, the term "sloped entry" is often misunderstood, and many employees assume it means a sloped entry to the pool area. A better term to use is a zero-depth entry pool.

Finally, a good place to look for information about properties that have accessible pools is from the companies that manufacture and sell pool lifts. Some maintain a list of customers on their websites, while others will share this information on request.

SHORT STATURE KITS

Some properties go well beyond the minimum access requirements and provide additional amenities for better access. Such is the case for the properties that offer Assistive Convenience Kits for their guests of short stature. Produced by Direct Access Solutions (www.lp-access.com), these kits include a stepstool, a reaching tool, a bar to lower the clothes rack, and a device to retrofit the latch-hook lock on the door.

Although these kits were designed for people of short stature, a few of the items are also useful to wheelchair users. The kits are available at Radisson Hotels and Resorts, Park

Plaza Hotels and Resorts, Country Inns and Suites, Park Inn Hotels, Hawthorn Suites, Microtel, Shiloh Inns and Suites, and Red Lion Hotels.

The list of properties that carry these kits keeps growing, as they are an easy and relatively inexpensive way to provide additional access. For an updated property list, visit the Direct Access Solutions website. Also, don't be afraid to ask if they are available, no matter where you stay as more and more hotels are taking advantage of this unique access product.

INNS AND B&Bs

Many people overlook small inns and B&Bs when searching for accessible lodging, but some of these owner-operated properties are nicely accessible. Although by law, many of the smaller properties aren't required to be accessible if they're owner-occupied, many are either because of need or design.

For example, if an owner, family member, or close friend is disabled, then it's quite likely the property will be accessible. Additionally, many of these small property owners don't want to lose any wedding business, so they've designed their facilities to accommodate everyone, including all the friends and family of the wedding party.

Additionally, some designs just lend themselves better to access than others. For example, many older homes have nice hardwood floors and wide double doors. In short, it never hurts to ask about access but again, be sure to ask the innkeeper to describe the access features.

One advantage to staying at a small inn or B&B is that the owners are very familiar with their rooms, and most can describe them down to the smallest detail. Additionally, many small inns and B&Bs have the ability to reserve specific rooms; in fact, that's standard practice at most B&Bs. So if you reserve an accessible room, you can rest assured that it will be available when you arrive.

Although there are many inn and B&B directories on the internet, only a few provide any meaningful access information. B&B On-line (www.bbonline.com) allows users to search for accessible properties and, in some cases, access details are also included. It's incumbent upon the innkeepers to enter their own access details, so the amount and quality of the access information varies from property to property. Still, it's a great way to narrow your search.

Many small inns are nicely accessible. Pictured here is the Knickerbocker Mansion Country Inn in Big Bear Lake, which features accessible pathways to most areas of the property.

And although it's not devoted specifically to inns and B&Bs, the Accessible Properties database at www.accessibleproperties.net, features a wide variety of accessible lodging options. Each listing includes lots of pictures and detailed access information, so it's very easy to determine if a property will meet your needs. Check back often, as properties are continually added to this growing database.

EMERGENCY FIX-IT KIT

Let's not forget about those little access features that make rooms more comfortable and useable—things like lever handles, lowered clothing hooks, properly placed grab bars, and accessible bedside lamps. Although these items are mandated in the ADAAG, they are often overlooked by the lodging industry. So what's a traveler to do? Many people carry an emergency fix-it kit to overcome these access obstacles.

Faucets and doorknobs without lever handles can create problems for many people. Fortunately this oversight is fairly easy to remedy. Great Grips (800–346-5662; greatgrips.com) sells accessible faucet and door grips which simply slip over the existing hardware. These grips all have a mini-lever and although they may require a little assistance to install (ask hotel personnel if you're traveling alone), it sure beats fighting with inaccessible hardware.

And if you continually run into problems with grab-bar configurations, then carry along a few Port-A-Bars (800–542-5076; grabitonline.com). These portable grab bars feature two heavy-duty suction cups that can handle up to 200 pounds of pull strength. They are especially useful if you require grab bars on a specific side or at a specific height.

And then there are those bothersome bedside lamps. When was the last time you could actually operate one from the bed? In most cases they require a good deal of manual dexterity; other times they are simply out of reach.

There are a number of products you can buy to make lamps more accessible, including a touch-lamp control switch. Just screw the adapter into the light socket of any metal lamp, and this portable device turns an ordinary lamp into a touch-control lamp. Alternatively, you might want to pick up a voice-activated light dimmer, which will turn the lamp on and off with a simple voice command. And last but not least, don't forget the Clapper, which allows users to operate lamps with a simple clap or two.

And finally, my favorite hardware store item to pack along on a trip is a simple suction cup hook. This inexpensive and lightweight device is the perfect solution for those out-of-reach bathroom robe hooks.

RESOLVING PROBLEMS

Of course, sometimes, even when you do everything right, you can still run into problems. What do you do then? What do you do when you arrive at a property and find out they don't have the appropriate room for you, even though you have a confirmed reservation? There are many answers to that question.

Firstly, if the property doesn't have any accessible rooms left, they must find you appropriate lodging at another hotel. Sometimes this is acceptable and sometimes not. For example, if you chose a hotel because of its location, you might also want to ask for a transportation allowance. If it's really a big inconvenience to you, ask for a voucher for a free stay on a future visit.

These are both reasonable requests. Do not, however, ask the property to foot the bill for your entire vacation. This is not considered a reasonable request, and in most cases, management won't even address your problem if you ask for something they view as being totally unreasonable.

In most cases, the solution is open to discussion and, in truth, there is no one right procedure for getting the best resolution, as it all depends on your own personal style. To illustrate this point, let me tell you a true story, about how three people handled the same problem in three completely different ways. The players in this little drama are Carol, John, and James. The scene was the check-in counter of an upscale business hotel on the first day of a disability conference. All three players held a confirmed reservation for a specific type of accessible room. They all arrived at different times, only to find that their confirmed room type was not available. Here's how they each handled it.

Carol was the first to arrive. Her reservation was for an accessible smoking room with a tub/shower combination. The desk clerk explained to Carol that the only accessible rooms left were non-smoking rooms. This was not acceptable to Carol. She quoted the law, and calmly explained her needs, and patiently reasoned with the clerk. In the end, the clerk handed her an astray and told her to ignore the no smoking signs in the room. Problem solved. As a non-smoker, I cringe when I consider the resolution, but I do applaud Carol's tenacity.

John was the next to arrive. He was accompanied by Phil, his personal care attendant. John's reservation was for an accessible room, with two beds and a roll-in shower. There were no accessible rooms with two beds available. Now John is a very astute businessman with a no-nonsense approach to life. After reviewing the law with the clerk, John quipped that he had no intention of sleeping in the same bed with Phil. He added that he was very tired, and that if they didn't provide him with an appropriate room, he would sleep on the sofa in the lobby. John then added, "I sleep in the nude." Problem solved. In short order, the clerk found an appropriate room for John and Phil.

There were no accessible rooms left by the time James arrived; however, this good looking,

20-something young man didn't let that stop him. He effortlessly explained the law, and slowly won over the clerk with his charm. His Southern accent didn't hurt matters either. James ended up with the accessible penthouse suite.

Who's the best problem solver? In truth, there's no winner, as they all achieved equally appropriate results. What's the most effective advocacy style? It's the one that works best for you. The first steps: Learn the rules, know the law, and understand your rights. Then find your style, fine-tune it, and add it to your advocacy toolbox. It may take some time and a bit of trial and error, so be flexible until you find a style that works for you. It's not an exact science, but it is effective. It's the way to get results.

Taking the Kids

AFTER THE STROLLER

Let's face it, we all start out life on wheels. In fact, most parents are quite adept at wheeling around their young charges in strollers and baby carriages. It's pretty easy to do when they are small. But what about when they get bigger? Can you imagine wheeling around a teenager in a stroller? That uncut curb that was once easy to bump up is no longer a piece of cake with a teenager onboard.

Although this example may be an oversimplification of the situation, it illustrates a very common problem. I've seen it played out time and again as children get bigger and make the transition from stroller to wheelchair. Mom and dad can no longer lift them and those "few steps" that were once easily navigable in a stroller become impossible in a wheelchair. Plus, mom and dad are getting older, too.

It's usually at this point that I hear comments from parents such as, "We used to be able to travel when John was small, but now that he weighs 100 pounds we just can't do it anymore." Although I understand the frustration, that's not exactly a fair assessment of the situation. Travel is still possible, even with a child in a wheelchair.

The truth is that most parents don't give access much thought while their child is in a stroller. After all, why should they? A stroller fits through standard doorways, it's not too heavy to bump up a curb, and, if worse comes to worse, they can always carry junior.

When a child graduates to a wheelchair, parents have to think about accessible hotel rooms, toilets, and transportation for the first time. Subsequently, it takes more time to plan, organize, and actually execute a trip. Although this can be frustrating to many parents who traveled easily before, the good news is that family vacations don't have to end just because your child uses a wheelchair.

CAR TRIPS

Car trips are a favorite family vacation option. It's just easier to travel by car when your kids are small. Let's face it—you take a lot of things with you when you travel with young children. That fact by itself makes the family vehicle (with plenty of room for luggage and extras) the ideal vacation transportation choice. Additionally, many toddlers aren't exactly ideal air passengers. They get bored easily and it's hard to keep them entertained on long flights. A road trip allows you the flexibility to make as many stops as you need along the way to relieve that boredom, plus you can pack along all those favorite toys without having to worry about airline baggage restrictions.

Car trips also present an especially attractive option for wheeler kids. As one mom says, "My son can't fly anymore because he can't really sit in an airplane seat. He just doesn't have enough head and back support. He can only sit in his wheelchair. So now we travel by van and he stays in his own wheelchair. We can stop when we want and he is safer and more comfortable this way. It's really a good solution."

Some families take it one step further and go camping. "We usually camp with our travel trailer," says another mom. "It's a great way to travel because we pull it with our lift-equipped van, so we have accessible transportation at our destination. Also, it's less expensive and we can bring along any piece of equipment we think we might need, like bath chairs, potty chairs, or special bikes."

No matter which option you choose, finding accessible rest stops along the way is a vital component to any car trip. To be honest, it's kind of a hit and miss process but you can improve your odds by seeking out fast-food chains that look as if they were built in the last five years. Most of these are built from cookie cutter designs and, although the food may not be nutritious, the restrooms are well done access-wise and they are fairly standard from location to location. The exception, of course, is older restaurants that have been retrofitted for access.

Unfortunately there aren't many resources that list accessible rest stops; in fact, I only know of one. The Oregon Department of Transportation website (www.tripcheck.com) lists the location of rest areas throughout the state, with the accessible facilities noted. Just click on the map, and details about the nearby rest areas will be displayed below. It's a very handy trip planning tool if you happen to be traveling in Oregon. Unfortunately websites like these are not commonplace, but it never hurts to look up the Department of Transportation website for your state to see if they have any rest area access information.

If you're not towing your own accessible trailer with you, you'll also have to find accessible hotels for your car trip. This perhaps is the biggest adjustment parents need to make when their child transitions from a stroller to a wheelchair. Although some parents can manage with a non-accessible room when their child is in a stroller, it's almost impossible with a wheelchair.

Wheelchairs are wider than strollers and non-accessible rooms present many access obstacles, including narrow doorways and tiny bathrooms. Plan ahead and make a checklist of your access needs, and be sure the hotel you choose can meet them. Even though it takes more time in the planning stage, booking an accessible room makes for a happier vacation in the long run.

AIR TRAVEL

Air travel has its benefits, but admittedly it's not for everyone. The major advantage of air travel is that it allows you to cover a long distance in a relatively short amount of time. The downside is that once you get off the airplane you need to find accessible transportation at your destination. This is sometimes hard to do; in fact, accessible ground transportation is the most often overlooked component of any trip.

Additionally, any time you travel by air, there is the very real possibility that the airline will damage your wheelchair. No one wants to have a wheelchair damaged, but for some people with highly specialized wheelchairs, this alone prevents them from flying. In short, it's just not worth the risk to these people. If your child falls into this category, choose another mode of transportation;

air travel is just not the idea choice for everyone.

But air travel does work for many people. In fact, when your child is small enough to use a car seat, it's a good choice. Car seats can help with head and neck support in young children. But what happens when they get too big for a car seat? Can you just make your own seating and support device? Not exactly.

In order to take a child restraint device on an airplane, it must be Federal Aviation Administration (FAA) approved. What makes the cut? Well, most car seats do, but home-made seating devices do not. Generally speaking, neck pillows, towels, and blankets are allowed, but one parent recently got a 30-inch piece of foam rubber "needed for back support" nixed at the cabin door. Generally speaking, unless it's FAA-approved, anything that straps to the seat or is too big and bulky will usually get the boot.

The Cares harness (800-299-6249; www.kidsflysafe.com) may be an option for some children. This FAA-approved harness straps to the seat and can be used for children over one year old who weight between 20 and 44 pounds and are up to 40-inches tall.

If your child can ride on your lap, the Baby B'Air flight vest (800-417-5228; www.babyba ir.com) might work for you. This cotton garment fits over the child's head and is secured by straps under the arms and between the legs. After takeoff, a seat belt can be attached to the back of the vest to secure the child. The FAA does not allow any harness to attach directly to the parent, but the Baby B'Air is designed to attach to the seat belt instead of the body.

Although designed for lap babies, it may work for children who need some extra support but who are not comfortable in a car seat. The company also promises a full refund if any airline refuses to let you use the vest. The major drawback, of course, is that the vest cannot be used during takeoff and landing.

Unfortunately, if your child is too big for a car seat and you can't provide appropriate neck or trunk support, flying may not be an option. It just doesn't work for everyone.

If you decide that air travel well work for you, be sure and familiarize yourself with the Air Carrier Access Act. It's important to note that the same rules and regulations that apply to adults also apply to children. The best course of action is to familiarize yourself with your rights so you will know what to expect before you take off.

CRUISES

The cruise industry has drastically changed over the years. At one time, this all-inclusive travel option was only attractive to seniors. Today cruising is a great family vacation idea, and many cruise lines have a plethora of special programs and activities for children of all ages, from toddlers to teens.

There are many advantages to cruising. First, you can visit a number of destinations without having to pack and unpack at every stop. Second, with the increasing number of home ports, almost everyone can drive to an embarkation point. This means you can take that exotic vacation without having to get on an airplane. And finally, with the wide variety of onboard kid-centric programs, not only do kids have some interesting and educational things to do, but their parents can also enjoy some much needed alone time. Everyone gets a vacation.

Of course the key to a successful cruise is in picking the right cruise line and the right ship. After all, you don't want to get stuck on a ship that only has limited wheelchair access or on a cruise line that isn't kid friendly. With that in mind, two cruise lines stand head-and-shoulders above the crowd: Royal Caribbean

Royal Caribbean features H2O Zones on all of their Freedom-class ships. There is level access to most areas of this water park, and a plastic wheelchair is available for loan, so everyone can enjoy this feature.

International (RCI) and Carnival Cruise Lines (CCL).

RCI offers the Adventure Ocean program. This complimentary program is open to kids between 3 and 17 years old and is designed to blend educational activities with just plain fun. Kids participate in age appropriate activities, learn about local customs, do science experiments, and make new friends. There are special play areas for kids and even a nightclub for teens on most RCI ships, but the Adventure Ocean program is not always restricted to one area.

Although children must be toilet trained to be accepted into Adventure Ocean, there is an exception for disabled children. If a child is not toilet trained because of a disability, he or she may still participate; however, it's important to note that the staff will not change diapers or provide one-to-one attention to program participants. Parents are required to carry a pager and be available to change their child's diaper as needed, and they must agree to remain aboard the ship (not on a shore excursion) whenever their child is in the program.

RCI ships also have some fun kids areas, such as the H2 O Zone water park on their Freedom-class ships. This level play area features fountains, pools, and geysers and lots of room to play in the water. RCI goes one step further and also provide plastic wheelchairs, so wheelchair-using kids can play in the water.

Camp Carnival is the kids program offered by CCL. This day program is open to kids between 2 and 15 years old. Like the RCI program, children are divided by age group and supervised by specially trained youth counselors. They participate in a variety of activities from bingo and sponge painting to teen dinners and dance parties.

CCL does not require children to be toilet trained in order to participate in the program, but they do require parents to provide diapers and toiletries if their child is still in diapers.

No matter which cruise line you choose, always pick the newer ships because in general they are more accessible. Talk with the special needs department about the specific features of the accessible cabins and then book the one that best suits your needs. Accessible can mean a number of different things, so do your research and make sure the accessible cabin will really work for your child.

DESTINATIONS

If you'd prefer to stay on dry land during your holiday, rest assured that there are many accessible family-friendly choices. Generally you will find better access in large cities, as most have some type of accessible public transportation and many even have accessible taxis. Your selection of hotels will also be bigger in a large city, which means you'll stand a better chance of finding an accessible hotel room that suits your needs.

Learning vacations are a popular family travel choice and Washington, D.C. tops the list of accessible educational destinations. Most of the public buildings in the nation's capital are accessible, but advance research is a must. Some venues (like the popular Smithsonian National Air and Space Museum) have barrier-free access at the front door, while others (like the White House) require advance arrangements for the accessible tour. As an added bonus, there is no admission charge to most Washington, D.C. attractions.

If you'd like to stay closer to home, then plan a trip to your state capital. Government buildings usually have good access, and it's a great place for kids to learn how the state legislature works. Many state capitals also have large museums and other accessible tourist attractions.

Colonial Williamsburg is a big hit with kids, especially when they are studying colonial history in school. Many of the buildings are accessible and there are many hands-on activities with guides and interpreters dressed in period costumes. Kids learn while they have fun. The Colonial Williamsburg Foundation publishes an excellent access guide that lists the accessible attractions and buildings. The best bet is to review the access guide before your visit so you can plan your activities in advance.

And for an experience they'll never forget, send your kids to space camp at the U.S. Space and Rocket Center in Huntsville, Alabama. There is wheelchair access to most of the facility, and many of their programs can accommodate wheelchair users with advance notice.

If you'd like to explore the outdoors, consider visiting a national park. Access varies from park to park, but most parks at least have an accessible visitor center. Many parks also have short accessible interpretive trails and lodging facilities. Visit the National Park Service website at www.nps.gov for access information.

SIGHTSEEING OPTIONS

The City Museum in St. Louis features lots of fun diversions, including a wheelchair-accessible tidepool.

As far as tourist attractions go, look for aquariums, zoos, and museums for the best access. And although I'm not a big fan of theme parks, most have good access and many even publish detailed guides about their accessible facilities and services. It's a good idea to review the guide before your visit so you know in advance which rides are accessible. Policies vary from park to park, but most parks have at least a few rides that are off limits to wheelchair users. Knowing this in advance can help avoid disappointment.

Many children's museums are also a good choice for a kid-friendly outing. These interactive-play places are popping up throughout the country, and the good news is that many are wheelchair accessible. For example, St. Louis is home to the nicely accessible City Museum, which features plenty of spaces to crawl, roll, or climb, lots of hands-on art and craft workstations, a working tidepool, and even a wheelchair-accessible cave.

If you'd prefer a museum with an emphasis on history, then head down to Alabama and visit the Early Works Museum in Huntsville. Billed as the South's largest hands-on history museum, Early Works offers a wide variety of interactive fun. Children can hear stories from a talking tree, play a tune on giant-sized instruments, or try building a house in the interactive architecture exhibit. There's something to suit just about every interest, including a 45-foot wheelchair-accessible keelboat.

And don't forget about factory tours. Many are free and most have at least partial access. Accessible favorites for kids include the Basic Brown Bear Factory (San Francisco, CA), Jelly Belly Candy Company (Fairfield, CA), Ben & Jerry's (Waterbury, VT), and The Crayola Factory (Easton, PA). A great resource for factory tours (including access details) is *Watch It Made in the USA* by Karen Axelrod and Bruce Brumberg.

WORDS OF WISDOM

Of course, the best advice about kid-focused accessible travel comes from parents who have already hit the road. With that in mind, here are some words of wisdom from a few real-life experts.

"Try to find equipment that can do double duty. For instance, I buy a cheap beach chair every year and attach a seat belt to it. Then we use it to sit in sand at the edge of the beach and also in the tub as a bath chair."

"If accessible transportation looks like it's going to be an issue, we'll usually opt for a manual wheelchair that can fold up and go into the trunk of a rental car. If we're flying to a destination, I've got to be really comfortable that there will be great accessible transportation when I get there to be able to take the power wheelchair."

"Allow tons of time. It will take three times as long to get something done! And don't forget to pack your patience and your sense of humor."

"I always pack a little personal backpack for my daughter with a couple of favorite books and a MP3 player. I also try to add several little things she hasn't seen before such as new books, a little art activity we can do together, a coloring book, or one of those little games with magnetic pieces that won't get away. She can't manipulate all of these things alone, but she enjoys making choices and playing games. She knows it's going to be fun to open the pack!"

"Don't be spontaneous. Plan ahead for everything. The romantic notion of just packing a bag and heading off to some destination with no plans just doesn't work for someone who needs accommodations for their disability. You need to approach it like an invading army."

Sailing Away

CRUISE TRAVEL

Cruising has long been touted as the most accessible vacation choice for wheelchair users and slow walkers. In fact, according to a 2002 Harris Interactive poll, 12 percent of disabled adults had taken a cruise in the previous five years, compared to 8 percent of the able-bodied population. Still, some cruises are more accessible than others.

Although there's a high level of accessibility in the cruise industry today, you can still end up on a very inaccessible ship if you don't do your homework. It's truly a situation of buyer beware. Don't assume all cruises are equally accessible. Just like any other mode of travel, you need to research all of your options before you make a cruise decision. Additionally, if you work with a travel agent, work with one who is well versed in accessible travel, not just in cruise travel. In the end, it takes a good amount of advance planning and preparation to ensure adequate access on a cruise holiday. But the good news is—it *is* possible.

ACCESS AT SEA

Every time I read an article that states that the Americans with Disabilities Act (ADA) applies to cruise ships, I get a little miffed. Technically that statement is correct, but it's also very misleading. In fact, access on cruise ships is somewhat up in the air right now, as two U.S. agencies are still sorting out the rules.

On June 6, 2005, the U.S. Supreme Court decided in favor of the plaintiffs in *Spector v. Norwegian Cruise Line,* and ruled that the ADA applies to foreign-flagged cruise ships that call on U.S. ports. But there's a catch: Even though we have case law requiring access, we still don't have any specific rules and regulations. Those are being sorted out by the U.S. Access Board and the Department of Transportation (DOT).

The Access Board is in charge of creating the architectural guidelines for ships, while the DOT is addressing nondiscrimination as far as services and flagged ships that dock at U.S. ports. And keep in mind that the majority of cruise ships are foreign flagged.

Currently the Access Board is stalled. They released a proposed draft of the guidelines and accepted public comments;

however, they are still evaluating those comments and have yet to release the final rules. Once they are released, they will be published in the *Federal Register,* along with the effective date.

To be fair, the Access Board has a tough job. After all, they have to take the same ADA Access Guidelines (ADAAG) that apply to land-based accommodations and apply them to ships. In some cases that's just not practical. Additionally, they have to take international law and passenger safety into consideration as they draft the guidelines.

What will the final guidelines say? Well, it's anybody's guess, but according to Supreme Court Justice Kennedy (who penned the majority opinion on *Spector v. Norwegian Cruise Line*), the structural changes will have to be readily achievable. Thomas Goldstein, who argued the plaintiff's case before the Supreme Court, believes that large-scale physical changes and retrofitting will probably not be required. And most everyone feels the regulations will probably only apply to newly built or newly designed cruise ships.

The Department of Transportation (DOT) also produced their own proposed guidelines on procedural issues regarding access. Their document clearly states that price discrimination against people with disabilities will be forbidden. In other words, cruise lines won't be able to charge disabled passengers more for accessible cabins. It's expected that this final rule will be issued in conjunction with the architectural specifications.

Rules and regulations aside, the good news is that most cruise lines already provide good access; in fact, they've had accessible cabins long before any rulings were ever issued. They've been very responsive to the market. Still the regulations will codify things, so keep an eye out for them. Visit the Access Board website at www.Access-B oard.gov for the latest updates.

CHOOSING A CRUISE LINE

The first thing you need to do when selecting a cruise is to choose a cruise line. There are several things you should take into consideration when making this decision, including passenger demographics, fleet age, and, of course, accessibility and attitude. Some cruise lines have a more proactive approach to access than others. Ultimately your decision will be based largely on personal tastes and budget; however, don't overlook the cruise line's overall attitude about access issues.

With a little help, many people are able to tackle the rock climbing walls on Royal Caribbean's ships.

Each cruise line has its strengths and weaknesses as far as access is concerned. For example, Royal Caribbean International (RCI) has been particularly proactive in addressing access issues; so much so, that they even named disability advocate Jean Driscoll godmother of the *Mariner of the Seas.* They were one of the first lines to have pool lifts, and their golf courses and outdoor areas are all nicely accessible. Additionally, wheelchair users who have some upper body control can even use the climbing wall. It's a very inclusive line.

Although the room stewards are very accommodating on just about every line, the ones on Holland America Line (HAL) stand out, not so much for the job they do, but for how they do it. Instead of using those big housekeeping carts that clog up the hallways, the HAL room stewards use hand-held carts. This frees up the hallway space, which makes the area easier to navigate for wheelchair users.

Norwegian Cruise Line (NCL) offers short stature accessibility kits aboard all their ships. These kits include a custom stepstool, a grabber, a door security latch adapter, an extension or "'push-pull" tool, and a closet rod adapter. Although these kits were designed for passengers of short stature, some of the items may also be useful to wheelchair users.

Last but not least, Carnival Cruise Lines (CCL) gets high marks for family cruises, as their children's program is very flexible. The staff goes out of their way to make every child feel included, and activities are adapted on an individual basis. If you are cruising with a disabled child, CCL is an excellent choice.

Of course things are constantly changing with cruise lines, so it pays to stay on top of things. Cruise Critic (www.cruisecritic.com) is a good resource, as this website has a good number of message boards including one devoted entirely to disabled cruise travel. It's a fairly active board and quite a few of the regular participants have some good knowledge about accessible cruising. It's a great place to get first-hand information about the accessibility of specific cruise lines, ships, and even ports.

So shop around for a cruise line that meets your access needs and has a proactive attitude about access. Remember: The best indication that a cruise line actually wants your business is if it has a separate access department that passengers can contact directly. Additionally, it's always a good sign when a cruise line has access information available on its website or in its collateral materials.

CHOOSING A SHIP

After you've decided on a cruise line, you then need to select a ship. Even within the same line, ships can differ regarding to amenities, size, and even accessibility. Choosing a cruise ship is analogous to choosing a hotel—it's where you'll live, sleep, and play for the length of your holiday at sea. Suffice it to say, it's a very important decision.

For best access, choose a large ship built within the past three years. Access continues to improve so the newer ships generally boast the best access.

Many ships now have pool lifts. Pictured here is a pool lift aboard Royal Caribbean's Adventure of the Seas.

Of course, a picture is worth a thousand words, so don't hesitate to check the photo gallery on www.wheelchaircruising.com for some great access photos. Operated by Connie George Travel Associates, this site is continually expanding, with new photos added often. It's nicely organized by cruise line and ship class, and it even includes some port shots.

Once you've narrowed your choices, contact the cruise lines directly regarding access on each specific ship. Ask to speak to the special needs department or to an access specialist. This is the time to ask specific access questions about each ship.

One of the first things to ask the access specialist is if they have any accessible cabins on the ship in question. But don't stop there. Ask how wide the doorway clearance to the cabin is, and if there is a sill or lip at the threshold. Some ships still have sizable threshold lips called coamings (a marine term not in the vocabulary of most customer service agents). Ask about the square footage of the accessible cabin compared to a standard cabin and request a detailed floor plan if available. Don't forget to also ask about the width of the corridor outside of your cabin. It really doesn't matter how wide your cabin doorway is if the outside corridor isn't wide enough for you to turn into the doorway.

Next, you need to inquire about the bath-room in the accessible cabin. Ask for specific measurements, including the bathroom doorway clearance and the dimensions of the bathroom. Ask if there is a lip at the bathroom door. If so, ask if they provide a portable ramp. If a portable ramp is used, ask about the height of the bathroom lip. Do the math. A 1:12 grade means that you need one foot of ramp length for every inch of rise; so a six-inch lip would require a six-foot long ramp. Make sure there is enough room in the cabin to accommodate the ramp.

You also need to ask about the bathroom fixtures, including the toilet and shower. Ask if there are toilet grab bars installed on the wall. Some cruise lines provide a raised toilet seat with grab bars attached to the seat. Although this configuration is preferred by people who have difficulty standing, it's unsuitable for many wheelchair users as it makes lateral transfers impossible.

Here are some more things to keep in mind when you're talking to the access specialist.

- Don't assume all accessible cabins are the same. If you need a specific feature, such as a roll-in shower, ask if it's available.
- Don't forget to inquire about access to the public areas of the ship, especially those of

prime interest to you. For example, if you really like the nightly shows, ask about the availability and location of wheelchair seating in the showroom.

- If you'd like to enjoy the water, ask if any of their ships are equipped with pool and Jacuzzi lifts.
- When you book your cruise, remember to request a table near the restaurant entrance but out of the main traffic flow; this will make for a more pleasant dining experience.
- Don't forget about airport transfers. If you book your flight through the cruise line, you can also purchase transfers from them. However, if you fly in the day before departure, you'll have to arrange your own transfers. If you purchase transfers from the cruise line, be sure and let them know you need a lift-equipped or ramped vehicle.
- If you use a power wheelchair or scooter, ask about the electrical supply on the ship. If it's not compatible with your battery charger, bring a converter. For easier recharging, also pack an extension cord and a power strip.
- If you need any special equipment, such as a commode chair or a shower chair, ask if the cruise line can provide it. Provide a detailed description and a photo of the type of equipment you need.

- Ask about tender ports before you choose an itinerary. In some ports, cruise ships anchor offshore and ferry their passengers to the docks in small boats called tenders. In most cases the cruise lines will not tender passengers in power wheelchairs. To avoid being stuck onboard, bring along a manual wheelchair for use in tender ports.

BOOKING AN ACCESSIBLE CABIN

Once you've found a ship that suits your needs, it's time to book your cabin. Accessible cabins are in short supply so try to book at least 6 to 9 months in advance to get your first choice of sailing dates. Accessible balcony cabins on Alaska cruises sell out extremely fast, so book those as soon as they become available.

Most cruise lines block their accessible cabins to prevent them from being booked by able-bodied passengers who merely want more room. Because of this, they are usually only available through the access department. Granted, some slipups do happen and some passengers just outright lie. Case and point are people like the Smiths, who were reported to me by Paul, an angry reader.

"One morning we had breakfast with the family that booked the accessible stateroom we needed (I'll just call them the Smiths)," says frequent cruiser Paul. "They were all able bodied, and they confided in us that they had to lie about being disabled in order to get their cabin. After all, Mr. Smith said, 'It's the only cabin that could accommodate our family of four.' He added, 'I had to instruct our travel agent to lie to the cruise line and tell them that we were disabled. I told her that I'd take my business elsewhere if she didn't. She knows which side her bread is buttered on!'"

Accessible cabins are usually larger than standard cabins in the same class.

It's not right, but it does happen. The cruise lines try to do whatever they can while staying within the law to ensure that it doesn't happen. They now ask passengers who want to book an accessible cabin to submit a simple letter stating their access needs; for example, a roll-in shower or grab bars in the bathroom. You don't have to state a specific diagnosis or go into detail about your medical issues unless you require special services such as supplemental oxygen.

Previously, many cruise lines required a doctor's statement from people who wanted to book an accessible room, but because that violates parts of the ADA the cruise lines have moved away from that requirement. The DOT also strongly opposes requiring medical certification of disabled passengers.

In the end, the cruise lines just want to make sure disabled passengers get the accessible rooms they need. In other words, if you use oxygen but do not use a wheelchair, then most likely you won't need a room with a roll-in shower. The goal is to make sure that limited resources are distributed to those that really need them, and self-declaration accomplishes that goal.

Once you've asked all the questions, chosen a ship, and booked your cabin, there's one more thing to remember. Be sure to have your reservation marked "no upgrade." Although upgrades are usually a good thing, when it comes to cruise ships they can be an access nightmare. I've had a number of complaints from readers who booked accessible cabins, only to be upgraded on sailing day to non-accessible cabins. This seems to happen across the board at all cruise lines, and the only way to prevent it is to specify "no upgrade" on your reservation.

If you do this, your reservation will be flagged accordingly and you won't even be considered for an upgrade. Accessible cabins sell out quickly and it's very unlikely that you will be upgraded into another accessible cabin, so this method is the best way to protect yourself and ensure that the cabin you need is not given away to another passenger. A little advance planning can make things go a lot smoother on sailing day.

WORKING WITH A TRAVEL AGENT

Although you can certainly research a cruise yourself and book it directly with the cruise line, there are advantages to working with a good travel agent that specializes in accessible cruises. The main benefit is product knowledge. The true experts know about the features of accessible cabins, and many can even make arrangements for accessible shore excursions. Additionally, contrary to popular belief, it

220

doesn't always cost more to work with a travel agent; in fact, a savvy one can even save you some money.

It should be noted that unofficially some of the cruise line's special-needs agents "prefer" not to talk to passengers directly. The reason given for this is that the passengers "bog down the special needs agent with general cruise questions in addition to access questions." Although there's no official policy regarding this, be aware you may encounter resistance from some special-needs agents. If that happens, just call back and speak to another agent.

You should also be aware that if you book through a travel agent, most cruise lines will refer you back to that travel agent if you have questions or need changes. Some cruise lines will answer simple inquiries, or verify that you have an accessible cabin reserved. If, however, you discover that your travel agent didn't reserve an accessible cabin, the cruise line will inform you that your travel agent is the only one who can make changes to your reservation.

And if you do work with a travel agent, make sure that the cruise line debits your credit card directly. Why? Well, for one thing it protects you from the few unscrupulous agents who re-price cruises or doctor the tickets and then don't pass on the savings to their clients. It's not all that common but it does happen. If you pay the cruise line directly, your agent won't be able to pocket any savings that belong to you.

Although it's standard practice for cruise lines to charge credit cards directly, some agencies credit the funds to their agency and then use the money as working capital. Legally there's nothing wrong with that, as long as the agency actually turns around and pays the cruise line. But the point is, who wants to work with an agency that is that tight for capital? It's just not a good practice, especially in these economic times. Additionally, there's always the chance that the agency won't pay the cruise line, then closes their doors leaving you holding the bag.

And remember, always pay for all of your travel services with a credit card. This protects you in case the travel agency, airline, or even the cruise line goes bankrupt. If you pay with a credit card and don't receive the services you purchased, your credit card company will refund the money to you. This isn't always true with debit cards, so check with your bank about that. It's best to be on the safe side, though, and always pay with a credit card.

GETTING ON AND OFF THE SHIP

Some ports offer roll-on gangway access, but remember that's not always the case.

Ship accessibility is only part of the equation when it comes to cruising, as getting on and off the ship is another big concern. How does the whole embarkation and disembarkation process work? How do you get on and off the ship at the various ports of call?

To be honest, embarkation and disembarkation in general can be a real zoo. After all, the goal is to get thousands of passengers and their luggage on or off the ship in a matter of hours. So, if you have any kind of physical disability, make sure it is noted in your file, even if you do not need an accessible stateroom. Embarkation assistance can range from fast-tracking disabled passengers through the process, to providing wheelchair assistance. If you are unable to stand for long periods of time or use any type of assistive device, it's important to request embarkation assistance when you book your cruise.

Wheelchair assistance is also available during disembarkation. Different cruise lines have different procedures for disembarking people with mobility disabilities. Some cruise lines gather people needing assistance together in one area, while other lines let them disembark before the other passengers. If you need assistance during disembarkation, make your needs known to the purser when the disembarkation procedure is announced.

Although home ports generally offer roll-off access, that's not the case in every port of call. How do you get off the ship if you are in a wheelchair? Do you just roll down the gangway? Well, sometimes that's the case, but often it's a bit more complicated and passengers needing assistance may have to be lifted and carried. This is especially true at smaller ports outside of the United States.

If you're cruising to Alaska, be aware of the huge tidal fluctuations. While you may be able to roll off in the morning, the gangway may be very steep when you return in the afternoon.

Many recreational activities are accessible on cruise ships, like this accessible golf course on Royal Caribbean's Liberty of the Seas.

And then there's the issue of tendering. Some ports are just not accessible to large ships, and sometimes even the larger ports are too crowded to allow all ships dockside access. In these cases, the ships must anchor offshore and tender their passengers to the docks. Tendering is the process of ferrying passengers by small boats, or tenders, from the cruise ship to the main dock. Most cruise lines can provide a list of tender ports, but depending on traffic and tide conditions, any port is a potential tender port.

Tendering is handled differently by the different cruise lines, but in most cases, it involves hand-carrying wheelchair users onto the tender. Indeed, sometimes tendering can be a white-knuckle experience, especially in rough seas. It should also be noted that some cruise lines will not tender power wheelchairs at all, so it's always a good idea to bring along a manual wheelchair for shore excursions.

Some ships have a more accessible method of tendering passengers. Currently Holland America and Royal Caribbean have lift-equipped tenders on some of their ships. This system allows most wheelchair users to roll on and off the tenders. Check with the cruise lines directly for availability and specifications.

The downside to this process is that the most of the lifts cannot accommodate power wheelchairs or scooters and are only available for lightweight wheelchairs. Additionally they usually need to be reserved ahead of time, and sometimes wheelchair passengers are only tendered after the main rush of passengers. Check with the cruise line directly for their procedures.

In the end, how you get off the ship depends on the port, the incline and access of the gangway, and what the cruise line considers the safest procedure for the conditions. The final decision on the safest procedure always lies with the captain of the ship. If the captain deems it too dangerous to carry a passenger, then so be it. Additionally, he may discontinue tendering for all wheelchair users if conditions are too dangerous.

EXTRA WHEELCHAIR OR SCOOTER?

As previously mentioned, you might also want bring a manual wheelchair along to use in some of the more inaccessible ports. As accessible travel specialist Connie George says, "While a scooter or power wheelchair typically gives you comfort and more independence in day-to-day life, it's the manual wheelchair that can give you more comfort and independence in some ports."

It should be noted that even though most ships carry some manual wheelchairs, they are not allowed to be taken ashore. They are used for embarkation and debarkation and for emergencies. Additionally, they are not for the exclusive use of any passenger. So if you need a wheelchair fulltime, you either must bring your own or rent one and have it delivered to the ship.

If you rent a wheelchair or a scooter, be sure and get exactly what you need. Several national companies can arrange for rentals; however, it pays to shop around for rates and equipment availability. You can also deal directly with your cruise line; otherwise they will not accept delivery of the medical equipment.

Don't be afraid to ask questions about the size, model, and features of the equipment you plan to rent. Ask them to send pictures so you can see what it looks like. Don't be afraid to ask for specific measurements; after all, you want to be sure the equipment will suit your needs.

Also, read the contract carefully to ensure the company guarantees delivery of the specific model your ordered. One passenger recently reported that, although she ordered a compact travel scooter that would fit in her standard cabin, a full-size scooter was delivered instead. She was unable to use it. The company later issued a statement saying that they will no longer guarantee delivery of specific makes or models of equipment. So read the fine print and deal with a company that is able to meet your needs. There are a lot of choices out there. with a local supplier in your home port. This takes more time, but will save you some money. Additionally, be sure your provider is an approved vendor

Scootaround (888-441-7575; www.scootaround.com), Care Vacations (877-478-7827; www.cruiseshipassist.com), and Special Needs at Sea (800-513-4515; www.specialneedsatse

a.com) are the major equipment rental companies but not necessarily approved vendors on all cruise lines.

Additionally, I've received a number of reports from passengers who had other passengers abscond with their rental wheelchairs because they thought they were the ship's wheelchairs. Most of the thefts happened when the wheelchairs were left outside the dining room entrance, although one occurred while the renter was in the restroom.

The bet way to prevent this is to mark your wheelchair so others do not assume it's the property of the cruise ship. The best bet is to put a cushion, a name tag, or a brightly colored personal item on the wheelchair so there will be no doubt it's yours.

And no matter what kind of assistive device you bring on the ship, be sure there's room for it in your cabin. In other words, make sure it can fit through the doorway and be stored inside, as equipment is not allowed to be stored in the hallway. It's also important to note that some cruise lines now have restrictions on the size of assistive devices allowed in standard cabins to eliminate the problem of passengers parking their full-sized scooters in hallways. So, check with the cruise line before you book to be sure your assistive device will fit inside your cabin.

LIFE BOAT DRILLS

Under U.S. Coast Guard regulations, all passengers, including disabled passengers, are required to participate in a life boat drill before sailing. Basically, passengers must show up at their designated muster stations with their life vests on when the alarm sounds. A roll call is then taken, followed by a short safety demonstration, while crew members check all cabins and public areas to ensure everyone is ondeck.

Everyone is required to participate. If you can't do stairs or stand for long periods of time, the procedure can be problematic.

Some cruise lines allow wheelchair users and slow walkers to forego the on-deck life boat drills and instead meet in a designated place to receive instruction about how things would be handled in a real emergency. Ask your room attendant if this is an option. Other cruise lines have no alternate plans for wheelchair users and everyone is expected to show up at their muster stations during life boat drills.

Since passengers are not allowed to use the elevators during these drills wheelchair users are advised to show up at their muster stations at least 15 minutes before the alarm sounds. This is pretty easy to do, as the time for the drill is announced throughout the day, and it's even posted in the ship's newspaper.

In the end, it's important to know what would happen in a real emergency, so be sure and ask your cabin steward what you should do in that case. Don't be afraid to ask too many questions; after all, it's your safety that's at stake.

ROLLING ON THE RIVER

The River Explorer offers a very accessible way to explore the rivers of America's Heartland.

Although ocean cruises are probably the most accessible option, a small number of river and canal cruises are also available. Unfortunately they are pretty limited in the United States and only sporadically available in Europe.

The most accessible U.S. river vessels, the *Empress of the North* and the *American Queen,* are not currently sailing, as they were seized for overdue debts when Majestic American Lines closed its doors. They will probably be sold to satisfy the debtors, so keep an eye open for them to reappear under new ownership. Although the ownership may change, it's unlikely they will eliminate the access features.

The most accessible river option for now is the *River Explorer,* a barge which cruises the rivers of America's Heartland. Operated by River Barge Excursion Lines (888-462-2743; www.ri verbarge.com). This unique vessel has three wheelchair-accessible staterooms with roll-in showers.

In Europe, there are a few more accessible river options, including canal boats, river boats, and self-drive barges.

You can cruise the canals of northwest England aboard *New Horizons,* an accessible narrowboat. *New Horizons* is operated by the Stockport Canalboat Trust (+44 161 430 8082; www.newhorizons.org.uk), and staffed with a skipper and volunteer crew. It features a boarding ramp and lift, plus wheelchair access throughout the boat.

The Lyneal Trust (+44 1743 252728; www .lyneal-trust.org.uk) provides accessible canal boat holidays on the Llangollen Canal, from their base at the Lyneal Wharf (near Ellesmere). This U.K. charity operates two accessible canal boats, the *Shropshire Lass* and the *Shropshire Lad.* The *Shropshire Lass* is a 70-foot residential canal boat which sleeps eight, and the *Shropshire Lad* is a 45-foot canal boat designed for day trips.

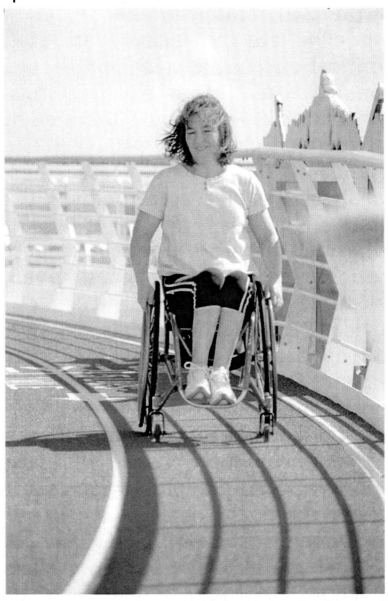

If a workout is in your daily schedule, find out if areas like jogging tracks offer barrier-free access.

You can also cruise the waterways of Ireland on the *Saoirse ar an Uisce* (+353 45 529410; www.kildare.ie/FreedomOnTheWater). This fully equipped barge has central heating, a full galley, and a large bathroom and shower. It is accessible to wheelchair users via a boarding ramp. Day cruises, which depart from Bell Harbor in Monasterevin, are available for groups and families. This is not a self-drive option.

Operated by Peter Deilmann EuropAmerica Cruises (800-348-8287; www.deilmann-cruises .com), the 110-passenger *MV Dresden* makes weekly cruises between Hamburg and Dresden on the Elbe River in eastern Germany. There is one wheelchair-accessible cabin with a roll-in shower. This riverboat was built in 1991 and refurbished in 1996, so all public rooms are barrier-free except for the gift shop and the beauty shop.

And finally, you might consider a French barge holiday. Le Boat, Inc. (800-734-5491; www.leboat.com) operates accessible barges on the Canal du Midi in southern France. If you prefer to leave the driving to somebody else, they also have a wheelchair-accessible barge with full service and a crew (*La Reine Pedauque*). Says one veteran barger, "If you think a trip to Europe won't be accessible enough for you, then barging may be the way to go. Floating slowly through the canals of France was a very accessible and a totally enjoyable experience for me!"

SERVICE ANIMALS

Can you take your service animal aboard a cruise departing form a U.S. port? Absolutely! The Department of Justice rule regarding service animals is pretty explicit. It states that public accommodations must modify their policies, practices, or procedures to accommodate service animals. And, yes, this includes cruise ships that dock in U.S. ports. That's the short and easy part; the more difficult part is the documentation, preparation, and (of course) the paperwork.

It's important to realize that you can't just stroll on board a cruise ship with your service animal. You must inform the cruise line when you book your cruise that you will be traveling with a service animal. All cruise lines require a health certificate for service animals, which must be presented at embarkation. Some cruise lines require additional forms.

Some ports of call require even further documentation, and as mentioned in an earlier chapter, some countries impose quarantines on imported animals. If you dock at a country that has such a quarantine, your service animal will not be allowed off the ship. Be sure and find out about quarantines, restrictions, and all required documentation in advance. This simple step will save you a lot of heartache.

What are your options if you can't take your service animal ashore? Basically you have two choices. You can stay onboard while the ship is in port, or you can go ashore without your service animal. Of course the latter is a realistic option only if you are traveling with an able-bodied companion, but it's something to consider if you really want to see the port.

One of the biggest concerns about service animals and cruises is the toileting arrangements (for the service animal, that is). Is there really a poop deck? Well, there will be the week you cruise! Seriously, ask about the cruise line's toileting policy well in advance. It's also a good idea to get the policy in writing. Policies vary from cruise line to cruise line. Some cruise lines provide a wood box filled with mulch, while some provide Astroturf.

It's a good idea to get your dog used to non-grass toileting prior to your cruise. I'm reminded of my friend Karen's predicament when she took a cruise. Her service animal just wouldn't (or couldn't) do his business for days. Finally her husband took the dog out for a vigorous run around the deck, just to shake things up a bit. It worked like a charm; doggy did his business but hubby was pooped (no pun intended). The moral of the story is that it pays to familiarize your dog with toileting conditions similar to what you'll find on the ship.

It also pays to be prepared for the unexpected. Learn how to deal with problems when they arise. One cruise passenger reported that he left his service animal in his cabin while he went ashore, only to discover his cabin steward refused to clean his cabin. Apparently the cabin steward was afraid of dogs. If you have an incident such as this, report it to the purser. Remind the purser that it's an access issue, and request that appropriate accommodations be made. In the above case, an appropriate accommodation would have been to arrange for a different another cabin steward to clean the cabin.

Finally, a word of warning if you book a cruise and air package. Never rely on the cruise line to relay information about your service animal to the airline and never trust the cruise line to make access arrangements with the airline. Always contact the airline directly to confirm all access arrangements.

OXYGEN

Different cruise lines have different policies regarding the use of therapeutic oxygen (liquid or compressed gas). Some cruise lines allow it and some don't. In nearly all cases, a physician's statement is required for passengers who use therapeutic oxygen.

Some cruise lines may be able to arrange for the delivery of oxygen, but remember—this is not a free service. You can also arrange for oxygen delivery yourself with one of the cruise line's approved suppliers. Contact the special services department for a list of approved suppliers. Be sure you bring enough oxygen to last for the duration of the trip. Alternatively, you can arrange for refills at the ports of call.

If you are driving to the port, you might want to consider bringing your own oxygen supplies. In most cases, this is the most economical option. Check with the special needs department to see if there are any limitations on the types of equipment you can bring onboard.

Alternatively, you might want to check with your doctor to see if you can use a potable oxygen concentrator (POC) while onboard. Check with the cruise line for their POC policies and procedures. If you just need supplemental oxygen occasionally, then consider renting a POC and having it delivered to your cabin. Of course, check with your doctor first to be sure a POC will work for you.

If you are flying to the port, be sure you also make arrangements with the airline for in-flight oxygen use. If your travel agent is making both your cruise and air arrangements, remind them that you will also need in-flight oxygen. This crucial step is often overlooked by many cruise travel agents.

DIALYSIS AT SEA

Special arrangements can be made on some cruises for passengers who require hemodialysis. Although cruise ships do not have dialysis equipment routinely onboard, a few tour operators organize special dialysis cruises. These tour operators make all the arrangements for dialysis equipment, supplies, and medical personnel. These cruise packages are not cheap, but many people enjoy having somebody else take care of all the details. The major drawback: Unless enough people sign up, these specialty cruises are usually canceled.

Some people opt to arrange dialysis on shore. This can be a risky (and sometimes an expensive) plan of action, as evidenced by Linda's experience. "When I booked our seven-day Caribbean cruise I carefully chose our itinerary so I could arrange for dialysis at the U.S. ports of call, as our insurance only covers dialysis in the United States," says Linda.

"When we boarded the ship we were informed of a last minute change of itinerary. Instead of docking at St. Thomas, we docked at St. Maarten. That port change cost me $738 because dialysis on St. Maarten wasn't covered by my insurance."

Most cruise contracts state that the cruise line is not responsible for additional charges due to last minute port changes. Although in Linda's case the port change happened before they boarded the ship, it's important to note that it can (and does) also happen while en route. Always have a backup plan if you opt to get dialysis ashore.

Two good on-line dialysis resources are Dialysis Finder (www.dialysisfinder.com) and Global Dialysis (www.globaldialysis.com). Dialysis Finder features a database that contains dialysis clinics around the world, while Global Dialysis is a U.K.-based web site with lots of information on dialysis travel.

It should also be noted that portable hemodialysis machines designed for home use are not permitted on cruise ships. Although the NxStage System One unit model was allowed aboard a cruise ship during clinical trials, none of the major cruise lines have cleared it nor any other user-operated hemodialysis machine for use on board. The reason cited for this decision is passenger safety.

On the other hand, peritoneal dialysis is a different story. Most of the cruise lines have taken a different view on that, as they feel it's not as risky as hemodialysis. In short, they do allow peritoneal dialysis, but you must contact the special needs department to make special arrangements for the delivery of your supplies to the ship. Check directly with the cruise line for its current regulations, and be sure you specify you are inquiring about peritoneal dialysis, not hemodialysis.

FREE PARKING?

Oddly enough, one of the most common cruise questions I get is about parking—free parking at Florida cruise ports, to be specific. There is a lot of misinformation circulating about this subject, so I'm including the regulations here.

Florida state law requires that free parking be maintained at cruise ship terminals only for passengers who have vehicles with ramps, lifts, hand controls, or State of Florida toll-exemption permits. That is the minimum law, but there's no statute prohibiting the ports from offering free parking to a larger class of people. Such is the case with the Miami Seaport, which allows disabled passenger with a valid placard to park for free. You need to fill out a form and show your placard when you enter the lot.

All other Florida ports only offer free parking for passengers who have an adapted vehicle. This means a vehicle equipped with a ramp, a lift, hand controls, or a State of Florida toll-exemption permit.

All Ashore

ACCESSIBLE SHORE EXCURSIONS

No matter how luxurious the stateroom or how decadent the food, if you can't get off the ship it's just a long boat ride. Now some people can live with that; in fact, some people love the idea of just staying on the ship and being pampered. They even enjoy the port days, when the bulk of the passengers are ashore and the ship's facilities are less crowded.

On the other hand, if you want more from your cruise experience—like being able to enjoy the ports—you have to jump in and do some research. Whether you go it on your own or opt for one of the shore excursions offered by the cruise lines, you need to ask a lot of questions before you sign up for any shore tour.

IS IT REALLY ACCESSIBLE?

Most cruise lines provide a lot of detailed information about their official shore excursions; in fact, many even rate the accessibility of their shore tours. Unfortunately, some cruise lines do better than others in that respect.

The big problem lies in the fact that the cruise lines use pictograms to rate their tour accessibility. There's nothing inherently wrong with that if the pictogram criteria are adequately defined; however, more often than not, that's not the case.

In most cases, when a tour is rated as wheelchair accessible, the tour operators assume that disabled passengers will use a manual wheelchair. They also assume that passengers will be able to climb the steps of a standard tour bus, and that their wheelchairs can be folded and stowed underneath.

So the number one rule is, before you book any shore tour, find out what kind of vehicle will be used. If you need a ramped or lift-equipped vehicle, be sure to specify this when you book your tour. Don't just ask for an accessible vehicle, as you will probably get a standard bus. Again, the assumption is that all wheelchair users can walk at least a few steps.

This is true at all ports (even those in the United States), but it's more prevalent at Caribbean and Mexican ports where accessible transportation is extremely limited. So, don't just ask for an accessible tour. Instead, describe the access features you need. Additionally, it never hurts to ask for photographs of the "accessible" vehicles. In this day and age, that's pretty easy to provide, even in the less-developed nations.

If you are working with a travel agent, be sure they understand the access features you need in a shore tour. Don't just settle for the standard "it's accessible" reply. Again, make sure the tour will be accessible to *you.*

SHIP SPONSORED ORINDEPENDENT?

You basically have two options when it comes to shore excursions. You can book one of the group tours offered by the cruise lines, or you can book an independent tour directly with a local tour operator. There are pros and cons to each method. Some people prefer to deal directly with the tour operator, while others love the convenience of booking a ship-sponsored tour. Here are some of the benefits of each option.

CRUISE LINE SHORE EXCURSIONS

- Passengers on ship-sponsored shore excursions usually get priority boarding on tenders.
- If there is a delay getting back to the ship, they won't sail without you.

- If the ports are changed due to weather or other issues, your money is promptly refunded.
- You can just charge the tour to your cabin.
- Exclusivity agreements prohibit some local tour operators from accepting direct bookings from passengers, so some tours can only be booked through the cruise lines.

Tio Taxi Tours offers accessible tours of Curacao in their lift-equipped Bluebird Bus.

INDEPENDENT SHORE EXCURSIONS

- Independent shore excursions are usually cheaper, as the cruise lines charge local tour operators a hefty percentage to carry their tours.

- Many smaller tour companies are willing to work with passengers to create specialized tours based on the participants' interests.
- It's easier to get accurate access details when you deal directly with the tour operator.
- Some local operators do not take credit cards, so you will have to pay in cash.
- Independent tours can be customized to go at a slower pace.
- You take the tour with your own group—be it family or friends—so you won't feel like you are holding up the whole bus.

A third, hybrid option involves working with a travel agent who can book independent accessible tours for you. If you go this route, be sure you work with a travel agent that specializes in accessible travel. Planning accessible shore excursions is a time-intensive task, and most general travel agents don't have the skills or the contacts to do this. The expertise comes from doing it time after time and knowing the local suppliers.

The one thing you shouldn't do is book your cruise on your own and then contact a travel agent to plan your accessible shore excursions. Like I said, it's a time-intensive process, and most of the small accessible tour providers don't offer commissions. You can't expect a travel agent to work for free. So be sure and plan for your accessible shore excursions when you book your cruise.

ACCESSIBLE CRUISE LINE TOURS

For the most part, the shore excursions that cruise lines offer are not totally wheelchair accessible. By that I mean that most of the accessible excursions are best-suited for passengers that can at least walk a few steps. The good news is, a few cruise lines have started offering wheelchair-accessible shore tours in ramped or lift-equipped vehicles. They aren't well publicized, and they are pretty limited, but they are out there.

Royal Caribbean International and Celebrity Cruises offer a limited number of these shore excursions at some of their European ports. These are not private tours, but because of the vehicles used, the groups are smaller than those on the standard bus tours. All of the tours are conducted in ramped or lift-equipped vehicles.

The fully accessible tours are appropriate for power wheelchair-users and include Easy Tenerife, Easy Lanzarote, Easy La Palma, Easy Athens, Easy Malaga, Easy Barcelona, Easy Palma, Easy Istanbul, and Easy Ephesus. These tours are available on a first-come basis and they can only be purchased onboard at the shore excursion desk.

Holland America Line (HAL) also offers a few fully accessible shore excursions in select ports. They are called Signature Tours and include a van plus a guide for the day, so you are free to set your own itinerary. Only a few of these tours are available with a ramped or lift-equipped van, so contact the shore excursion manager to see if they are available in your ports. I've had good reports from readers who have taken these tours in Tallinn and Helsinki. Currently HAL is looking to expand their offerings, but growth is slow due to the limited availability of accessible vehicles in many ports.

Hopefully more cruise lines will follow suit, and begin offering truly accessible shore excursions in as many ports as possible.

ACCESSIBLE SHORE EXCURSION PROVIDERS

For the most part, people who need truly accessible shore excursions end up planning them on their own. And it's getting easier to that do that, especially with the evolution of the internet. To make things a little easier for you, I've included this list of accessible shore excursion providers. Not only does it include tour operators who have accessible vehicles, but it also features things like accessible boat and helicopter tours, attractions, and city tours within walking distance of the pier.

I didn't include every single tour and attraction, but it's a good starting point. Let's just say, I hit the highlights. The focus is on accessible vehicles, so for the most part I didn't list taxis or tours that require a transfer. There are a few exceptions, and I included those because they were unique or hard to find.

The list also comes with a few cautions. It was compiled from a combination of personal visits and reader recommendations. I did not personally take each and every tour, but had adequate feedback to determine their access levels. That said, things can change over time, especially in the Caribbean and Mexico. Sometimes accessible vehicles break down and are not repaired, while other times companies just go out of business. Like I said, the list a good starting point.

Also be aware that accessible vehicle standards vary outside of the United States. Be sure and ask about the availability of tie-downs and raised roofs when you contact the tour operator.

Last but not least, be sure and ask a lot of questions as far as access is concerned. Although you may not find the level of access you are accustomed to in many foreign ports, most of the tour operators are very honest about their shortcomings. Be patient, though, and allow a long lead time, as sometimes they are hard to reach or slow to answer their e-mail. Persistence will pay off in the end, as there are a lot of accessible options out there.

ALASKA

JUNEAU

- The Mount Roberts Tramway (907-463-3412) features roll-on access and is within walking distance of the pier.
- The lift-equipped Juneau Trolley (907-586-7433; www.juneautrolley. com) stops at 13 attractions as it makes a 30-minute loop through the downtown area. It stops at the cruise ship pier.
- ERA Aviation (800-843-1947; www.flights eeingtours.com) provides accessible transportation to their heliport and offers lift boarding for wheelchair users.
- Orca Enterprises (907-789-6801; www.or caenterprises.com) offers a variety of accessible whale-watching expeditions with lift-equipped ground transportation to the boat.

SKAGWAY

- The White Pass & Yukon Route Railroad (800-343-7373; www.wpyr.com), offers a three-hour rail excursion from Skagway to White Pass summit. There is lift access to one rail car, which has two wheelchair spaces but no tie-downs.
- The Klondike Gold Dredge (907-983-3175; www.klondikegolddredge. com) also offers accessible tours with transportation to and from the pier. This excursion includes a tour of the dredge plus a chance to try your hand at gold panning.

KETCHIKAN

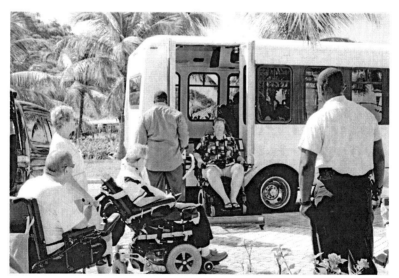

Louis Jeffers can provide wheelchair-accessible tours in his lift-equipped bus on St. Maarten.

252

- The Great Alaskan Lumberjack Show (907-225-9050; www.lumberjacksports. com) is located in the waterfront area, just a short walk from the cruise ship pier.

HAWAII

- Polynesian Adventure Tours (808-833-3000; www.polyad.com) offers a variety of tours in lift-equipped buses on Oahu, Maui, Kauai, and the Big Island.
- Sunshine Helicopters (808-270-3999;) features portable lift boarding for their helicopter tours on Maui and the Big Island.
- Lahaina Divers (808-667-7496; www.la hainadivers.com) operates a variety of dive trips from Maui on their wheelchair-accessible *Dominion.* All staff members are certified Handicapped Scuba Association (HSA) dive buddies, and co-owner Akiyo Murata is a certified HSA instructor.
- Ron Bass (808-572-6299; www.maui.ne t/~kayaking/access) teaches kayaking to wheelchair-users on Maui.

CARIBBEAN

BAHAMAS

- Majestic Holidays (242-322-2606; www
.majesticholidays.com) in Nassau provides accessible tours and airport transfers in their lift-equipped bus in Nassau.
- Expert Tours (242-351-4004) in Freeport
has one lift-equipped van. They provide
island tours.

BELIZE

- Experience Belize Tours (+501-225-
2981; www.experiencebelizetours.com)
offers tours of Belize City, the countryside, and out to Altun-Ha. They are
conducted in an air-conditioned minibus
with lift access and wheelchair seating.

BERMUDA

- Access Bermuda (441-295-9106; www.
access.bm) can provide airport transfers
or island tours in an accessible van with
a lowered floor and tie-downs.

CAYMAN ISLANDS

- Shore Trips (414-964-2100; www.shore
trips.com) can arrange day tours in a

lift-equipped van on Grand Cayman Island. This Wisconsin-based company contracts with the local vendors, who are sometimes difficult to reach individually.

- Elite Limousine (+345-949-5963) can provide airport transfers or tours in a lift-equipped van on Grand Cayman Island.
- Max Taxi Tours & Transfers (+345-917-0133) has one large air conditioned van with a wheelchair lift for tours on Grand Cayman Island.

COSTA RICA

- Vaya con Silla de Ruedas (+506-2454-2810; www.gowithwheelchairs. com) offers day tours in accessible vans from the Atlantic port of Limon (Moin) and the Pacific port of Caldera (Puntarenas).

CURACAO

- Tio Taxi Tours (+599-9-560-5491; www .tiotaxi.com) provides tours of the island in their lift-equipped Bluebird Bus. The bus normally holds 30 people, but capacity varies depending on the number of wheelchair users aboard.

DOMINICA

- Hibiscus Tours (767-445-8195) offers a 3.5-hour Accessible Dominica & Rain Forest Drive tour in a ramp-equipped bus.

JAMAICA

- Noel Wilson (+876-870-6545) can provide a customized Ocho Rios tour in a lift-equipped Toyota van.
- Lincoln Campbell (+876-779-9211) has one lift-equipped and two ramped vans. He offers a variety of tours from Ocho Rios.
- A-Z Jamaica Planners (+876-994-1960; www.a-zjamaicaplanners.com)hasseveral ramped and lift-equipped buses. Their *Take It Easy Tour* is the best choice for full-time wheelchair-users.

PUERTO RICO

- Countryside Tours (787-593-9014; www .countrysidetourspr.com) provides customized walking tours of Old San Juan for wheelchair users and slow walkers.
- Wheelchair Transportation and Tours (800-868-8028) provides accessible island tours in wheelchair-accessible

vans. The company owner formerly operated the Wheelchair Getaways franchise on the island; however, self-drive rental vans are no longer available through this company.

ST. KITTS

- Kantours (+869-465-3054; www.kantours.com) has a lift-equipped Coaster bus, which can accommodate two wheelchair-users and 14 able-bodied passengers. Although the bus is accessible, access may be difficult at some of the sites, so it's best to bring along a manual wheelchair.

ST. MAARTEN

- Louis Jeffers (+599-524-9204) can provide a three-hour tour in his lift-equipped bus.

U.S. VIRGIN ISLANDS

- Accessible Adventures (340-344-8302; www.accessvi.com) offers a historic tour of St. Thomas in a lift-equipped, open-air trolley.
- St. Thomas Dial A Ride (340-776-1277) can provide customized tours in their lift-equipped air conditioned bus.

MEXICO*

[* When calling a cell phone in Mexico from the United States, insert a 1 after the country code.]

ACAPULCO

- Shore Trips (414-964-2100; www.shoret rips.com) offers a Limited Mobility City Tour and Quebrada Cliff Divers excursion in a lift-equipped van.

CANCUN

- Accessible Cancun (+52-998-883-1978; www.cancunaccesible.com) provides a variety of shore tours in their ramped vehicles.

Sunshine Helicopters features portable lift boarding for their helicopter tours on Maui and the Big Island.

COZUMEL

- Accessible taxis are usually available at the port for day tours. To reserve one in advance, call +52 987 872 0236 and ask for a vehicle equipped with the electric winch.

ENSENADA

- Tour guide Gabriela Altamirano Sosa y Silva (+52-1-646-128 7206) offers a number of wheelchair-accessible shore excursions in Ensenada in a lift-equipped, 15-passenger bus.

MAZATLAN

- Victor Chavez (+52-669-102-1448) offers day tours in his lift-equipped van.

PUERTO VALLARTA

- Accessible Mexico (+52-322-225-0989; www.accesiblemexico.com) offers customized tours in their full-size lift-equipped van.
- Transportes Brianchi (+52-322-222-8384) offers accessible tours and airport transfers in lift-equipped vans.

EUROPE

BARCELONA

- Accessible Barcelona (+34-93-428-52-27; www.AccessibleBarcelona. com) offers two accessible city tours. One is a walking tour; the other uses accessible public transportation. Both tours avoid steps and (whenever possible) cobbled streets. The tour guides are also happy to offer assistance if needed.
- Disabled Accessible Travel (+34-605-918-769; www.disabledaccessibletravel.com) offers accessible shore excursions in Barcelona and Palma Mallorca. They may also be able to locate and book other hard-to-find accessible European shore excursions through local operators.

COPENHAGEN

- Customized tours in a lift-equipped bus are available from Harbirk´s Bustrafik (+45-44-44-32-66; www.harbirk.dk).

FLORENCE

- A taxi van with a manual lift is available through SO.CO.TA (+39-055-410133; www .socota.it) for sightseeing trips. Reservations must be made at least 48 hours in advance.

HELSINKI

- Nexttravel (+358-94342-590; www.nexttra vel.fi) provides tours in a van with an attached trailer. The trailer carries scooters and wheelchairs, but passengers must be able to transfer to a van seat for the tour.

LISBON

- Accessible Portugal (+351-217-203-130; w ww.accessibleportugal.com) offers a variety of day tours from Lisbon in lift-equipped mini vans.

LONDON

- Eddie Manning (+44-7970-761-505; www.li mo.co.uk) provides accessible transfers to and from the Dover, Southampton, or Harwich Cruise Terminals from Heathrow, Gatwick, or central London. His accessible vehicle, a VW Transporter, has ramp access and space for one wheelchair user and five able-bodied passengers. Airport transfers to and from London are also available.

OSLO

- Citysightseeing Tours (+47-9710-4742; ww w.citysightseeing.net) offers a city tour in a lift-equipped bus, which departs from the

Cruise Terminal. Although the buses stop at sights along the way and allow passengers to get off and reboard, this isn't a feasible option for wheelchair users since there is only one accessible bus. This tour only operates from May to September.

STOCKHOLM

- Seascape Tours (+46-8-441-3963; www.se ascapetours.se) provides a variety of day tours in a lift-equipped bus.

ST. PETERSBURG

- Liberty Tours (www.libertytour.ru) offers a variety of accessible tours of St. Petersburg in an accessible minibus with folding ramps and tie-downs.
- On some of their tours, DenRus Tours (+561-459-5534;www.denrus.ru)canaccommodate manual wheelchair users who use folding wheelchairs. These tours include transportation in a lift-equipped van.

When Things Go Wrong

NO GUARANTEES

Anybody who tells you that your travels will be trouble free is either a liar or a fool. There are no guarantees in life, and travel by its very nature is unpredictable. There are numerous variables involved on any given trip, and theoretically something could go awry at any stage. Add accessibility issues to this equation and your odds of experiencing a travel mishap greatly increase. I'm not trying to scare or discourage you; I'm simply trying to prepare you. Expect something to go wrong at some point in your travels. It may not happen on your first trip; it may not even happen on your second trip. But odds are it will happen. So the best defense is proper preparation.

BE PREPARED

One of the best ways to prepare for your trip is by playing a healthy game of "what if" before you depart. Ask yourself questions like "What if my wheelchair breaks while I'm on vacation?" Having some well thought-out solutions to these "what if" scenarios will come in very handy when disaster strikes. For example, a good solution to the question would be to gather the phone numbers of a few wheelchair repair shops in your destination city. Of course, it's easy to go overboard with the "what if" game—remember, I said a *healthy* game of "what if." Sometimes there is a fine line between obsession and preparation.

So, what do you do when disaster strikes while you are on the road? Well, your immediate goal should be to solve the problem and salvage your vacation. Next you should try to mitigate or prevent further damage. Sometimes these two goals overlap, and sometimes they even conflict with one another. For example, if your wheelchair is damaged, your first priority should be to make it useable so you won't have to cancel the remaining portion of your trip. However if using your chair could further damage it, it's best to sacrifice a few days of your trip in order to get it properly repaired. In the end it's a judgment call on your part.

You will also have to learn how to effectively communicate your needs to customer service personnel. For example, if your power wheelchair is damaged in-flight, you will have to explain to airline personnel why a manual wheelchair is not an appropriate loaner. Try not to lose your temper, although admittedly that's difficult when dealing with service personnel who don't or won't understand. Threatening to sue or file a formal complaint never really helps; it just creates an adversarial situation. Concentrate on maintaining your composure, and try to calmly explain your needs. It also helps to explain the reasons behind your needs; tell the clerk exactly why you can't use a manual chair. In the long run this is usually the quickest way to an appropriate resolution, but sometimes easier said than done.

You may also want to address your financial loss at the time of the incident. Bear in mind, you may not get a final resolution to this matter, but at least you will have set the ball in motion. You may get an upgrade or some other minor perk for your troubles. Not that I'm implying that a first class upgrade is payment enough for a mangled wheelchair, but if an upgrade it offered on the spot, take it. If you later learn your actual damages are substantial, you can address that problem when you get home.

Be sure and keep all documentation of your actual damages, such as extra hotel nights and airline cancellation charges. Many companies will reimburse you because it's good public relations. In any case, be realistic when you ask for compensation. If your trip was delayed for one day and you had to pay a $100 cancellation penalty to re-book your flight, don't ask for $1500. You have a much better chance of receiving prompt compensation if your demands are realistic.

Save your official complaints for when you get home. Remember to collect documentation along the way, save receipts, and get names. You might also want to jot down the details of the incident while they're fresh in your mind. Then, go away on your vacation and try to enjoy yourself. I know this is not easy, but there's no sense ruining your entire trip over an unfortunate incident. Dwelling on the matter won't accomplish anything. When you get home, you can start the official complaint process. Most likely there won't be a swift resolution to your official complaint, and in some cases it won't even be acknowledged. After all, we are talking about government agencies here.

So why take the time to file an official complaint? In most cases this is the only way to enforce U.S. access laws and to effect change. Filing an official complaint is a very personal decision, but you must also bear in mind that access requirements overall won't improve until more people come forward and complain. Although some agencies don't respond to individual complaints, they do look at trends. So if a particular business is getting a lot of the same type of complaints, there is a chance the enforcement agency will look into it. The first step in filing an official complaint is determining how and where to file it. This varies and depends upon the nature of your complaint.

AIR TRAVEL

The Air Carrier Access Act (ACAA) covers access regarding air travel on all U.S. airlines and on any foreign-flagged flight departing or arriving in the United States. The enforcement agency for the ACAA is the Department of Transportation (DOT). A common misconception shared by many is that air travel is covered under the American with Disabilities Act (ADA). It is not. Air travel is addressed in the ACAA, which was established in 1986 and actually predates the ADA. It was most recently revised on May 13, 2009.

Although a lawsuit was filed in 2003 alleging that U.S. airlines were subject to the Rehabilitation Act of 1973 because of the $3.2 billion federal bailout they received after the 2001 terrorist attacks, it was later dismissed by the U.S. District Cour? Again, the ACAA is the only access law that applies to air travel.

I stress this fact because you need to know the law in order to advocate for yourself. If you spout off to an airline employee that you are unhappy with their service and that you are going to file an ADA complaint, this will only prove your ignorance. The airlines know the rules better than most of us, so you need to be educated on the law in order to be taken seriously.

Although there is much debate about the effectiveness of the ACAA, it does offer some protection and many essential services to people with disabilities. One of the most useful mandates of the ACAA is the creation of the Complaints Resolution Official (CRO). All U.S. carriers must have a CRO available during airport operation hours to specifically address alleged ACAA violations and to solve customer complaints.

The CRO is an airline employee specifically trained in airline duties and passenger rights under the ACAA. The CRO must be available either in person or by phone. So if you encounter a problem en route regarding a violation of the ACAA, and you can't solve the problem with front-line personnel, ask to speak to the CRO immediately. Bear in mind that the gate agent or ticket agent may not know who or what the CRO is, especially if they are new employees. In that case, just ask to speak to a supervisor. Anybody in a supervisory position should be very well educated on the role of the CRO.

CROs also have authority over third-party contractors. This is important to remember because many airlines use third-party contractors as wheelchair pushers (in the airport) and for assisting non-ambulatory passengers with boarding and deplaning. When a problem arises with one of these services, airline employees may claim there is nothing they can do because the service is provided by a third-party contractor. So, if you are unable to resolve a problem regarding a third-party contractor, be sure and point this out to the CRO.

You can also file a written complaint with the airline after you return home. This is your best (and sometimes only) route to monetary compensation for damages. Watch your deadlines here, however, as airlines are not required to respond to complaints postmarked more than 45 days after the violation. For complaints filed in a timely manner, the airline must respond in 30 days.

You also have the right to file a complaint with the DOT; however, this must be filed within six months of the incident. You can download the complaint form on the DOT website (http://airconsumer.ost.dot.gov) or simply submit a letter outlining the details of the incident to the DOT at the following address:

U.S. Department of Transportation
Aviation Consumer Protection Division,
C-75-D

1200 New Jersey Ave. SE
Washington, D.C. 20590

Once the DOT receives the complaint, they investigate and determine what compliance or enforcement action, if any, is warranted. They will acknowledge your complaint and advise you of its disposition when their review is completed. DOT complaints usually result in an adjustment to airline policies and practices, and sometimes fines to the airlines. They do not include monetary compensation for damages to the complainant. You must address this issue directly with the airline within the required time period.

And finally, when dealing with violations of the ACAA, you may also file a civil lawsuit. Although this is probably the most lengthy process, outside of addressing the carrier directly it's the only way to recover monetary damages directly from the airlines.

AIRPORTS

It would be nice if there were one federal agency or department set aside to deal with access in U.S. airports. This unfortunately is not the case, as the presiding enforcement agency is dependent upon many factors, including when the airport was built, where it is located, and what type of funds were used to construct the facility. It's also not uncommon to have different areas within the same facility fall under the jurisdictions of different enforcement agencies. It's confusing at best, but here's the basic rundown of how it all works.

Airports that receive federal funding are subject to Section 504 of the Rehabilitation Act of 1973 and the implementing regulations developed by the DOT. Airports that are owned or operated by state or local governments (considered public entities) are subject to Title II of the ADA. This regulation applies even if the airport in question also receives federal funding. Title II also covers any fixed route transportation system (such as airport parking shuttles) within a public entity airport. Complaints addressing violations to either of these regulations may be filed with the Federal Aviation Administration at the following address:

Federal Aviation Administration
800 Independence Avenue SW, Room 1030
Washington, D.C. 20591

Privately owned, public-use airports are subject to Title III of the ADA. Violations found in these facilities should be addressed to the Department of Justice (DOJ) at the following address:

U.S. Department of Justice
Civil Rights Division
950 Pennsylvania Avenue NW
Disability Rights Section—NYAV
Washington, D.C. 20530

And finally, all terminal facilities owned, leased, or operated by an air carrier at a commercial airport are subject to provisions in the ACAA. (See the "Air Travel" section in this chapter for details on how to address an ACAA complaint.)

GROUND TRANSPORTATION

Ground transportation accessibility is covered under the ADA. Regarding enforcement of the law, ground transportation is divided into two categories: publicly owned transportation and privately owned transportation.

Access standards for public transportation in the United States are mandated under Title II of the ADA. For the purpose of this discussion, public transportation includes city bus lines, paratransit services, commuter rail lines, subways, and Amtrak. The U.S. Access Board developed the access guidelines for public transportation mandated under Title II of the ADA, and public transportation authorities must follow these guidelines and adhere to the accessibility requirements for newly purchased vehicles.

The Federal Transit Administration (FTA), a division of the DOT, provides for enforcement of Title II of the ADA with respect to public transportation. Call the FTA ADA Assistance Line at 888-446-4511 for more information or download a complaint form at www.fta.dot.gov . You can also write a letter outlining your complaint to the FTA at the following address:

Director, FTA Office of Civil Rights
East Building—5th Floor, TCR
1200 New Jersey Ave. SE
Washington, D.C. 20590

Privately owned vehicles, such as those owned by hotels and private bus companies, are covered under Title III of the ADA. Title III complaints should be directed to DOJ:

U.S. Department of Justice
Civil Rights Division
950 Pennsylvania Avenue NW
Disability Rights Section—NYAV
Washington, D.C. 20530

You may also enforce your rights under Title II and Title III of the ADA through a private lawsuit. Provisions in the ADA allow for the payment of reasonable legal expenses on Title II and Title III cases. Many advocacy organizations that specialize in disability rights law will either help put your case together or represent you outright. Alternatively, you may hire a disability rights attorney of your choice to litigate this matter for you.

CRUISE SHIPS

Technically cruise ships are covered under the ADA; however, at the present time, compliance is difficult to enforce. The reason is that the U.S. Access Board has not yet established any accessibility standards for cruise ships. Look for that to change in the next few years, however, as the U.S. Access Board is currently working to remedy this matter.

The U.S. Access Board is responsible for developing the American with Disabilities Act Accessibility Guidelines (ADAAG). To that end, the Access Board created the Passenger Vessel Access Advisory Committee (PVAAC) to make recommendations for the cruise ship ADAAG. After studying the issue for many years, the PVAAC finally released their draft guidelines for public comments on November 26, 2004.

In most cases in the past, after the Access Board reviewed the public comments, it issued the final guidelines. That's not how it worked this time, as there was a very strong response from the deaf community regarding emergency alarm issues. In response to that, the Access Board opted to create an advisory committee to examine the issue instead of issuing the final guidelines. So the wait continues. Suffice it to say, it's now stuck in committee

When completed, the final cruise ship ADAAG will be published in the *Federal Register,* along with the effective date.

As you can see, even though the rule-making process has begun, it may still be some time before official rules are on the legal books. Once the regulations are developed, passenger vessels operated by private entities (including foreign-flagged cruise ships docking at U.S. ports) will fall under Title III of the ADA, and passenger vessels operated by state and local governments (including some ferries) will fall under Title II.

For more information on U.S. Access Board activities, including updates of the PVAAC, visit the U.S. Access Board website at www.accessboard.gov.

HOTELS, RESTAURANTS, AND TOURIST ATTRACTIONS

The lion's share of tourist facilities are covered either under Title II or Title III of the ADA. Title III covers public accommodations, those facilities which are privately owned but open to the general public. This includes privately owned hotels, restaurants, bars, theaters, recreation areas, museums, and tourist attractions. Title III of the ADA is enforced by the DOJ, and complaints should be sent to this address:

U.S. Department of Justice
Civil Rights Division
950 Pennsylvania Avenue NW
Disability Rights Section—NYAV
Washington, D.C. 20530

There is no official Title III complaint form, so just submit a signed letter that details the alleged ADA violation. Remember to include all pertinent information such as dates, names, and addresses. You may also include other documentation, such as receipts and photos, with your letter. Never send original receipts or documentation, as they won't be returned and you may need them for future action.

Title II of the ADA covers access to services, programs, activities, facilities, and buildings owned or operated by state or local governments. This could include facilities such as state-owned museums, recreation areas, or tourist attractions. Additionally if you are unlucky enough to end up in a local or county court (watch those speed traps!), those facilities are also covered under Title II. You can get a copy of the Title II complaint form on the DOJ website at www.usdoj.gov/crt/ada/publicat.htm.

You may also enforce your rights under Title II and Title III of the ADA through a private lawsuit.

NATIONAL PARKS

There's a lot of confusion about access requirements for U.S. national parks and there is also a lot of misinformation. You may have heard that the ADA does not cover access in U.S. national parks, which is true. However, some people interpret this fact to mean that U.S. national parks are not required to be accessible. This is not true—U.S. national parks *are* required to be accessible.

Access in U.S. national parks is covered under Section 504 of the Rehabilitation Act of 1973, legislation that actually predates the ADA. Additionally, concessionaires in U.S. national parks are responsible for providing appropriate access to all programs, services, and facilities. This is important to remember as many U.S. national parks have concessionaires that provide lodging, food, and tour services. The National Parks Service (NPS) is ultimately responsible if these concessionaires are in violation of any access laws.

So, where do you go if you encounter an access problem in a U.S. national park? Common sense would tell you to talk to the access coordinator for the park, and that's fine if you just want to talk about access. The access coordinator is actually a NPS employee, and although the coordinator may be interested in access solutions, he or she is not in any position to implement them.

Consider the access coordinator something akin to an access advisor, able only to make recommendations. Many access coordinators have great ideas and are very helpful, but when it comes to action, most coordinators don't have enough influence to actually facilitate access improvements. Access mandates come from above and are usually the result of official complaints.

Official complaints about access issues in national parks should be directed to the Department of the Interior at the following address.

U.S. Department of the Interior
Office of Equal Opportunity
1849 C Street NW, Room 1324
Washington, D.C. 20240–0002

Write a letter describing your access problem and state that you are making an official complaint under Section 504 of the Rehabilitation Act of 1973. Try to be as inclusive and detailed as possible when describing your access problem, and be sure to include your name, address, telephone number, and the date of the violation. The complaint must be filed within 180 days of the alleged violation.

For more information about filing a complaint with the Department of the Interior, visit www.doi.gov. Technical assistance and general information about access in U.S. national parks can also be obtained by calling the National Center on Accessibility's Technical Assistance Line at 812-856-4422. The National Center on Accessibility has done a great deal of work in this area and is really the most expert resource. It has a very informative website at www.ncao nline.org.

OFTEN OVERLOOKED LAWS

Many people think only of the ADA when addressing access violations in the United States, however, the ADA is far from the only law mandating access. It's one of the newer access laws and perhaps that's why it gets so much press. In truth, many laws actually predate the ADA, and sometimes these useful laws are overlooked when addressing access violations. It pays to be on the lookout for all access laws that may apply to your particular case. Remember, sometimes more than one law may apply. Here are a few often-overlooked access laws you might want to consider.

The Architectural Barriers Act of 1968 (ABA) mandates accessibility in certain buildings financed or leased by the federal government. Buildings that were constructed or altered with federal funds may be subject to this legislation. The key words here are federal funds, so follow the money trail to determine if a building falls under ABA jurisdiction.

The current access standards for the ABA are detailed in the Uniform Federal Accessibility Standards. The U.S. Access Board is responsible for enforcement of the ABA. To file a complaint, write a letter stating the name of the facility and describing the access barriers you encountered. Additional information about the facility, such as when it was built or known sources of federal funding, is helpful but not necessary. Send your complaint to the following address:

U.S. Access Board
Compliance and Enforcement
1331 F St. NW, Suite 1000
Washington DC 20004–1111

Alternatively, you can use the on-line complaint form at www.access-board.gov to file your complaint electronically. Technical assistance is also available from the U.S. Access Board by calling 800-872-2253.

If the U.S. Access Board determines there is a violation of the ABA, they will notify the responsible agency and request removal of the access barriers. The U.S. Access Board monitors the progress of the removal and updates the complainant of the status. In rare cases, the Board has sought court action to enforce ABA violations, but that's usually not necessary because the U.S. Access Board has an excellent record of achieving voluntary compliance.

Another often-overlooked access law is Section 504 of the Rehabilitation Act of 1973. Although I touched on this law briefly is earlier sections of this chapter, be aware there are many avenues to enforce Section 504. Section 504 states that no qualified person with a disability shall be denied access to programs or services that receive federal financial assistance. So once again, follow the money trail to determine if your access problem is covered under this law.

The confusing part about Section 504 is that each federal agency has its own set of 504 regulations that apply to its particular programs. Each department also has its own contact person, and Section 504 complaints must be filed with the appropriate federal agency. Section 504 complaints can also be pursued in civil court. For information on how to file a Section 504 complaint with the appropriate agency, contact the DOJ at the address below.

U.S. Department of Justice
Civil Rights Division
950 Pennsylvania Avenue NW
Disability Rights Section—NYAV
Washington, D.C. 20530

Finally, don't overlook any state or local civil rights laws that may pertain to your access complaint. For example, in California the Unruh Civil Rights Act prohibits businesses from discriminating against certain individuals, including people with a disability. So a California tourist attraction would be in violation of the Unruh Civil Rights Act if it charged people with disability a higher admission price or refused them access or entrance to their establishment. Many states have some type of civil rights legislation that may pertain to discrimination against people with a disability. Check with your State Office of Civil Rights for more information.

LAWYERS AND COURT

Since Title II and Title III cases provide for the payment of reasonable legal fees, more and more attorneys are willing to take these types of cases on a contingency basis. In fact, many law offices actively solicit these types of cases through fancy websites and slick disability rights pamphlets. Although I'm in favor of the distribution of accurate disability rights information, be forewarned that you do need to exercise some caution when searching for an attorney to represent you.

First and foremost, always remember that you are the boss, even if you don't pay your lawyer any money up front. The attorney you hire is working for you even if you have a contingency arrangement. Some attorneys may imply that they are taking your case (at no cost to you) out of the kindness of their heart. Remember, they will recover their expenses and fees if they win the case. It's also not unusual for attorney fees to sometimes exceed the plaintiff's award. Just keep things in perspective and remain in control of your legal proceedings. Your lawyer works for you.

And now some words about choosing an attorney: Be careful. Obviously you shouldn't choose an attorney just because he or she agrees to take your case on a contingency basis. Ask for references and ask what types of disability rights cases the attorney has tried in the past. Try and find an attorney who has experience with cases that are similar to yours. Disability rights is a very broad category. Finally, don't be afraid to ask your attorney what percentage of disability rights cases he or she has won. If the cases are closed, the settlements should be a matter of public record, so also ask for specific case names. Spend some time selecting your attorney and don't let anybody rush you into a decision.

Alternatively you can represent yourself and file your own Pro Se ADA Complaint in Federal District Court. The Pennsylvania Coalition of Citizens with Disabilities has compiled some easy-to-understand instructions along with the forms required to file your own complaint. You can find these on the internet at www.ragged-edge-mag.com/archive/pro-se.htm.

FOR MORE INFORMATION

There's a lot of good information available about disability rights legislation. Here are a few of my favorite resources.

ACCESSIBLE AIR TRAVEL

This free guide is published by the United Spinal Association. It explains consumer rights and airline responsibilities under the ACAA in simple language. It also includes some good photographs of airline boarding procedures for non-ambulatory passengers. A free PDF version of this booklet is available at www.unitedspinal.org; a print version can also be ordered by calling the United Spinal Association at 800-444-2898 at a $1.95 charge.

DOT AVIATION CONSUMER DISABILITY HOTLINE

The DOT operates an aviation consumer disability hotline at 866-266-1368. Travelers are invited to call to obtain information and assistance if they experience disability-related air service problems.

THE AMERICANS WITH DISABILITIES ACT: YOUR PERSONAL GUIDE TO THE LAW

Published by the Paralyzed Veterans of America, this helpful publication contains general information on the different titles of the ADA. Information about ADA enforcement is also included. It can be downloaded free at www.pva.org.

A GUIDE TO DISABILITY RIGHTS LAWS

This free guide presents a good overview of eight federal access laws including the ADA, ABA, the Rehabilitation Act of 1973, and the ACAA. It also contains a helpful list of disability rights resources. It can be downloaded at www.pueblo.gsa.gov or ordered by calling the Federal Citizen Information Center at 888-878-3256.

ADA INFORMATION

For general ADA information, answers to specific technical questions, free ADA materials, or information about filing a complaint, call the ADA Assistance Line at 800-514-0301. Free technical assistance materials are available at www.ada.gov/publicat.htm.

TAKING ACTION

This handy self-advocacy guide includes a list of self-advocacy do's and don'ts, with some excellent real life examples, sample letters, and a list of helpful websites. Call 800-444-2898 to order your print copy for $1.95, or download it for free at www.unitedspinal.org.

Beyond the U.S.A.

OUTSIDE OUR BORDERS

Access doesn't magically disappear once you venture beyond U.S. borders; however, it does change. These changes can be good or bad, depending on your perspective. With that in mind, there are a number of things to consider if a foreign destination is on your travel calendar.

First, you should become familiar with the access laws of your destination country. The Unites States is not the only country that has rules and regulations that govern access; in fact, some countries have even stricter laws with higher access standards. It's true that the Americans with Disabilities Act (ADA) won't protect you on foreign soil, but don't rule out the existence of local access laws.

Other countries, of course, are at the opposite end of the access spectrum and have no human rights or access legislation. Whatever the case, it pays to find out about the laws (or lack thereof) before you hit the road. This not only helps you understand local customs, but more importantly, it also gives you a good idea of what to expect in the access department.

CANADA

Because of its proximity to the United States, Canada is a popular destination for many Americans. Canada presents a welcome air of familiarity, as English is widely spoken throughout the country. But there are many differences, too. As far as access laws go, it's a 50–50 split; some are very similar to U.S. regulations, while some are drastically different. Here's a breakdown of what to expect.

On the strikingly familiar side is the Canadian Transportation Act of 1996 (CTA), which covers access on transportation throughout Canada. Among other things, the CTA mandates access at airports and on Canadian airlines (on aircraft with 30 or more seats). The air transportation regulations under the CTA are very much like our own Air Carrier Access Act (ACAA). Basically the regulations mandate access and prohibit disability-based discrimination at Canadian airports or on Canadian airlines.

Although Americans are not protected by the ACAA on Canadian airlines, most travelers feel comfortable with the protection afforded them under the CTA air transportation regulations. For more information about the regulations, visit www.cta-otc.gc.ca/access/regs/air_e.html.

The biggest difference between the United States and Canada as far as accessible air travel is concerned is Canada's new one-person/one-fare rule. This groundbreaking regulation, which took effect on January 10, 2009, allows "people with severe disabilities" to travel with an attendant at no extra charge, on domestic flights within Canada.

Of course, there are some limitations. The attendant must be required for the in-flight personal care or safety of the passenger, which; and it doesn't apply if you simply prefer to travel with a companions or if you only require attendant care at the destination. Additionally, it only applies to Canadian airlines. To find out if you qualify for free attendant airfare under this rule, contact your airline directly.

There are some glaring differences between Canadian access laws and the ADA. For example, although disability-based discrimination is prohibited under the Canadian Human Rights Act of 1976–1977, there are no building codes that address physical access. This results in much confusion for uninformed Americans who assume that Canadian access standards are identical to those mandated under the ADA.

In order to address this problem and institute some uniformity, the Hotel Association of Alberta founded Access Canada, a voluntary rating program for Canadian hotels and motels.

The Access Canada rating system is divided into four levels, with level four having the highest level of access. Level one has basic pathway access, while level four properties have a roll-in shower and a trapeze bar over the bed. In actuality, there are very few level four properties.

Participating establishments pay a fee and are then inspected by an Access Canada specialist to determine their access rating. After inspection, the property can display the Access Canada logo along with their access rating. Although not widely used, Access Canada is the only official access rating system for Canadian hotels. More information about this voluntary program can be found on the Alberta Hotel Association website at www.albertahotels.ab.ca.

In the absence of official access regulations, sometimes it's best to take the cue from disability organizations within the country. What do they consider accessible when it comes to hotel rooms? Well, here's the access criteria that the Canadian disability organization Keroul uses to define an adapted room.

"[An] accessible entrance is ground level or gently sloped, the threshold is less than 2 cm high and the door is wider than 76 cm. The bathroom has a door at least 76 cm wide, enough space to circulate (1.5 m by 1.5 m), grab bars and enough clearance under the wash basin (68.5 cm or more). If there is one bedroom, it is large enough to move around in easily."

As you can see, it's not exactly an ADA definition of accessible, but it's pretty much what you can expect to find when you see that little blue wheelchair pictogram in Canada. One important final note about access in Canada: Roll-in showers are not as commonplace as they are in the United States. It's somewhat unusual to find a property that has a roll-in shower, so even if a property touts a guest room with an accessible bathroom, be forewarned that a roll-in shower is probably not considered part of the access package. Remember to always ask specific questions about access. Never assume anything.

A good Canadian travel resource is the Access To Travel website at www.accesstotravel. gc.ca. Developed by the Canadian government, this informative website includes detailed access information on bus, rail, air, and ferry transportation, and gives visitors the heads-up on accessible public transportation, paratransit options, and even accessible van rentals.

EUROPE

Europe is another popular vacation spot, and thanks to the work of organizations like the European Network of Accessible Tourism (ENAT), a high degree of access is found throughout the European Union. Composed of regional tourist boards like Visit Britain and the Athens Ministry of Tourism, as well as disability organizations such as Tourism for Alla, ENAT fights for the removal of architectural barriers and works to improve access to public transportation. And on the customer service side of things, the organization also encourages the adoption of higher standards of service for disabled customers.

On the other hand, there are still a few differences between access in Europe and access in the United States. It goes without saying that it pays to be aware of those differences.

Thanks to the strengthening of Britain's Disability Discrimination Act in October 2004, there are now many more accessible things to do in London.

In 1995, Britain passed the Disability Discrimination Act (DDA), which made it illegal for most providers of goods, services, and facilities to discriminate against any person with a disability. The DDA applies to public accommodations such as hotels, airports, and entertainment venues, as well as to most ground transportation providers. In October 2004, the DDA was further modified and strengthened to include even the smallest businesses.

Although the DDA doesn't apply to British air carriers, the European Union Passengers with Reduced Mobility (EUPRM) regulations cover access on all flights departing from European Union (E.U.) airports, as well as flights on European airlines arriving in the E.U.

These regulations, which went into full effect on July 26, 2008, prohibit E.U.-based airlines, travel agents, or tour operators from refusing service or denying boarding to disabled passengers. They also prohibit E.U. airlines from charging for the transport of wheelchairs or service animals, or for wheelchair assistance in airports. And finally, the regulations make it the responsibility of the airport authority to provide assistance for disabled passengers from the time they arrive at the airport until the moment they are seated on the airplane.

Disabled passengers who are refused boarding or are denied any of the required

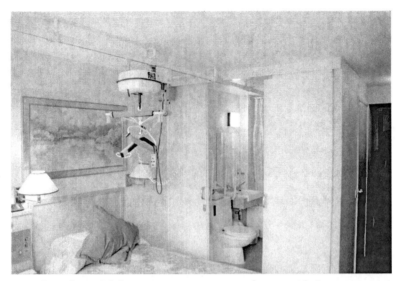

Rooms in the M4 category, such as this one at the
Copthorne Tara in London, offer the highest level of
access.

access accommodations can file a complaint
with the Equality and Human Rights Commission
(EHRC). The EHRC will investigate the complaint
and, if warranted, refer the matter to the Civil
Aviation Authority (CAA). The CAA has the
power to prosecute; if found guilty, the airlines
can face unlimited fines.

As far as accessible lodging goes, the United
Kingdom also has a voluntary access rating
program. The National Accessibility Scheme
(NAS) works much like the Access Canada program. Properties are first inspected by a trained
professional in order to determine their access
rating. This rating is then noted in guide books,
tourism department publications, lodging
brochures, and travel websites.

There are four mobility categories in the newer NAS scheme, with category M4 having the highest level of access.

*   *M1:* Typically suitable for a person with sufficient mobility to climb a flight of steps but would benefit from points of fixtures and fittings to aid balance.
*   *M2:* Typically suitable for a person with restricted walking ability and for those that may need to use a wheelchair some of the time.
*   *M3:* Typically suitable for a person who depends on the use of a wheelchair and transfers unaided to and from the wheelchair in a seated position.
*   *M4:* Typically suitable for a person who depends on the use of a wheelchair and transfers to and from the wheelchair in a seated position. They also require personal/mechanical assistance to aide transfer (e.g., carer/hoist).

Like the Access Canada rating system, this NAS is voluntary. But because participation in the U.K. program is more widespread, there is a greater availability of detailed access information on hotels, inns, and vacation rentals in the region.

The United Kingdom also gets a big thumbs up for the availability of accessible ground transportation, particularly taxis. In fact, all

London black cabs are now required to be accessible, either by a portable ramp or a fold-down dickie seat.

Another access service unique to the United Kingdom is the National Federation of Shopmobility UK—Shopmobility, for short. This U.K.-based charity provides manual wheelchairs, power wheelchairs, and scooters to the anybody with limited mobility so they can shop and visit leisure and commercial facilities throughout town. Shopmobility schemes (a scheme is something akin to a local chapter) are located throughout the United Kingdom and each scheme has different rules.

Some locations provide for the free use of equipment, while others charge a nominal rental fee. Some require advance notice or reservations and others have equipment available on a walk-in basis. And although this service was originally designed for daily use, many schemes now offer weekly rental, which is the ideal option for visitors. Best bet is to contact a Shopmobility scheme in advance to see what they offer. If they are not able to meet you access needs, they will most likely refer you to a local provider who can.

And then there are accessible public toilets. The good news: There are thousands of accessible public toilets throughout the United

Kingdom. The bad news: They are locked and are only accessible with a National Key Scheme (NKS) key. NKS keys are available from The Royal Association for Disability and Rehabilitation (RADAR) for £4.11 in the United Kingdom (about $6.00) and £5.40 (about $8.00) in the United States. It's best to plan ahead and purchase a NKS key before you set off on your trip. A directory of NKS toilets is also available from RADAR for £12.25 ($18.00).

If your travels include the Republic of Ireland, a different key is available from J Williams & Son in Dublin for 20 Euro (about $26.00). This key will open 99 percent of the locked accessible public toilets in the Republic.

A good general resource about accessible travel throughout the United Kingdom is the Disabled Travel Advice website (www.disable dtraveladvice.co.uk), which contains a growing collection of articles about the accessible travel from a British perspective. It features accurate, first-hand information and helpful travel tips.

And if you'd like some destination specific access information about London, visit the Access in London website at www.accessproj ect-phsp.org/london. Although it's a bit dated (most of the information is from the 2004 edition of the printed guide), the website is sporadically updated and includes information on accessible tourist attractions, toilets, accommodations, recreation, and transportation in the London area.

On the Continent, access standards and laws vary from country to country; however, some things apply across the board. Although different from the United States, access terminology is pretty standard throughout Western Europe, although the differentiation between an adapted room and an accessible room is a new concept for most Americans.

An *accessible room* is defined as a room that presents no obstacles to entering and moving about in a wheelchair, but offers no other specific access amenities. An *adapted room* is a room in which the bathroom, shower, and toilets are adapted to comply with access standards. So, if you need a roll-in shower or a raised toilet, don't ask for an accessible room. Roll-in showers are quite common throughout Europe, but you need to specify your needs. They are sometimes called level entry or no-rim showers. Also remember that in Europe, the first floor is not at street level. If you want a room at street level, ask for a room on the ground floor.

One of my favorite European resources is *Rick Steves' Easy Access Europe.* This 2004 release contains general information about

European travel and includes listings for accessible hotels, restaurants, and attractions in London, Paris, Bruges, Amsterdam, and Frankfurt. All listings are rated for access, but because of the off-the-beaten track focus of Steves' titles, the majority of the listings are appropriate for slow walkers only. Still it's a useful resource for budget travelers and for people who can make do with less than perfect access.

DOWN UNDER

With the passage of the Disability Discrimination Act (DDA) of 1992, access for people with disabilities in Australia has greatly improved in subsequent years. The DDA states that it is unlawful for providers of goods, services, and facilities to discriminate against a person with a disability. This includes public accommodations such as restaurants, lodgings, transportation, and entertainment venues.

The Human Rights and Equal Opportunity Commission (HREOC) is the enforcement authority of the DDA, and like many other government agencies, they are able to grant exemptions to the law. For example, in 2008 the HREOC granted Regional Express Airlines (Rex) a five-year exemption from parts of the DDA. Under this decision, airline employees are not required to manually lift passengers from aisle chairs to aircraft seats if the transfer cannot be preformed safely due to space limitations in the aircraft cabin. This exemption is conditioned upon Rex's trial use of sliding boards and lifting devices, with the ultimate goal being improved access. That's generally the case with all exemptions—they work toward the bigger picture of improved access.

In practice, Australia offers good access to lodging and most tourist facilities. And although accessible ground transportation can be difficult to find in some of the remote regions of the continent, Australia has some very unique access resources.

At the top of the list is NICAN, a national database which contains access information on accommodations, tourist attractions, and recreational facilities throughout Australia. Free access information is available from NICAN by phone, or online at www.nican.com.au.

Another great Australian innovation is the mobility map. These city maps depict the access features of local business districts and they are usually available through city tourism departments. The maps include information on accessible routes, telephones, toilets, and parking. They also include local landmarks, tourist attractions, and street gradients.

The city of Melbourne publishes an excellent mobility map, which is also available online at www.accessmelbourne.vic.gov.au.   Printed copies are available from the City of Melbourne at +61-3-9658-9658. I'd love to see this concept catch on in other countries, but so far Australia is the only place that has really developed this access resource.

Australia also has an accessible public toilet key scheme called the Master Locksmith Access Key (MLAK) scheme. Patterned after Britain's NKS, the MLAK scheme was introduced in Australia in 1994. Anybody with a disability can purchase a MLAK key from a locksmith who is a member of the Master Locksmiths Association of Australia. For more information on this program, contact Spinal Cord Injuries Australia at +61 2 9661 8855 or visit their website at www.scia.org.au.

ASIA

This region is massive and technically includes many sub-regions. But the one unifying fact throughout the area is that change is in the air as far as access is concerned.

That said, currently Asia presents some major access obstacles to anyone with a mobility disability. Generally speaking, Laos, Myanmar, and Cambodia have a lesser degree of access than Japan, Thailand, Malaysia, Singapore and Hong Kong; however, gaps in accessible services are still present even in the more accessible countries.

Outside of a few major metropolitan areas, there is also a lack of accessible ground transportation. Although some hotels have accessible guest rooms, narrow doorways are routinely present even in rooms with roll-in showers. So when visiting this region, ask a lot of questions about accommodations.

On the plus side, in places where physical access is limited, personal help is usually enthusiastically offered. This is especially true in the more remote areas of the region.

On the civil rights front, China, India, and Thailand have endorsed the United Nations' Convention on the Rights of Persons with Disabilities, which establishes the right of people with disabilities to participate in sports, leisure activities, and tourism. India recently released its first online access guide, Thailand hosted the Second International Conference on Inclusive Tourism in November 2007.

As noted earlier, change is on the horizon in the access department. For example, according to the Beijing Tourism Commission, more than 120 Beijing hotels were remodeled to accommodate disabled guests for the 2008 Olympic games. It's definitely *the* region to watch, as exciting things with accessibility are happening there.

MIDDLE EAST

The Middle East is another up-and-coming region as far as access is concerned. Like Asia, many parts of the area are highly inaccessible; however, there are a few pockets of good access. And the good news is, those pockets are expanding.

Israel is a prime example of this expansion. Although there are some accessibility laws, in most cases these laws only fully apply to buildings constructed after 1995. So it's quite possible to encounter things like narrow doorways, steps, and small elevators in older buildings. On the plus side, the country as a whole is responding to the aging population, which has resulted in bevy of access information. With a printed access guide, several excellent websites, and a few organizations that provide access information, there are a lot of information resources.

Access Israel is one of these organizations, and their focus is providing access information to Israel's tourist sites. Their website (www.aisrael.org) contains a searchable database of accessible tourism facilities throughout Israel, with detailed access information included with each entry. And the good news is, this site is continually growing.

Other exciting access improvements in the Middle East include the introduction of accessible taxis in Bahrain. And there are not just a few vehicles either—by the time the project is completed, there will be 300 accessible vehicles in the fleet. These aren't special vehicles; they are the standard taxis operated by the Arabian Taxi Company. Access is just one of their features, just like GPS and tamper-proof meters. Again, they are looking ahead and responding to the market.

And then there's Dubai, a country that recently launched a "Tourism for All" campaign in order to improve access to tourism sites. It's slow going and many improvements need to be made, but at least there is recognition of the problems and shortcomings with access.

For the most part, the rest of the region lacks truly accessible services and facilities, but hopefully that will change in the future.

DEVELOPING COUNTRIES

What about travel to developing countries? Is this really a possibility for wheelchair-users and slow walkers? It depends; there really isn't a pat answer to that question.

I know a number of wheelchair users who love this kind of off-the-beaten-track travel, but they admit it's not easy. It takes a lot of planning and, in the end, these adventuresome folks set out well prepared with very realistic expectations. On the other hand, I also know people who have attempted this type of travel with grossly unrealistic expectations and even a certain degree of naïveté. These poor souls set out very ill prepared for what they will encounter along the way, and as expected, don't fare very well. Indeed, the key to any successful trip lies with proper preparation, and proper preparation in this case also means familiarization with the access realities of your destination.

What should you realistically expect as far as access goes in developing countries? Well, in many cases, human rights and access laws are scant or nonexistent, so you have to be prepared for access obstacles. In most cases, you should be prepared to be carried up steps and through narrow doorways. Accessible toilets and bathrooms are few and far between. and accessible transportation is usually nonexistent.

That's the downside. The upside is that in many cases there are work arounds. As far as physical access goes, it's best to travel with a lightweight manual wheelchair whenever possible. It's also a good idea to travel with a companion who is able to lift and carry you and bump you up stairs. Alternatively, you can hire a local (usually for a very low price) to assist you.

As far as transportation, you will have to transfer (with help or by yourself) to a standard vehicle, as accessible vehicles are very rare in most developing countries. Take along a transfer board and whatever manpower (or womanpower) you need to accomplish this task. Many drivers and tour guides are also willing to help, but you should be sure to tip them for their assistance.

You might also consider taking along a portable suitcase ramp to help make some of those two-or three-step entrances more accessible. Handi-Ramp (www.handi-ramp.com) manufactures a wide variety of sizes and styles of portable ramps.

Although access information is sorely lacking for most developing countries, one volume stands out: *Access Africa: Safaris for People with Limited Mobility.* Penned by Gordon Rattray, this unique guide was published in 2009 and contains accessible safari information on Kenya, Tanzania, Zambia, Botswana, Namibia, and South Africa.

Last but not least, the best all-around resource for travel in developing countries is *The Practical Nomad: How to Travel Around the World* by Edward Hasbrouck. This comprehensive volume includes authoritative information on everything from air and surface transportation to baggage, budgets, and health issues. Although the book contains a few paragraphs and lists some resources on accessible travel, it's not really an accessible travel title. Still it's a must-read for any off-the-beaten path traveler. Additionally, Mr. Hasbrouck has a very enlightened attitude about accessible travel in developing countries—an attitude which serves to encourage rather than discourage people from giving it a try.

ELECTRICITY AND CONVERTERS

Access standards aren't the only differences you'll encounter when you travel outside of the United States. One difference of major importance to many wheelers is the electrical voltage outside of North America. In short, if you travel with a rechargeable battery you will need to learn how to safely recharge your battery while you're on foreign soil. It goes without saying that you also need to formulate a contingency plan, just in case something goes wrong.

The United States, Canada, and most countries in the Western Hemisphere operate on 110-volt electricity; most other countries operate on 220-volt electricity. Additionally, some countries also have plug configurations that are different from those used in the United States.

So, you need two things to safely charge your battery overseas. First, you need a converter or transformer to safely convert the foreign electricity. Second, you may also need an adapter so that your U.S.-style plug will fit in the foreign socket. What happens if you don't use a converter? Quite simply, you will fry your battery charger. Although it sounds pretty basic, many people get into trouble because they don't think before they plug in their equipment.

For example, some countries have that familiar two-prong outlet found across the United States but they operate on 220 voltage. The plug fits in the socket nicely, but if you don't use a converter you'll fry your charger.

Remember, the only thing an adapter does is change the shape of the plug. It does nothing to convert the electricity. Just because the plug fits into the socket doesn't mean that it's safe to plug in your equipment. Before you plug in your battery charger, always ask yourself, "Do I need a converter?" Don't plug in your equipment until you know the answer. Nothing ruins a vacation faster than a fried battery charger.

What kind of a converter do you need? Well the first thing you need to do is to find out the voltage, amperage, and wattage of your battery charger. This information is usually written on the charger, but if you can't locate it consult your owner's manual. If you still can't find this information, write down the make and model of your wheelchair, then call the manufacturer and ask for the technical support department.

You'll probably also need also some adapters to go along with your converter. Which adapters should you buy? That depends on where you plan to travel. A good information resource for adapters is Magellan's, a mail-order catalogue for travel supplies. They have a good look-up chart on adapters plus lots of valuable information on their website and in their printed catalogue. Additionally they will answer individual questions about specific needs. Of course, they also carry just about every adapter known to man.

If you travel a lot or just don't want to bother with thinking about converters and electricity, you might want to consider buying a universal battery charger. They are available through a variety of companies, and can be installed on your wheelchair. Check with your wheelchair manufacturer to see what model will work best for you.

The advantage to a universal charger is that you don't have to carry a special converter in order to use electricity in a foreign country.

You may still need some adapters to use with your universal charger, however, depending on your destination. A universal charger is a good idea if you plan to travel overseas frequently.

Other helpful suggestions include carrying a photo of a battery charger and the words "battery charger" written in the local language. These items will help you if you fry your battery charger and need to go in search of a replacement in a country where you don't speak the language.

OTHER CONCERNS

Medical issues are a concern no matter where you travel, but they take on an added importance when you travel outside of the country. While your medical insurance will most likely cover you throughout the United States, it may not cover you in a foreign country. Check with your insurance company before you depart. If your insurance does cover you outside of the United States, be sure and carry the appropriate medical cards and insurance forms. And find out how to file an overseas claim. Although nobody plans to seek medical care while on a vacation, accidents do happen. The best strategy is to be prepared.

You'll also want to find out if your destination country has some sort of national health care program that also covers travelers. Some countries do, and they provide free emergency medical care to anyone, even visitors. It pays to ask a few questions, as it may prevent you from buying unneeded medical insurance.

If you don't have any other coverage, you may want to buy some travel medical or health insurance that will cover you overseas. Some travel agents sell this, but it's really best to check with your own insurance agent. After all, agents are the experts about insurance issues. Make sure that any travel insurance you purchase doesn't exclude pre-existing conditions.

One of the biggest costs of a medical emergency overseas is the cost of medical evacuation. If you should have an accident and can't fly home on a regular airline, you'll need to hire an air ambulance. Some types of insurance already cover this. For example, my Travel Medical Protection Plan from American Express covers up to $100,000 for emergency medical evacuation. The premium is incredibly affordable and it covers me for the entire year, no matter where I travel. Of course I carefully inspected the policy before I made my purchase decision.

Check with your insurance company about travel insurance plans. They are affordable and some even include trip cancellation and accidental death coverage. Again, it's very important to ensure that your policy does not exclude pre-existing medical conditions. Additionally, it's usually more economical to buy a policy that covers you year round, as opposed to a short-term policy that only covers you for just one trip.

Many travel agents also sell all sorts of trip cancellation and travel insurance. Some travel agents even make you sign a form stating that you declined to purchase coverage from them. Although they make a commission on the travel insurance policies they sell, most travel agents don't like to see folks go without it, just in case something happens. After all, they want happy clients.

Of course, there are a handful of those dishonest travel agents who will push anything off on their clients just to make a commission. Such agents don't seem to stay in business too long, however. Although most travel agents are reputable, it's best to see your own insurance agent regarding any travel insurance issues. Again, they are the experts in all insurance matters.

Of course, always take a copy of all of your prescriptions with you when you travel. Pack them in your carry-on baggage. Some people also take a brief medical history with them in case they have a medical emergency and are unable to communicate. You might also want to check into getting a Medic Alert bracelet if you have a special medical condition or unique medical needs. And finally, if you are going to a foreign country, learn a few words of the language. At the top of the list is "wheelchair." If you can't manage the pronunciation, then just write it down and carry with you. It may come in handy.

WHERE TO BEGIN

Where do you begin your research for your overseas trip? Well, the first rule of thumb is to try and deal directly with organizations or people in your destination country. Although many people in the United States are experienced with overseas travel, the locals have the most updated and accurate information.

Wherever you travel, there will most likely be some set of rules governing access, and the best way to find out about these is through a national disability organization. Disabled Peoples' International, an international cross-disability network, has a good list of worldwide disability organizations on their website at www.dpi.org.

Another good resource are the foreign counterparts of U.S. disability organizations. For example, if your travels take you to the United Kingdom, you might want to check out the Multiple Sclerosis Society of the United Kingdom. The internet is a great tool for this type of research. Post a few notices in travel forums and on disability focused websites,. The goal is to find a local contact. Generally speaking, if you ask enough people, sooner or later you will find a good contact.

And finally, don't forget about foreign tourist bureaus. Some offices now have access information and some even publish access guides. It never hurts to ask, as they may even be able to give you a local access contact.

The Travel Agent

FRIEND OR FOE?

You've finally decided that it's time for a vacation, so what's the first thing you need to do? Well, according to most other books about accessible travel, you need to "find a good travel agent." To be honest, that's pretty useless advice. After all, nobody wants to find a bad travel agent.

Sarcasm aside, there are several things you need to understand before you go in search of that perfect travel agent. First, you need to determine if you even need a travel agent. To do this, you need to understand how travel agents work and what they can and can't do for their clients. In the long run, this will also help you work more effectively with your agent.

Of course you also need to know how to find a travel agent that best suits your needs. To do this, you also need to learn a little bit about the industry, so you will know how to recognize a good travel agent. Additionally, you need to be able to recognize a bad travel agent, along with some of the pitfalls and scams that seem to proliferate in this industry. As with everything else, it's definitely a case of buyer beware.

TRAVEL AGENT 101

Travel agents work in a variety of ways, but in the simplest terms, they book travel for clients and receive commissions from suppliers (cruise lines, hotels, airlines, tour companies, etc.). The products they offer are dependent upon their business relationships and commission arrangements with the suppliers. So in theory, two different travel agents could work with a number of different suppliers, and as a result, offer their clients different travel options. I say in theory, because it doesn't always work that way.

In practice, many mainstream travel agents only work with the suppliers that pay the highest commissions. Unfortunately, there are only a limited number of suppliers that provide accessible services, and since most of them don't pay large commissions, they are somewhat unknown to mainstream agents. Those agents that specialize in accessible travel are ultimately the ones that are familiar with these specialty providers. The big problem is finding these specialist agents. More on that later.

The truth is that many small accessible tour operators would like to be able to pay commissions, but they just can't afford it. So, these small guys are effectively left out of the booking loop. Travel agents can't afford to work for free, of course, so they must work with suppliers that can pay commissions. Small tour operators need to make a living, so most can't afford to pay out commissions—a vicious circle.

But it's not just the small tour operators that don't pay commissions to travel agents. Years ago, most airlines paid out hefty commissions, but over the years, those commissions have also dwindled. Today it's difficult for many travel agents to even pay for their reservation software with the meager commissions offered by most airlines. The result is that some agents no longer work with air-only clients, while others now charge a minimal processing fee for domestic air tickets. Generally speaking, travel agents still receive a decent commission on international airline tickets, so most are still willing to offer this service.

As a result of dwindling commissions, many travel agents found new and different ways to address the travel market. The professional organizations encouraged travel agents to find profitable niche markets, such as accessible travel. Many travel agents became accessible travel specialists overnight, by simply printing "accessible travel specialist" on their business card.

Others listened to the industry experts and took advantage of training courses to become "niche specialists." Currently one company offers an "Accessible Travel Specialist" certificate, but the requirements for getting it are minimal. You must be a travel agent for one year, pass an online test, and demonstrate some "disability life experience" by performing tasks such as subscribing to a disability publication, attending a disability conference, or volunteering at a disability organization. Although there's nothing wrong with encouraging volunteerism, it should be noted that travel agents can get this certification without ever planning a trip for a disabled client.

On the other hand, there are a number of genuinely qualified accessible travel specialists out there; and most of these experienced agents have served this niche market long before it was ever fashionable. But, with so many Johnny-come-latelys popping up, sometimes it is difficult to recognize the qualified accessible travel experts.

Then there are the destination specialists and itinerary planners. These are highly trained experts, and I encourage you to actively seek them out. Destination specialists focus on a particular destination and they are experts about everything related to that destination. Many of these destination specialists are also knowledgeable about access, and some also do itinerary planning.

Itinerary planners charge their clients for their services. Sometimes they also get commissions from suppliers, but these travel agents don't exclusively work only with suppliers that pay out commissions. These travel professionals are worth their weight in gold, but be on the lookout for impostors. No one can be a destination specialist for all areas of the world, so be wary of any travel agent who makes that claim.

In truth, I know a lot of good travel agents; in fact, some of my best friends are travel agents. I've also heard horror stories about bad travel agents, so I know they are out there. Good travel agents work hard for their money and offer their clients valuable, first-hand knowledge about products, services, and destinations. The bad ones? They can ruin your trip and make you swear off travel forever.

DO YOU NEED ONE?

Do you need a travel agent? There's not really a blanket answer to that question as it depends on many factors, including your travel needs and your own personality type. This book gives you the tools to cut out the middleman and, in a sense, be your own travel agent. But do you really want to do that? Some people do and some don't.

Many people work with travel agents because they want someone else to take care of all the details. So if you don't want to deal with the hundreds of minor details that can pop up before, during, and after your trip, then by all means delegate the task to a competent travel agent. But planning and knowledge are two different things; so remember: Just because you delegate trip planning to a travel agent, it doesn't mean that you shouldn't also educate yourself about the logistics of accessible travel and the accessibility of your destination.

No matter who makes your travel arrangements, you still need to know your rights and understand the process. Why? Because the real proof of a competent accessible travel specialist lies with their knowledge about the rules, regulations, and realities of accessible travel, and the only way to judge their expertise is to become an expert yourself.

As I pointed out earlier, many travel agents don't want to bother with domestic air-only tickets because it's simply not profitable. So if you are just looking for the lowest fare to Cincinnati, then it's usually best to bypass the travel agent. Let's face it, sometimes the logistics of accessible travel are time intensive, and most agents just can't afford to spend this time with clients pro bono. Like everyone else, they need to be paid for their time, and if the airlines won't pay them, they simply can't afford to work for free.

On the other hand, travel agents can be quite helpful with international travel, package tours, cruise travel, or group tours. These are pretty competitive markets, so be sure your agent is well versed in the finer aspects of accessible travel. In other words, don't just rely on that "Accessible Travel Specialist" certificate as proof of their expertise. For example, if you are planning a Caribbean cruise, be sure the agent you choose also has recent experience with arranging accessible shore excursions at your ports of call.

Additionally, don't feel you are married to one agent forever, as different agents have different specialties. One agent may be a great cruise agent but know very little about land tours in the United Kingdom. Again, no one can be an expert at everything, so choose the expert that works best for your particular trip.

In fairness to travel agents, some agents go above and beyond the call of duty for their regular clients. As one travel agent confides, "I've done some ridiculously time-consuming things for long-term clients, just as favors because they've used me for years." Truthfully, the best reason to work with any travel agent is to take advantage of their destination and access knowledge. A good travel agent is a very valuable resource.

THE SEARCH

The search for a travel agent begins much the same way as the search for any other professional. The best strategy is to gather a list of potential candidates and then interview them over the phone. Where do you find the candidates? Well, personal referrals are great, so ask your friends and family if they know of any good travel agents. Be sure and specify that your definition of a good travel agent is an agent that is well educated about accessible travel.

Scan through national disability magazines, search the internet, ask people in your support group, and look for advertisements in the phone book. Learn to read between the lines of advertisements, though. I recently spied an advertisement in a national disability magazine that didn't even list a phone number, company name, or address. The only contact information for this company that touted accessible tours of Ireland was an e-mail address.

After a little investigation I learned that this individual was ill equipped to organize accessible tours, as the agent wasn't even aware of the accessible transportation situation in Ireland. The big tip off should have been the lack of contact information. Skip over any advertisement that just doesn't have a professional look. The same goes for websites.

Soon your list of candidates will grow and you'll be ready to begin the interview process. Before you pick up the phone, remember that it's important to ask all the candidates the same questions. Try to talk to at least five candidates. Even if you absolutely love the first candidate, continue to call everyone on your list. You never know; you may just find somebody you love even more.

Feel free to eliminate anyone you just don't like, even if they seem to have the appropriate professional qualifications. Go with your gut feelings. This is a personal service and you need to feel comfortable with your travel agent. You don't have to become best friends, but you can't really work effectively with somebody if you have a personality conflict.

Be sure and inquire about what kind of training the agent has, as well as how long they have worked with accessible travel. Nobody is born with this knowledge, so remember that we all have to learn it at some time in life. Don't rule out real-life experience either, as some agents are very experienced in accessible travel because they have a disability and they personally love to travel. This type of experience is valuable, but by itself is not enough.

The agent also must be familiar with the travel industry. Ask about their professional qualifications. If they have a lot of "initials" (credentials) after their name, ask what they mean and how they got them.

It's also a good idea to throw in a test question, just to ensure they have the requisite knowledge about accessible travel. Now, I'm not saying you should cross examine and badger each candidate, but ask at least one question that tests their accessible travel expertise.

If you have a specific destination in mind, ask about their expertise on that destination. Additionally, ask them how many clients they book to that destination annually, as well as when they last visited that destination.

Most importantly, ask them if they have experience dealing with clients with your specific disability. Ask for references, then contact those clients and inquire about their travel experiences.

You may run into some travel agents who won't give you references. Says one long time travel agent, "I used to give out references (with my clients' permission), until I had a bad experience. A few years ago a lady requested references and then she badgered the heck out my client. She kept calling her up and just wanted to chit-chat and be her best friend. My client didn't want anything to do with her, and she had a hard time getting rid of her. I don't give out references any more. I just can't risk another experience like that one."

So, don't automatically disqualify a potential candidate just because they won't provide you with references, as sometimes there is a very good reason behind this decision. And let's face it, no travel agent is going to use the client that had the disaster trip as a reference.

In the end, you'll just have to rely on your own judgment in this matter. But-if the travel agent doesn't have the time to answer your questions, then move on, as answering a few personal questions is easy compared to the intricacies of researching and arranging accessible travel.

SOME RED FLAGS

Once you've completed the interview process, how do you evaluate the answers and pick the best travel agent? The personality factor will serve to screen out some candidates. In fact, you will probably run across a few agents that you just don't like. They are easy to scratch off the list. But what about the rest? Your final decision should be based on the candidates' destination and access knowledge; but there are also a few responses that should throw up a red flag.

Be wary when an agent claims he or she is a "certified" accessible travel expert. Again, a travel agent can get this certification without having any hands-on experience booking accessible travel. Ask how long the agent has been in the industry, how long he or she has been working with accessible travel, and how many disabled clients the agent has booked.

Watch out for candidates who tout their membership in a professional organization as their primary qualification as an accessible travel specialist. Ask about the organization's membership requirements. There are a large number of professional organizations for travel agents; while some have rigid membership criteria, others merely require members to write out an annual check.

A red flag should go up if a candidate guarantees you something that is simply not within his or her power. For example, if someone guarantees you bulkhead seats "no matter what," this only serves to illustrate that agent's ignorance about the Air Carrier Access Act. Additionally, be wary of any agent that guarantees you a problem-free trip. Travel is unpredictable, and no one knows when problems will arise.

Stay away from an agent that uses that dreaded "h" word. It's all right to use this word to describe horses and golfers, but not to describe people with disabilities. It shows a general lack of knowledge and sensitivity about the market that usually doesn't stop at terminology. Most likely this person is also lacking in essential knowledge about the logistics of accessible travel.

Some agencies advertise that they are "owned and operated by a person with a disability." Although there's nothing really wrong with stating that fact, be wary if that in itself is the agent's only qualification. Of course you should also ask what their disability is, given that they make it a point to include this fact in their advertisements. Look for somebody who is experienced and knowledgeable about your specific disability. Just because a person is blind, doesn't mean they have a good working knowledge about wheelchair travel.

Watch out for agents that use broad generalizations, such as "everything is accessible." This indicates a general lack of knowledge on the subject.

Finally, be wary of travel agents who don't travel. If they don't travel, ask them why (sometimes there is a good reason), and then ask them what they do to keep up with the industry. Ideally the agent should have also traveled to your destination recently, although this isn't always possible.

On the other hand, be wary of travel agents who always travel. Some people get into the travel business just so they can write off their own travel expenses. Although there's nothing wrong with that per se, your travel agent should be available to answer your questions and deal with problems as they arise, and that's just not possible if they are always on the road.

BUYER BEWARE!

There are a few things that you need to be extra cautious about when searching for a travel agent. I hate to blatantly call them scams; however, they deserve more attention than the red flag items. By far the worst one of these items is the "you too can be a travel agent" scam. Yes, I do classify this one as a scam.

Also known as a card mill, this scam is incredibly damaging to consumers and professionals alike. Many people unknowingly fall prey to it even if they aren't in the market for a job. In fact, the biggest market for card mill operators is people who like to travel, not just people who need a job. This scam works in a variety of ways, and indeed some are quite slick.

Typically the con man (or woman!) tries to convince you that it's in your best interest to become a travel agent, because you can save money on your own travel. He or she will also tell you about how you can book travel for your friends and family and make big bucks with little or no effort, and then will rave about the free and discounted travel you'll receive as a official card-carrying travel agent. What's he or she selling? Not much; usually just a card saying you are a travel agent and maybe a manual of some sort. Both items are pretty worthless.

Card mills can present themselves in a variety of ways, including self-employment opportunities. This is perhaps the most straightforward approach, as at least you know what they are selling. Other approaches aren't so straightforward and can include advertisements that read "travel for free" or "save big money on travel."

Additionally, card mill operators take full advantage of the underemployment in the disabled community and actively solicit people with disabilities. They entice their "marks" with promises of a turn-key, home-based business that makes big bucks. Be careful when somebody offers you something that sounds too good to be true.

The truth is, real travel agents work very hard for their money and most have had some kind of hands-on training. It's not easy work, and many travel agents take years to turn a profit and establish their business. As for the travel agent discounts and family trips, travel suppliers are familiar with card mills, too, so card mill travel agents are routinely screened out of most offerings.

So, be wary of anyone who tries to sell you a home-based travel business, as they could in fact be a card mill operator. Unfortunately, many people fall for this scam, and as a result there are a number of card mill travel agents out there. Worse yet, some of these untrained travel agents specialize in accessible travel. All the more reason to carefully screen your travel agent candidates!

Another thing to be on the lookout for are travel agents or tour operators that operate as non-profit agencies. This practice isn't something that I actually classify as a scam, but it can be pretty misleading. True, there are some legitimate non-profit organizations that do offer accessible trips and tours; however, some businesses operate as non-profits in name only. It's merely an accounting method for some; they still make money and take a salary. There's really nothing wrong with that, unless they imply otherwise.

So if your tour operator or travel agent claims non-profit status, ask about the services they provide for the community.

If the best they can come up with is, "We negotiate good deals on travel," then you may be dealing with a non-profit in name only. Remember, operating a non-profit organization doesn't necessarily guarantee altruistic motives and could just be a marketing tool. Ask a lot of questions whenever a travel agency or tour operator touts their non-profit status.

Finally, be wary if something just doesn't sound right. Recently a travel agent told me this horrifying story. A man called her after he had booked a group tour to Europe with another travel agent. The man used a power wheelchair and required assistance to transfer. He was feeling a little anxious about his upcoming tour because no arrangements for accessible transportation or lodging had been mentioned. He confronted his travel agent with his fears and she told him, "Don't worry, all of Europe is completely accessible." This should have sent up a big red warning flag! Fortunately the second travel agent told the man the truth.

So ask around and do your research; if something just doesn't sound right, use your common sense and investigate further. And if somebody tells you, "All of Europe is completely accessible," run (or roll) away as fast as you can in the opposite direction!!

TRAVEL AGENT ETIQUETTE

Choosing a travel agent is only half the battle. Now that you understand how the travel industry works, you can use this knowledge to work more effectively with your travel agent. Here are a few pointers to help you along the way.

First and foremost, don't waste a travel agent's time. For example, don't call up a travel agent and just ask for a list of accessible hotels. Remember what travel agents do. They book trips and use their expertise for their clients They are not a public information resource.

Do I wish they would freely share their resources? Sure, but that's not the way it works. In fact the travel agency business is pretty cut throat, so resources are somewhat guarded. Says one travel agent, "Last week one caller took up about three hours of our time. She wanted detailed information on accessible ships, accessible ports, and ports where her service dog could come ashore. She asked for multiple rates on different ships and cabins. Then her traveling companion decided she felt more comfortable booking locally, so she took all the information she gleaned from us and booked with another travel agent. I now understand why so many specialists require non-refundable goodwill deposits."

Of course, if your travel agent is making travel arrangements for you, then it's perfectly acceptable to ask for a choice of hotels in a particular city; but don't just call up any agent, ask for the information, and make the arrangements yourself. If you want to make your own travel arrangements, find another information source.

Be well prepared when you first contact your travel agent. Have at least some idea of where you want to go, when you want to go, and how long you want to stay. Have a general idea about your travel budget. It's perfectly fine to present your travel agent with a few choices and ask for an opinion, but don't just walk in and expect them to find the right trip for you. Do some advance research and make a list of destinations that interest you, then inquire about their suitability when you talk with your travel agent.

Be honest with your travel agent (and yourself) about your disability. It won't benefit anybody if you hide important information; in fact, anything short of full disclosure can be disastrous. Consider the plight of Judy B., who ended up stranded at Denver International Airport because of a failure to disclose. Judy, a 52-year-old woman with multiple sclerosis, was no longer able to travel independently due to progressive cognitive difficulties. Unfortunately, when Judy's daughter made the travel arrangements she neglected to mention her mom's cognitive difficulties to the travel agent. She only said that her mom needed some wheelchair assistance.

After Judy landed in Denver, she got confused and didn't know where she was. She missed her connecting flight to Bismark. Of course she assured everybody she was all right and that she was just waiting for her daughter. Finally, security stepped in and came to Judy's aid. Unfortunately by this time Judy's pants were soaked with urine, and her daughter was worried sick in Bismark. The whole situation could have been easily avoided with a little honesty.

Now, I'm not saying that you need to give out a complete medical history, but don't hide important facts. For example, if you can't transfer independently, then you need to be honest with your travel agent about this fact. It won't prevent you from going on a trip, but it will help your travel agent plan a trip that is appropriate for you. Most likely your travel agent will have a questionnaire for you to complete. Try to answer all the questions as honestly and completely as possible; if a particular question makes you uncomfortable, talk it over with your travel agent and ask why that information is necessary.

Don't call your travel agent for daily updates about your travel arrangements. Remember, you are not the only client. Admittedly you will have questions, so write them down and consolidate them into one phone call. Now, I'm not saying you should never call your travel agent. For example, if your agent promised to call you back on a certain date, and that time has passed, then by all means pick up the phone.

On the other hand, calling for daily updates only tends to frustrate travel agents, as time is a very important commodity to them. Give them a fair chance to do their job. If you don't trust your travel agent to make the appropriate arrangements, then perhaps it's time to find somebody that you do trust.

Remember, "I don't know," is sometimes an acceptable answer; in fact it's better than a wrong answer or a guess. Nobody knows all the answers, but a good travel agent has the resources to find them. Allow your travel agent time to research your question, and be glad you have a travel agent who is willing to do the research. However, if your travel agent continually answers "I don't know" to your questions and is unwilling to do the research, then perhaps you need to look elsewhere.

Don't blame your travel agent because your dream destination is not accessible. Instead, work with your agent to find a suitable alternative. The truth is, some countries are just not very accessible, and it will take more than your travel agent to change that fact. You should expect an honest evaluation about access from your travel agent, but don't blame your agent if it's not exactly what you want to hear. In other words, don't shoot the messenger!

If your travel agent is working on a package tour or cruise for you, remember to inquire about the access of *all* facets of your trip. This includes transportation, transfers, accommodations, and day trips. For cruises, it's very important to ask about the accessibility of shore excursions. Outside the United States, there are few accessible shore excursions, so work with your travel agent to arrange your own accessible shore excursions.

Remember that it is standard practice for travel agents to ask for a deposit. If they are making independent travel arrangements for you, the deposit will be deducted from your final bill. If you cancel, they will most likely retain the deposit in order to cover fax and phone costs. If you're a booking a package tour or cruise, the deposit requirements are set by the supplier. Make sure you have a good understanding of the deposit agreement. Don't be afraid to ask your travel agent for clarification before you pay the deposit.

Finally, always use a credit card when paying for travel services. That way if the tour company or airline goes bankrupt, you can recover the funds from your credit card company. If you are working with a travel agent, ask them if the charge will be payable to the provider (airline, cruise line, etc.) or to the travel agency. If the latter is the case, then you might want to reconsider your choice of travel agents.

Standard practice is to make the charge payable to the provider, however some cash-strapped agencies credit the funds to their agency, and then use those funds as working capital. Although there's nothing inherently wrong with this practice, who wants to work with an agency that is that tight on funds? It's just not a good practice, especially in these economic times.

THE WAY IT SHOULD BE

Ideally, all travel agents should have a working knowledge of accessible travel. But what if your long-time travel agent doesn't have this knowledge? This question comes up often, from people who are recently injured or newly disabled and who want to work with the same travel agent they have been using for the past 20 years. What do you do in this case?

If your travel agent seems willing to learn and you feel comfortable dealing with him or her, then I say give it a try. But don't expect perfection overnight. Your agent will be learning something new and it may take a while to learn all the in's and out's of accessible travel. It is, as you know, an extremely complex subject. The advantage to working with your present agent is that you have developed a relationship over the years but remember—it will be incumbent upon you to update your agent about your new access needs.

Everyone has their own definition of the perfect society. My Utopia comes equipped with all the standard features (universal health care, courteous cab drivers, and an unlimited supply of chocolate), but it also has an few added options. In my Utopia, all travel agents (not just the specialists) have a good working knowledge of accessible travel and disability issues. Furthermore, every travel agent is able to book accessible tours, rooms, and transportation for anyone that happens to walk or roll into their office. That's just the way it should be!

As you may well know, that's not exactly the way things work today. Perhaps some day soon, all travel agents will have a working knowledge of accessible travel. Until then, take care when selecting your travel agent. Your research, time, and effort will pay off in the long run.

Point, Click, and Pack

SHOPPING THE NET

The internet is a great research tool, especially when it come to accessible travel. Not only can you find updated access information online, but you can also connect to travelers who can share first-hand experiences about your upcoming vacation destination. But when it comes to actually booking the trip, can you do it online if you require accessible services? The answer is a conditional yes. In reality, there isn't a one-click method, but you can use the internet to save money and ensure appropriate access.

FINDING A FLIGHT

Airline websites, travel portals, and booking engines are the best places to book air travel online, but you can also use these websites to do a little research and save some money.

Once you've decided on a destination, go to an airline booking engine, such as Orbitz, to find out what carriers fly to that particular destination. With a few mouse clicks you'll be able to see all the options. And while you may be able to save money with more layovers and interline connections, it's vital to understand that these factors may also influence access.

For example, nonstop flights may be more expensive but they are also usually more convenient for wheelchair users, as you only have to board and deplane once. Additionally, if you opt to use more than one carrier for your journey, you increase the risk of your luggage and medical equipment being misrouted and delayed.

It's important to note that the best price for your access needs may not necessarily be the cheapest price. Additionally, you'll also want to avoid small airplanes and regional airports if at all possible. In the end, you need to evaluate all the factors—convenience, access, and cost—before you make your decision.

Seating is another important access issue. Wheelchair users are not always guaranteed seating in bulkhead areas. Contact each airline directly to find out about their specific seating policies for wheelers. Some airlines will seat you in the bulkhead section and others will not. Do business only with those airlines that can provide you with appropriate seating.

Once you've found out which carriers serve your destination and can met your access needs, visit the airline website to see what kind of a deal you can find. Sometimes airline websites feature special fares that are not available on booking engines. When you find the best deal, book your flight.

After you receive your confirmation, call the airline to make sure your access needs are noted. This is also a good time to request special seating or an onboard wheelchair. Additionally, it's a good idea to reconfirm all access arrangements 24 hours in advance of the flight.

It's also good to remember that if an airline website is not accessible, the Air Carrier Access Act requires the carrier to offer their web-only fares by phone or another accessible reservation method. The airline must make these fares available to disabled customers at no extra charge, even if they routinely charge customers a fee for making reservations by phone. This applies to all U.S. airlines.

PIG-IN-A-POKE.COMS

As far as booking air tickets online, one kind of website to avoid is the auction or name-your-price websites. I also call them pig-in-a-poke.coms, as sometimes you really can't tell what you are buying.

At these websites, you enter your departure city and your destination along with your credit card number. Then you state how much you are willing to pay for the ticket. Finally, you receive a response indicating if your bid has been accepted. Once your bid is accepted, your credit card is immediately charged.

The catch is, you can't choose the carrier, routing, aircraft, or even the time of day you travel, which can all factor into the accessibility of the flight. What may seem like a good deal can quickly turn into an accessibility nightmare when you discover you're booked on a turbo-prop that makes seven stops between Boise and Atlanta.

Although buying an air ticket "sight unseen" may be acceptable for travelers who don't have access needs, it's a big gamble for anyone who does. Unfortunately, these websites are hyped heavily across cyberspace as being the best places to find cheap airfares. They may be cheap, but many times the tickets are not useable by people with disabilities. The sad part is that most people don't find this out until it's too late. Never give out your credit card number before you have selected a specific flight, as you need all the flight information to determine accessibility.

There is also a hybrid type of a website that includes both an auction interface and a traditional booking engine. While the booking engine may be safe to use (although I wouldn't

344

pay a fee or commission to use it), avoid the auction or name-your-price options.

So steer clear of pig-in-a-poke.com as, as they don't offer choices of airlines, aircraft, or routes, all of which are important factors in airline accessibility. Remember, a cheap airfare is no longer a bargain when you can't get on the airplane. And, of course, the tickets are non-refundable.

FINDING A ROOM

The hands-down best way to book an accessible room online is to make a reservation directly on the hotel's website, as you're more likely to be able to reserve a specific type of accessible room there. Additionally, like the airlines, many hotels have online specials on their websites.

First, visit a number of hotel websites and check their rates for the dates of your visit. Then, pick the best rates and then call those properties directly to inquire about their access features and to ask about their policy on blocking accessible rooms. And while you're on the phone, go ahead and inquire about their rates. If they offer you a better rate than on the internet, and the room suits your needs, then by all means make a reservation. If the rate quoted is higher than their online special, ask if they will give you the internet rate. If the answer is no, then go back to the hotel website and book your reservation online.

Make sure and specify your access needs when booking online. It never hurts to mention them twice, so go ahead and also list them in the comments section. Then, get your confirmation number and call the hotel directly to confirm that all of your access needs have been properly noted. If POINT, CLICK, AND PACK the reservation is not to your satisfaction, or you find out that the property doesn't block accessible rooms, then cancel the reservation. Of course, you'll have to start the whole process all over again, but in the end you're more likely to get the type of accessible room you need.

In truth, this whole process takes an awful lot of legwork. For better results it helps to work with properties that have previously demonstrated a progressive attitude toward access issues. Unfortunately it takes time and experience to recognize these properties.

So shop around and watch for the internet sales, but remember to reconfirm all access details by phone. The internet is great tool for travelers, but remember that it's not the only tool.

HOTEL CONSOLIDATORS

Although there are many useful internet sites out there for researching and booking hotel rooms online, there is one type of hotel booking site that may present problems for anyone with access needs.

Hotel consolidators buy blocks of hotel rooms and resell them to the public at substantial discounts. The good news is that you can save anywhere from 20 percent to 50 percent off the regular rate by booking through a consolidator. The bad news is that it's virtually impossible to book an accessible room through some hotel consolidators.

In fact, many hotel consolidators only treat reservations for accessible rooms as *requests* for accessible rooms. Even worse, they charge stiff cancellation penalties. They require prepayment but won't make refunds under any circumstances—even if you can't use the room when you arrive.

One of the worst things about dealing with a consolidator is that you don't deal directly with the hotel. If you call the hotel to confirm your reservation they usually can't find a reservation under your name. The consolidators book big blocks of rooms, so your reservation is technically under the consolidator's name until the last minute. It's therefore impossible to communicate directly with the property about your access needs, because as far as the property is concerned, your reservation doesn't exist.

Spotting a hotel consolidator is pretty easy. They all require prepayment with a credit card and most have pretty stiff cancellation fees. Most also offer super bargain rates. Don't be lured by those low rates, though, as it's not really a good deal if you can't book an accessible room.

But there is good news on the hotel consolidator front, too. As we go to press, a landmark settlement in *Smith v* Hotels.com was just announced. Hotels.com agreed to not only include access information on their website, but also to implement procedures that will allow disabled travelers to reserve accessible rooms online. Previously accessible reservations were only treated as requests. These changes, which are hailed as "cutting-edge," are set to go into effect in September of 2009.

Additionally, the proposed Americans with Disabilities Act Accessibility Guidelines for lodging address this problem. The preliminary draft proposes that third-party reservation systems make alterations in their policies and procedures so that people can reserve and block accessible rooms online. The American Hotel and Lodging Association opposes this change, so there's no telling what the final rule will be.

In the interim, be careful about doing business with hotel consolidators. In fact, never do business with any property or service that imposes an unreasonable cancellation fee. You really need the flexibility to cancel your reservation, especially when you're dealing with access issues.

CRUISES

More and more cruise websites offer some type of discount booking option these days, but what about access? Can you really book an accessible cabin online at those discount cruise sites?

According to accessible cruise expert and travel agency owner Connie George, none of the major cruise lines release their accessible cabins to the discount cruise websites. This is done to ensure that the accessible cabins go to people who need them. Says George, "If you want to book online, you have to book a non-accessible cabin and then call the cruise line or dot-com agency to see if an accessible cabin is available in that category. Then you have to change your reservation."

Is the savings worth the hassle? Well, that depends on how you define savings. Yes, you may pay a lower fare if you book with a discount cruise website, but that's only part of the total cruise price. Most dot-com agencies operate on volume and their agents (who aren't usually trained in disability travel) can't afford to spend time on the telephone fielding questions. In short, customer service is slim to nonexistent.

If you book through a discount cruise website, you'll have to follow through with the cruise line regarding any special needs, such as medical equipment allowed on board, rental equipment delivered to the ship, specific access features of the cabins, and accessible transportation to and from the port. You'll also have to research each port, determine its accessibility, and in most cases plan your own accessible shore excursions. The cost of these calls alone (many of which are international) can far outweigh any money saved by booking online.

When comparing savings, it's important to compare the bottom-line costs of both options. This includes the extra time and money it takes to make the accessible arrangements after you book your cruise. The cruise fare is just part of the total cruise cost. In most cases, discount websites don't really offer any substantial savings on accessible cabins. The best bet is to book directly through the cruise line or deal with a travel agent who specializes (*really* specializes) in accessible cruises.

Accessible Recreation

A WORLD OF CHOICES

For many people recreation is an integral part of travel. In fact, for some people it's the main reason for travel. People go to great lengths to enjoy their favorite recreational activities at home and while on holiday. In the past, most recreational facilities only focused on able-bodied travelers, but today many facilities are now accessible to people with disabilities.

Additionally, many companies, facilities, and services are now using universal design to achieve barrier-free access. These welcome changes allow travelers with disabilities many new options for vacation-time recreational fun. Although there's literally a world of choices, here's a sampling of some accessible recreation possibilities.

TRAILS AND BOARDWALKS

Let's start with the basics—accessible nature trails. They come in all shapes and sizes. It's great to be able to roll along a trail and get an up-close-and-personal look at nature. Unfortunately trail accessibility varies greatly, even throughout the United

States. Although the Access Board is working on accessibility guidelines for trails and outdoor areas that are under federal jurisdiction, it's a pretty complex process. In short, it's a challenge to make outdoor areas accessible without disturbing their inherent rustic nature.

Even when the guidelines are final, trail accessibility will still vary. In short, what may be accessible to one person might not work for another. For this reason, the best strategy is to ask specific questions relating to your particular access needs. This applies to the outdoor environment as well as to any unfamiliar place you are traveling.

On the positive side, more developers are voluntarily incorporating the principles of universal design into trail construction whenever possible. And even private organizations are hopping on the access bandwagon. Such is the case with the Wilderness on Wheels (WOW) boardwalk near Kenosha Pass in Colorado.

Billed as a model wilderness access facility, WOW boasts an accessible boardwalk plus camping and fishing facilities. All facilities were constructed by volunteers and most of the materials were donated.

Accessible campsite at WOW in Kenosha Pass, Colorado.

The WOW boardwalk is eight-feet wide and winds around a well-stocked trout pond. This fishing pond is reserved for people with disabilities, while a nearby stream is available for able-bodied fishermen. The boardwalk follows the contour of the land and it's lined with willow trees and natural vegetation. It's a great place to enjoy a picnic lunch and afternoon hike.

The WOW facility also offers accessible campsites for overnight guests. All campsites have raised tent platforms and one even has a covered dining area. There is no charge for admission or camping at the WOW boardwalk, but advance reservations are required. The WOW facility is only open from April to October, so plan ahead.

Many state, regional, and local parks also have accessible trails. Access information is usually available, but is sometimes hard to find. Some parks have access information on their websites and some even have printed access guides.

If you can't seem to find any access information online, then pick up the phone and ask to talk to the accessibility director or somebody that is familiar with the access features of the park or facility. Remember, just because access information isn't prominently displayed doesn't mean that it doesn't exist; in fact, sometimes it's hidden behind the counter or in a forgotten corner of the office. Always remember to ask for access information!

Rail trails are another good accessible trail option. Located across the United States, Rail trails are built on abandoned rail corridors, and many of them are accessible. Most Rail trails are flat or have a minimal grade so they are excellent for wheelchair users and hand cyclists. The Rails to Trails Conservancy (202-331-9696, www.railtrails.org) has several guide books plus online information about rail trails.

Additionally, you can search for accessible rail trails on the Trail Link Database at www .traillink.com. This searchable database contains information on rail trails throughout the United States. You can search the database by state or by activity ("wheelchair access" is included as an activity). Each entry includes a description of the trail, including the length and surface composition, along with parking and trailhead information.

And if you're looking for a great resource on accessible trails in northern California, check out *A Wheelchair Rider's Guide San Francisco Bay and the Nearby Coast.* This handy resource includes access details on over 100 trails and parks in northern California. All sites included in the guide were visited by the author and Access Northern California founder, Bonnie Lewkowicz. And the really great news is that this guide is free. Download your copy at the California Coastal Conservancy website (www.scc.ca.gov) or call 510-286-1015 to have a printed copy mailed to you.

NATIONAL PARKS

National parks can also be good places for accessible recreation, although some parks are better than others. Most parks have at least some facilities or services that are accessible, even if just a visitors center. Indeed, there are a very wide variety of accessible trails and facilities in our national parks.

No matter which national park you choose to visit, advance research is a must. The best place to start is the National Park Service (NPS) website at www.nps.gov. Some parks have access information listed, while others only have contact phone numbers. Sometimes you'll have to pick up the phone and talk directly to a park employee to find out about access.

Many national parks offer wheelchair-accessible viewing points, such as Glacier Point in Yosemite National Park.

When you visit a park, always ask for access information, either at the entrance or at the visitors center. Many parks have printed access guides; however, be sure and note when the guides were printed. Some are out-dated. In fact the best place to get the most up-to-date access information is on the NPS website. Additionally, there are a lot of private websites that offer access information on specific parks. Usually these are created by people who have visited the park and just want to share the information.

Park rangers can also be a good source for access information. For example, I've been going to Yosemite for over 40 years, but just last year I found out about Washburn Point from a ranger. Located about a half-mile below Glacier Point, it's nicely accessible, has a spectacular view, and is less crowded that nearby Glacier Point. The ranger knew about access because his sister is a wheelchair user. It never hurts to ask.

Finally, if a visit to a national park is in your future, be sure to get your free America the Beautiful Access Pass. This lifetime pass is good for free admission to all national parks, monuments, historic sites, recreation areas, and wildlife refuges. Pass holders also receive a 50 percent discount on campsites. The pass can be obtained at any national park entrance and, although there's no charge, proof of disability is required.

CAMPSITES AND CABINS

Many people like to stay in or near recreation areas. Accessible lodging choices range from camping and rustic cabins, to luxury lodges and resorts. Although camping is the traditional way to enjoy the great outdoors, campgrounds are not always accessible. Additionally, if a campground is listed as accessible, it's a good idea to inquire about the specific access features. Most often accessible means that the campground has a level campsite, accessible parking, and an accessible bathroom. Raised camping platforms are not the standard, so be prepared to sleep on the ground. Some campgrounds will reserve accessible campsites in advance and others won't; again, it pays to check in advance.

If pitching a tent isn't exactly your style, then consider a USDA Forest Service cabin. They're a bit rustic, and indeed some are very basic, but they're a great choice if you love the outdoors. They are located across the United States and some are accessible, depending on when they were built or remodeled.

For example, in Alaska there are barrier-free Forest Service cabins at West Point, Kah Sheets Lake, Heckman Lake, Green Island, and Virginia Lake. Each cabin includes a table and benches, plywood bunks, a wood or oil heating stove, a broom, and an outhouse. The cabins don't have electricity, bedding, or cooking utensils. Reservations for Forest Service cabins can be made up to 180 days in advance

358

Accessible yurts are available at many state campgrounds in Oregon.

through the National Recreation Reservation Service (877-444-6777; www.recreation.go v).

State parks are also good resources for accessible cabins. For example, the Wisconsin Department of Natural Resources (DNR) has accessible cabins available at Kettle Moraine State Forest, Buckhorn State Park, Mirror Lake State Park, and Potawatomi State Park. Each cabin has one bedroom equipped with two hospital beds and a Hoyer lift, a living room with a fullsize sleeper sofa and two cots, and a bathroom with a roll-in shower, a fold-down shower bench, and a shower-commode chair. All cabins have heating and air condi- tioning, lowered kitchen counters, an attached screened porch, and an outdoor fire ring. Best of all, the cabins rent for a very affordable $30 per night.

And then there are yurts. Although they are available at state and regional parks across the country, the most affordable and accessible ones I've found are located in Oregon. These permanent domed structures have plywood floors, framed doors, electricity, and skylights. Accessible yurts with ramped entrances and wide doorways are available; the Oregon yurts are priced at just $27 to $30 per night. Advance reservations are a must, and be sure and specify that you need an accessible yurt when you make your reservation.

And if you'd like to camp out African-safari style, then check out Safari West (707-579-2551; www.safariwest.com) in Santa Rosa, California. This 400-acre game preserve is home to a bevy of exotic animals and birds, most of which roam free inside the gated compound. Safari West has two accessible luxury tent cabins with hardwood floors, canvas sides and tops, indoor plumbing, and electricity. Just like the upscale safari camps in Africa.

Access features in each accessible tent cabin include a ramped entry, wide doorways, ample room to maneuver a wheelchair, a roll-in shower with a fold-down shower seat, a hand-held shower head, and grab bars in the shower and around the toilet. Both tent cabins have a roomy porch with great views of the giraffe enclosure. It's the ideal place to watch the sunset and enjoy a glass of wine.

An accessible tent cabin at Safari West game preserve in Santa Rosa, California.

Access features in each accessible tent cabin include a ramped entry, wide doorways, ample room to maneuver a wheelchair, a roll-in shower with a fold-down shower seat, a hand-held shower head, and grab bars in the shower and around the toilet. Both tent cabins have a roomy porch with great views of the giraffe enclosure. It's the ideal place to watch the sunset and enjoy a glass of wine.

HIT THE BEACH

A lot of recreational activities revolve around the water. Indeed, the beach is a popular recreational venue. You can choose to simply sit and enjoy the sand and surf, or opt for a refreshing dip in the ocean. Beach access varies and includes everything from beach chairs and hard-packed sand to barrier-free access via ramps. But, of course, there are still many beaches that are not accessible at all.

One way to access the beach is in a beach wheelchair. These specially made wheelchairs have wide plastic tires designed to navigate sandy beaches. The major drawback is that most beach wheelchairs are not self-pro-pelling, so you need someone to push you.

The exception to this rule can be found at San Diego's Mission Beach, home of the world's first motorized beach wheelchair, the Beach Cruzr. Although the Beach Cruzr looks like a standard beach wheelchair, it's powered by two 24-volt motors. This allows wheelchair users independent access to the beach. These motorized beach chairs are also available at Imperial Beach, Ocean Beach, La Jolla Shores, and Coronado Beach. Some are available on a first-come basis at the lifeguard stations, while others require advance reservations.

Contact Accessible San Diego at 619-325-7550 for more information.

Alternatively, there are a variety of companies that manufacture standard beach wheelchairs, and you can buy your own and take it with you to the beach. They are made to disassemble easily, so they fit nicely into a car trunk or in the cargo bin of an airplane. Remember, though; you will need somebody to push you.

Many state parks, beaches, and resorts also provide beach wheelchairs for loan. Although there isn't a master list of venues that provide them, some beach wheelchair dealers have this information, so be sure to ask if they have a list of recreation areas that use their equipment. Some dealers also provide this information online. Do an internet search for "beach wheelchairs" and see what you find. Additionally, many state beaches and national recreation areas have beach wheelchairs for loan. When in doubt, always ask.

Another way to access the water is via beach mats. Although this concept hasn't exactly taken off full throttle yet, some cities are installing beach mats at their public beaches. These portable rubberized pathways provide a firm and flat trail over the sand. Currently beach mats are available at Ala Moana Regional Park in Honolulu, several of Chicago's

Lake Michigan beaches, and Hilton Head Island's Coligny Beach Park. Hopefully this concept will catch on at other public beaches.

A very unique approach to beach access is can be found at the Yaquina Head Tidepools on the central Oregon coast. This coastal headland area was established by Congress in 1980; and in 1992 through1994, the Bureau of Land Management (BLM) reclaimed the Yaquina Head rock quarry and converted it to a rocky inter-tidal area.

The BLM also made the inter-tidal area wheelchair accessible—a first for the Oregon coast. Accessible pathways allow wheelchair users to roll along and explore the tide pools. Wheelchair users can park in the lower parking lot and just roll down to the tide pools. The paved paths go right into the inter-tidal area. There are also a few raised tide pools that are just the right viewing height for wheelers. Yaquina Head gets high marks for barrier-free design.

WATER SPORTS

Let's now turn our attention to water sports. From fishing to sailing, the water attracts professional athletes and weekend amateurs alike. Fishing continues to be a popular recreational activity. For those who prefer to fish from shore, there are many choices. In fact, access doesn't have to be elaborate. Over in Frasier, Colorado, the local Lions Club constructed a very simple accessible fishing area around their local fishing hole.

They did two things: First, they built an accessible dock so wheelchair users can just roll on and fish. Second, they constructed some safety barriers that allow wheelchair users to fish safely from shore. The wheelchair-height barriers have one rail across the top and, although they prevent wheelers from rolling into the water, they don't obstruct the view. Of course they are made of natural material so they blend in with the environment.

If you prefer deep sea fishing, then head down to Mexico and check out *En Caliente.* Billed as the first ever accessible sport fishing boat, *En Caliente* is the brainchild of avid fisherman Larry Cooper. A C-5/6 quadriplegic, Cooper designed the boat so he could continue sport fishing after he was injured in 1992.

Access features on *En Caliente* include wheelchair tie-downs on the main deck, hoist access to the flying bridge, and custom fishing tackle designed for anglers of all abilities. The crew is experienced in working with disabled anglers and they are happy to assist whenever needed.

The boat is docked in Los Barriles, just north of Cabo San Lucas, and is available for full or half-day charters. It can accommodate a maximum of six passengers. Larry also has an accessible villa for rent in Los Barriles. For more information visit www.bajaenterprises.com or call 866-727-7986.

Sailing is another fun way to enjoy the water. Passengers can sit back and enjoy a leisurely sail or can actively participate in the navigation of the vessel. If you are looking for instant gratification and want to enjoy sailing with a minimum of instruction, then look for disabled sailing clubs that have access dinghies.

These fun little boats are very user friendly and, depending on the model, can accommodate one or two sailors. They are difficult to capsize and come equipped with a concave hull for additional stability. Best of all, they are designed to be operated by a person seated low in the boat, which is a very stable position for wheelchair users. Access dinghies are also outfitted with a servo-assist joystick to operate the electric winches. Even if you've never set foot on a boat before, you'll be able to enjoy sailing an access dinghy with a minimum of instruction.

Many clubs, like the Bay Area Association of Disabled Sailors (415-281-0212; www.baads.org) have access dinghies as well as adapted keel boats. In fact, BAADS has eight access dinghies, three keel boats, and a safety boat.

This energetic group is composed of people who just love to sail, and they invite folks to join them every weekend at Pier 40 in San Francisco's South Beach Marina. BAADS sails usually last for four or five hours, although the length is dependent on the weather and sailing conditions. Everyone is welcome, but reservations are recommended. Check out the BAADS website for their weekend sailing schedule, as some days they sail the keel boats while other days they work with the access dinghies.

And if you've ever dreamed of sailing a tall ship, then check out the Jubilee Sailing Trust (JST), a British non-profit organization (+44 23 8044 9108; www.jst.org.uk). The JST operates two accessible tall ships, the *Lord Nelson* and the *Tenacious* and JST participants are not just passengers, they are members of the crew. Wheelers and able-bodied crew members work side by side. Each ship is able to take a voyage crew of 40, including up to eight wheelchair users. No experience is necessary, and it's a fun way to meet new people and learn how to sail.

Accessible features on board JST ships include flat, wide decks suitable for wheelchair users, lifts between the decks, wheelchair tie-downs, and accessible living quarters. JST stresses integration and inclusion in all of their programs.

Another British organization, the Disabled Sailors Association, is working hard to provide accessible sailing opportunities through their Ro Ro Sailing Project (+44 1329 317279; www .disabledsailing.org). Founded by Mike Wood, Ro Ro was created to increase ocean sailing opportunities for disabled sailors. To that end, the organization designs, builds, and rents fully accessible ocean sailing vessels; in fact, the acronym Ro Ro stands for roll-on, roll-off.

They currently have two accessible yachts for rent, the *Verity K* and the *Spirit of Scott Bader.* They also maintain a list of volunteer skippers to accompany inexperienced sailors, so you truly can enjoy the thrill of ocean sailing with no previous experience.

A good one-stop resources for sailors is The Sailing Web (www.footeprint.com/sailingweb). This comprehensive website includes loads of information about adaptive sailing, from sailing clubs and accessible sailboats to competitions and ports of call.

For those who want to explore the undersea world, scuba diving is a great choice. The Handicapped Scuba Association (949-498-4540; www.hsascuba.com) sets standards and trains instructors in adaptive techniques. They also arrange dive trips for members and are very knowledgeable about accessible dive resorts around the world.

And although it's not exactly a sport, if you want to get up-close-and-personal with a dolphin (or two), then check out the Dolphin Research Center (DRC) (305-289-1121 ext. 232; www.dolphins.org) in Grassy Keys, Florida. This marine research center offers an excellent half-day dolphin interaction program, which begins with a dolphin education workshop and culminates with a structured dolphin swim.

Access at the DRC is excellent, with an emphasis on integration and removing physical barriers. Says DRC's Marry Stella, "We don't have only one program that is accessible. Instead, if a person wants to participate in any of our programs, we do our best to make it possible."

Finally, if you're undecided and you just want to sample a variety of water sports, then check out Shared Adventures annual Day on the Beach, held every July on Santa Cruz's Cowell's Beach. Volunteers lay down 160 plywood sheets over the sand to create their own beach city where participants can enjoy live music and free food, and try out adapted water sports such as kayaking, scuba, surfing, and canoeing. There's no cost to participate, but advance registration is required. Space fills up quickly for this popular event, so sign up early.

FUN IN THE SNOW

Skiing is a popular winter activity and a ski vacation makes a great winter getaway. The good news is that there is a wide variety of adaptive equipment that helps people with all types of disabilities enjoy the excitement of downhill skiing and Nordic sports. Truly, there is something for just about everyone.

Downhill skiers can either stand or sit to ski, depending on their ability. Stand-up skiers use outriggers for balance, which are modified ski poles with mini skis attached to the ends. Three-track skiers use one ski and two outriggers, while four-track skiers use two skis and two outriggers. Sometimes a ski bra is also used in conjunction with this technique to help skiers control the position of their ski tips.

Sit-down skiers use either a mono-ski or a bi-ski. A mono-ski is a fiberglass shell with a monoshock mounted on top of a single ski. Mono-skiers use two shortened outriggers to steer and turn the mono-ski. Mono-skis are a good choice for people who have disabilities affecting their legs, but still have some upper body strength.

A bi-ski is constructed much like a mono-ski, except the bi-ski is mounted on two skis. This extra ski offers added stability and balance. Bi-skis are used by people who have limited upper body strength, along with limited or no lower body strength. A bi-skier may ski independently or may be tethered (pulled) by an instructor.

Cross country skiing is great exercise for both stand-up and sit-down skiers, and it can be adapted for a wide range of disabilities. It gets you away-from-the-maddening crowds and, depending on your luck and location, it can allow you an up-close-and-personal glimpse of the local wildlife. Remember to pack your binoculars, as you never know what you will see. Many hand cyclists and wheelchair racers take up cross country skiing to stay in shape during the winter, but you don't need to be a super athlete to enjoy this sport.

Participants who can stand use traditional cross country skiing equipment—long narrow skis with bindings that attach to the toe of the boot. Skiers who can't stand or walk, or have problems maintaining their balance, use a sit-ski. Sit-skiers propel themselves with shortened ski poles in this adapted, sled-like device.

Equipment makers are now developing new sit-skis that add kick to each push, resulting in more slide for each arm movement. Of course, most adaptive ski schools are pros at altering and tweaking existing equipment to meet individual needs. For best results, check with the facility in advance, explain your disability in detail, and find out what equipment is available.

Adaptive snow sports are available in the United States, Canada, Europe, New Zealand, and Australia. Disabled Sports USA (www.dsus a.org) is a good resource for recreational adaptive skiing programs. Check their website for a chapter near you, and then inquire about the local programs. Additionally the *Emerging Horizons* website (www.EmergingHorizons.com) has an updated list of adaptive ski schools around the world.

A good, all-around resource for recreational activities and accessible fun is *Access Anything: Colorado,* by Craig P. Kennedy and Andrea C. Jehn (now Andrea Kennedy). This resource-filled volume includes detailed information about accessible outdoor fun and activities throughout Colorado. It includes information about adaptive sporting activities for all seasons—from snow skiing and dog sledding to hiking, biking, fishing, and camping. Also included are lodging and dining suggestions, plus lots of resources. It's a great primer on accessible recreation.

BEFORE YOU GO

It goes without saying that advance research is necessary before you hit the road. But there's another important aspect to consider whenever recreation is a major part of your holiday.

Always remember to take any recreational equipment or adaptive devices with you.

Says wheelchair athlete Sharon Myers, "Athletes who use wheelchairs need to be aware that some airlines may charge them a fee for bringing along their extra sports wheelchair. These chairs would be in the same category as a surf board, ski or other device used for sports by the able-bodied."

Indeed, sometimes figuring out how to take all of your equipment with you can take just as much planning as your travel arrangements. But it's well worth the added effort. This point is aptly illustrated by the following story from Patty, an above-the-knee amputee who wanted to enjoy the water on her family vacation.

"We planned to spend a week at a lakefront resort in upstate New York. My son's baseball team was playing a tournament in Cooperstown, so this wasn't only a family vacation, but also a vacation for the families of all my son's teammates. As we made our plans, I realized that most of our nonbaseball time would revolve around fun in the pool and lake. We have two young boys and I didn't want to be a spectator to their activities, but as a bilateral above the knee amputee, I wasn't sure how much I could participate.

"Sure I swim at home. In fact, I have a set of water legs that are specifically designed for water activities. My water legs allow me to swim, water ski, jet ski, sail, and generally enjoy the water. I used my water legs at home, but I had never traveled with them before. My problem was pretty simple; I just couldn't figure out how to transport my water legs from California to New York.

"I couldn't imagine my husband carrying them down the aisle of the airplane. I wasn't even sure if they'd fit in the overhead bin. If not, I wondered if they would survive the trip in the cargo bin. I've had nightmare airline experiences with my wheelchair and I didn't want to repeat those with my water legs. Would insurance cover damage to my water legs? Who would take responsibility if they were damaged? I had a lot of questions, and very few answers. So, I called my prosthetist.

"'How do I get my water legs to New York?' I asked. 'Simple,' he responded, 'we'll ship them.' As instructed, I delivered my water legs to my prosthetist one week before we left. Upon arrival, they were waiting for me when I checked into the hotel. There was also a return-shipping label, a roll of packing tape, and even a pair of scissors inside the box. It was obvious they had done this before! I enjoyed my water legs during my vacation. I spent a considerable amount of time in the pool, and I was glad I brought them."

So, even if it takes a little extra work before and after your trip, make sure you take along everything you need to make your vacation enjoyable. You'll be glad you did. And, don't be afraid to ask others for advice. They may have just the solution you need!

Budget Travel

IS IT REALLY POSSIBLE?

Is it really possible to travel on a budget? Well, of course it depends on your budget. Seriously, though, it never hurts to stretch your travel dollar. To some people, budget travel simply means getting the best deal possible, while to others it means not spending over a specific amount per day or per trip. The good news is, it's possible to cap travel expenses without sacrificing access. Like everything else, budget travel requires planning and research, and sometimes a little compromise, but in the end, access and affordability don't have to be mutually exclusive.

THE BUILDING BLOCKS OF BUDGET TRAVEL

Generally speaking several factors—destination, timing, and vacation type—can all have a serious impact on your budget. So if you want to hold down those travel costs, your money-saving approach begins in the early planning stages.

When choosing a destination, remember that the availability of accessible transportation is a major factor in determining the cost of any trip. For example, if you choose a developing-country destination that has only a few accessible tour vehicles, then chances are you are going to pay a premium for them. On the other hand, if you can accept physical assistance and get by with standard transportation, your costs will be much lower. Generally speaking, labor is very cheap in these countries, so hiring an attendant to help lift and carry you is cheaper than hiring an accessible vehicle. Admittedly this option is not for everyone, but I do know people who have gone this route.

Timing is also a major factor in cost containment. Avoid travel during the holidays whenever possible, as it's the most expensive time to fly. If you must travel around the holidays, then start shopping early for your air ticket. Watch the airfare sales and snap up your ticket early in the year. Don't wait until the month before Thanksgiving to buy your air ticket.

The most economical time to travel is in the shoulder season at your destination. Remember, the low season is usually the low season for a very good reason. Many times it's weather related. Additionally, in some resort areas, many of the attractions are closed during the low season.

Last but not least, the best way to cut your travel costs is to deal directly with a local tour operator. Tour operators usually pay commissions to travel agents, which raises the overall tour prices. When you deal direct, you can often negotiate a better deal. Keep in mind, however, that you'll need to be proficient in the native language, and it may involve a number of e-mails and phone calls. Still, if you have the time to devote to the process, it's a great money-saving method.

Finding local tour operators can be a challenge, however. Sometimes tour brochures mention the names of the local tour operators or there is a photograph of a tour vehicle with the local company logo. It doesn't hurt to ask the agent the name of the local tour operator, but don't expect any type of useful reply. In fact, you may meet with some resistance, but it never hurts to ask. Sometimes agents are willing to give out this information, even if it's only to get you off the phone.

And finally, ask friends, family, and business contacts if they have any resources. Don't forget to investigate every possibility, as you never know when something will pan out. The goal is to find somebody at your destination that has access to information on local tour operators. Sometimes this involves quite a number of contacts, but don't give up, as the internet has truly opened up the world. The best advice is to be persistent and methodical in your quest.

FINDING THE LOWEST AIRFARE

Sometimes there's no rhyme or reason for airline deals and discounts. In truth, two people sitting right next to one another on a flight can pay drastically different prices for the same ticket. Although there's no sure-fire method for always getting the lowest rate, generally speaking the key to finding a bargain is flexibility. Here are a few things to remember when shopping for your next airline ticket.

- Tuesdays and Wednesdays are usually the best days for lower airfares, as they are the least attractive days to business travelers.
- The first flight of the day is usually more expensive than the flight just two hours later, as the former is also the choice for most business travelers.
- Be flexible about your destination and shop the sales on the airline websites. Chances are that if the airlines have a sale, you'll also find bargain hotel rates at the same destination.
- The best deals on airfares are usually found early Saturday mornings.
- If you keep getting higher quotes after several visits to the same airline website, try it

from another computer. Some websites use cookies to track visitors, so you'll end up getting a low fare on your first try and higher fares on the same routing on subsequent visits.

- The best times for bargain airfares are between Labor Day and a week before Thanksgiving, and during the first full week of January.

AIRFARE DISCOUNTS

One of the most frequent questions I receive about accessible travel involves the availability of airline discounts for disabled passengers. Unfortunately these discounts are few and far between, and are not offered by any North American carriers. There are also a number of restrictions, so check with the carrier directly before you make your reservation to be sure you qualify for the discount.

Turkish Airlines offers a 25 percent discount on domestic and international airfares to passengers who have at least a 40 percent disability. Documentation, including a doctors certificate, is required to receive the discount. If the doctor's statement also states that the passenger must travel with a companion, a 25 percent discount is offered to the companion. This discount does not apply to flights departing from the United States or on code-share flights where Turkish Airlines is not the operating carrier. It is also not available on fares booked on the Turkish Airlines website.

Malaysia Airlines offers a 50 percent discount on domestic tickets for disabled passengers, and a 25 percent discount for their escorts. These discounts are available to passengers who the airline defines as "physically challenged," which includes ambulatory passengers who use crutches and canes, as well as non-ambulatory wheelchair users.

Quantas Airlines offers the Qantas Carer Concession Card scheme, which enables people with high support needs and their attendants to travel at reduced rates. Through this scheme, both the person with high support needs and their attendant receives a 10 to 50 percent discount on domestic travel within Australia and New Zealand.

In order to be eligible for this fare, you must require one-on-one support with meals, drinks, transferring to the bathroom, and communicating with the crew. People who only need assistance boarding and deplaning or wheelchair assistance at the airport are not eligible for this fare. The Qantas Carer Concession Card scheme is administered by NICAN. The fee for the card is $27.50 (Australian) and the card is valid for three years.

And although it's not technically an airline discount, the one-person/one-fare law allows "people with severe disabilities" to travel with an attendant at no extra charge, on domestic flights within Canada. See the "Beyond the U.S.A." chapter for details on this new access law.

HOTELS

Another way to stretch your travel dollar is to rein in those ever-escalating lodging costs. First, consider the location of your hotel. Generally speaking you'll pay more for downtown hotels than for suburban properties. However, be sure it won't cost you more in transportation to get downtown if you choose a suburban hotel. Sometimes it's just more economical to pay the higher downtown hotel rates if accessible public transportation is not available.

Additionally, don't forget to ask about senior discounts, auto club rates, or other special deals when booking a room. Sometimes special discounts aren't widely advertised and it never hurts to ask.

Many hotel chains, such as Microtel and Motel 6 offer accessible rooms at very reasonable rates. Microtel gets the highest marks for consistent access, as all Microtel properties are constructed from the ground up with access in mind. They also offer accessible equipment in their on-site fitness centers.

Motel 6 also offers good access in their newly constructed (post-ADA) properties. The best bet is to look for Motel 6 properties constructed after 1992, as some of their remodeled properties have access obstacles.

And if your travels take you across the Big Pond, you can't beat Premiere Travel Inns for access and value in the United Kingdom. They're not luxury properties, but they are clean, affordable, and accessible.

OTHER LODGING OPTIONS

Housed in the lighthouse keeper's quarters, the Pigeon Point Lighthouse Hostel features an accessible dorm and a bathroom with a roll-in shower.

It pays to get creative when you look for lodging, as hotels are not the only choice.

Although some of these options were considered inaccessible in the past, times have changed. So think outside the box when looking for budget lodging solutions.

Hostels are an often overlooked accessible lodging option. Although hostelling first gained popularity in the 1970s as an inexpensive way for young people to see the world, today most hostels are open to travelers of all ages.

Traditionally, hostels provide inexpensive lodging in dormitory-style bedrooms, with separate quarters for males and females. Today many hostels also have private family rooms that can be reserved in advance.

Accessible hostels are not limited to the United States; in fact, I've also found them in Europe, Australia, and New Zealand. Access varies from hostel to hostel, so contact each property directly for detailed access information. For more information, visit the Hosteling International website at www.hihostels.com.

The YMCA is another budget lodging option that's often overlooked by disabled travelers. Although sometimes grouped with hostels, the thing that sets the Y apart is the availability of on-site recreational facilities at most locations. Most Ys have swimming pools; some even have weight rooms; and many offer excellent access.

For a zero-cost lodging bill, consider a home exchange. The principles behind home exchanging are pretty simple. The idea is to find somebody with a lifestyle similar to yours in another part of the country or world, and then simply exchange homes with each other during your vacation. The big benefit of home exchanging is that you each pocket the money you would have otherwise spent on lodging arrangements. As an added bonus, most home exchangers also exchange tourism information about their local areas.

Unfortunately, most home exchange directories don't list accessible homes; however, the Institute on Independent Living in Stockholm has a great message board filled with accessible options. There's no charge to view or post a listing, and this helpful resource keeps growing. A list of accessible vacation rentals is also contained on their website at www.independentliving.org/vacex/index.html.

Last but not least, for a 50 percent discount at national park campgrounds across the United States, get your America the Beautiful Access Pass. It's available at all national park entrances to any U.S. resident with a permanent disability. The pass also provides free admission to all U.S. national parks and national monuments, and best of all, the price is right—it's free.

FREE TOURS

Another way to save a few bucks on your travel costs is to be on the lookout for free tours at your destination. Again, be creative and think outside the box when looking for these.

Factory tours top the list of free attractions; in fact, a wide variety of businesses offer them—from jelly bean factories to breweries—and many are accessible. A good resource for searching out accessible factory tours is *Watch It Made in the USA,* by Karen Axelrod and Bruce Brumberg. This handy guide contains detailed information on over 300 factory tours across the United States. Every listing includes general information about the tour, plus details on everything from free samples to wheelchair access.

Many major museums also have free days every week or month. Find out the schedule for these to cut down on sightseeing costs. Check the museum website in advance for information on their free days, and then adjust your schedule accordingly.

Many college campuses also boast some top-notch museums. For example, the University of Missouri in Columbia boasts two excellent museums—the Museum of Anthropology and the Museum of Art and Archeology—and neither charges any admission. Both also have excellent access.

A lot of campuses offer self-guided or hosted walking tours. Some are better than others, especially if the majority of the campus buildings were designed by a famous architect. Such is the case at Florida Southern College in Lakeland, which features the largest one-site collection of Frank Lloyd Wright architecture in the world. The tour itself follows an accessible pathway, and there is level or ramped access to most of the buildings. As an added bonus, you can take self-guided tours like these at your own pace.

Many large campuses have a visitors center for prospective students, parents, and the community. These visitors centers are an excellent resource, so don't be afraid to contact them for details about campus attractions, as well as access information about the campus itself.

Finally, many major cities offer some great introductory tours—at no charge. The Chicago Greeter (312–744-8000; www.chicagogreeter. com) tops the freebie list, with over 40 free tours available to visitors. This volunteer-based program, which is overseen by the Chicago Office of Tourism, offers customized tours conducted by local volunteers. A typical walking tour lasts two to four hours and is conducted on public transportation. Because of the customized aspect of the program, most tours can be designed to be accessible.

Based in New York City, The Big Apple Greeter (212–669-8159; www.bigapplegreeter .org) offers a similar volunteer-staffed tour program. They have accessibility-trained guides and actively recruit disabled volunteers. All of their customized tours are free, and most can be modified to be accessible. The Big Apple Greeter also maintains an excellent list of local access resources on their website.

A good resource for free tours is the local convention and visitors bureau (CVB). Not only are these tourism organizations up to speed about all the local happenings, but they also know about the free museum days. Additionally, they can provide visitors with free maps and information about local attractions, lodging, and transportation. You can search for CVBs on the national chamber of commerce database at w ww.ChamberofCommerce.com.

CRUISES

Cruises are a popular travel option and, like everything else, it pays to be flexible with your travel dates and destinations for the best cruise deals. Additionally, there are a few things you should understand about cruise pricing in order to maximize your savings.

First, the brochure price of a cruise is comparable to the sticker price of a car. In short it's like the suggested retail price and most cruise passengers pay less than the brochure price. In fact, some passengers pay substantially less than the brochure price. How do they do that? The best way to get a good price on your dream cruise is to work with a travel agent that monitors cruise prices (at least) weekly.

It's also important to remember to compare like products when shopping for a cruise. Although many discount cruise websites offer bargain-basement cruise fares, it's important to note that these internet companies don't offer any level of service beyond booking the cruise. In order to get information on accessible cabins, airport transfers, and shore excursions you need to work with a travel agent who specializes in accessible cruises. A knowledgeable travel agent can be your ticket to the best overall cruise deal.

Cruise prices rise and fall like the stock market and the general public isn't always aware of these fluctuations. It's a simple case of supply and demand and most price fluctuations are based on cabin availability. Once you book a cruise, you're locked into that price; however, if your travel agent finds a lower rate before you sail, she can re-book you, lock you into the lower price, and save you big bucks.

Of course this plan of action only works if your travel agent monitors cruise prices frequently. Additionally it works best when you book your cruise at least six months to a year in advance. It's also important to note that even though your cruise price can't go up once you're locked into a specific rate, other fees such as government taxes, port charges, and airline fuel surcharges can still increase.

Another way to save some dollars on a cruise is to look for repositioning cruises. These are fairly well publicized by the cruise lines and they usually occur at the end of the season when the cruise lines move (reposition) their ships to different routes. The cruise lines have to get their ships from port A to port B to start their new cruise schedule, and it's a great marketing move to also sell the cabins at bargain prices. The downside of a repositioning cruise is that open jaw airfares (when you fly into one city and out of another one) are sometimes pretty pricey. In fact, these higher airfares can sometimes offset any cruise savings.

And finally, if you have a group that will book at least eight cabins, you can qualify for group cruise discounts. You can either work with a travel agent or deal directly with the group cruise department at the cruise line. In most cases, you'll get one free berth for the first eight cabins you book, and an accessible cabin for the next eight. You can choose to use the discount yourself as the group leader, or pass along the savings to your group.

If you decide to go this route, it's important to remember not to book your cabins until after you've contacted a travel agent or the group cruise department. Putting a group together is easier than you think, so don't be afraid to get the word out. Of course, if you work with a travel agent, make sure he or she is an access specialist. It doesn't cost any more to use a travel agent, and an access specialist will be also be able to locate accessible ground transportation and shore excursions.

Resources

TIMES HAVE CHANGED!

Years ago, travel opportunities for people with disabilities were pretty limited. Today, things have changed, and more and more wheelers are hitting the road. Because of this, the demand for accurate access information has reached an all-time high, and (fortunately) new access resources are popping up every day. So where do you begin your search for these resources?

Of course my favorite resource is *Emerging Horizons.* In fact, that's why I founded the magazine—to provide updated information on barrier-free travel. And as of this writing we've been doing that for over 12 years. That's a lot of research. Through the course of this re-search, I've stumbled across a number of sources of access information. Here are some of my favorites.

At the top of my research list are the local Centers for Independent Living (CILs). Check with the CIL in your destination city to see if they have any access information on local transportation, attractions, and lodging.

You might also want to contact some nation-al disability organizations to see if they have any access information. Be sure to check with any disability-related organizations that recently held a conference (or are planning to hold a conference) in your destination city. Many such organizations collect local access information for their conference attendees. Don't forget about airports and public transportation providers, as sometimes they also provide printed access guides.

And finally, don't rule out the local Convention and Visitors Bureaus (CVB). Some CVBs incorporate access information in their own tourism publications, while others work with local organizations to provide this information in separate access guides.

PRINTED ACCESS GUIDES

Although printed access guides are few and far between, the folks that produce them put a lot of time and energy into ensuring that their information is accurate. California seems to lead the pack as far as printed access guides go, with San Francisco, Santa Cruz, and San Diego all publishing them.

Access San Francisco contains access details on over 100 San Franciscoarea attractions, restaurants, and hotels, plus information on accessible transportation, local disability organizations, wheelchair rentals, and medical supply dealers. It was first published in 2000, and the latest edition is available at the San Francisco

Visitors Information Center on Market Street. A free copy can also be obtained by calling the San Francisco Convention and Visitors Bureau at 415–391-2000, and a PDF version can be downloaded at www.onlyinSanFrancisco.com. Additionally, updated access information can be found on the Access Northern California website (the organization that researched the guide) at www.AccessNCA.com.

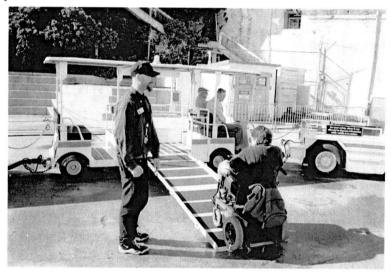

Get your copy of Access San Francisco to find out about access to Alcatraz Island (pictured here), as well as other local attractions.

Published by Shared Adventures, *Access Santa Cruz County* is the state's first bilingual (Spanish and English) access guide. This 64-page booklet contains access information on over 100 restaurants, hotels, parks, and facilities throughout Santa Cruz County. It is available for a $3 shipping charge from Shared Adventures at 831–459-7210. Additional access information can be found online at www.scacc essguide.com.

Accessible San Diego produces annual updates of *Access in San Diego,* which contains access information on selected hotels, restaurants, public transportation options, and tourist attractions. A PDF or printed version can be purchased on the Accessible San Diego website at www.accessandiego.com.

The Golden State is not alone in publishing printed access guides. *Easy Access Chicago* contains detailed access information on hotels, transportation, tourist sights, and restaurants in the Windy City. A project of the Open Doors Organization, this free access guide is available from the Illinois Bureau of Tourism at 800–266-6328. It is also available as a PDF download at www.EasyAccessChicago.org. This website also includes updated access information, along with an accessible hotel search feature.

Additionally, plans are in the works for more Illinois access guides. Check the Open Doors website at www.opendoorsnfp.org for updates on these projects.

INTERNET RESOURCES

Although printed guides are great, the best place to look for the most updated information is still the internet. However, even though it's easier to update online information, it still doesn't mean that every website is as good as gold. In fact, I've found a good number of outdated websites with some downright incorrect information on the internet. So check around carefully and see when the website was last updated. Also check to see if it has a lot of links that don't work. And be wary of any website that makes seemingly outrageous claims or just sounds too good to be true.

So where do you find access information on the internet? Although an internet search under "accessible travel" will return a bevy of selections, sometimes it's best to start in a more directed way. Check out some of the disability portals, as travel is a popular subject. Of course websites can come and go quickly, so look for those that have been around for a while to contain the most accurate information. My favorite accessible travel websites are:

- Rolling Rains Report (www.RollingRains.com)
- Gimp on the Go (www.GimpontheGo.com)
- Global Access (www.globalaccessnews.com)

Scott Rains (who pens the Rolling Rains Report) also operates Tour Watch (www.tournet.ning.com), a social networking site dedicated to presenting the best practices and opportunities for accessible services in the hospitality industry. This member-only site is geared more toward tour operators, travel suppliers, and travel agents; however, it's a good place to find new access resources in seemingly inaccessible and remote areas of the world.

I also try to provide the latest accessible travel news on my Barrier Free Travels Blog at www.barrierfreetraverls.com and to list travel discounts, deals, and freebies for wheelchair users and slow walkers on my Barrier Free Travel on the Cheap Blog at www.bftontheche ap.com. Additionally, I write regular columns and accessible travel content for Disaboom (w ww.disaboom.com), Frommers (www.Frommer s.com), Trips & Getaways (www.tripsandgetaw ays.com), Travel World International (www.tra velworldmagazine.com), and Stroke Smart (w ww.strokesmart.org).

And if you have an accessible travel question, then submit it to me on my *Emerging Horizons* "Ask the Expert" page at www.emerg inghorizons.com/expert. You might want to scan the past questions first, to see if someoneasked your question previously. It's also important to note that, because of the volume of questions I receive, I can't promise to reply personally; however, I do try to post all inquiries and responses to the column.

Last but not least there is *Emerging Horizons.* Of course we have a website! In fact, we have a searchable database of accessible travel resources at www.EmergingHorizons.com. Feel free to drop by and browse our travel resources, and drop me an e-mail if you have a resource to suggest. Bear in mind that we don't accept any advertising on our website, and all *Emerging Horizons'* resources must contain specific information on accessible travel.

RESOURCES

Here's a chapter by chapter rundown of the resources (along with complete contact information) that are mentioned throughout the book.

UP, UP, AND AWAY

- Department of Transportation Aviation Consumer Protection:
- *Federal Register:* www.gpoaccess.gov/fr
- United Spinal Association: 800-404-2899; www.unitedspinal.org
- Seat Guru: www.seatguru.com
- DOT Aviation Consumer Disability Hotline: 866-266-1368
- Transportation Security Administration: 877-336-4872; www.tsa.gov

ON A WING AND A PRAYER

- Haseltine Flyer: 888-445-8751; www.haseltine.com
- FedEx: 800-463-3339; www.fedex.com

OTHER AIR TRAVEL ISSUES

- *Breathin' Easy:* 925–891-5017; www.breath ineasy.com
- International Ventilator Users Network IVUN): 314-534-0475;
- PETS Travel Scheme Helpline: +44 870-241-1710
- Hawaii Animal Quarantine Station: 808-483-7151; rabiesfree@hawaii.gov
- Pets Welcome Database: www.petswelcome .com/milkbone/quarmap.html
- National Federation of the Blind Worldwide Service Animal Regulations: www.nfb-nagd u.org/laws/laws.html
- Freedom Shores: 951-801-2716; www.isla-aguada.com

GETTING AROUND ON THE GROUND

- Super Shuttle: 800 258-3826; www.supers huttle.com
- Project Action: 202-347-3066; www.project action.org
- ILRU Program at TIRR: 713-520-0232; ww w.bcm.edu/ilru
- Renting Cars With Hand Controls; www.use rs.actcom.co.il/~swfm

- Accessible Vans of America: 866-224-1750; www.accessiblevans.com
- Wheelchair Getaways: 800-642-2042; www.wheelchairgetaways.com
- Freedom Rentals; www.wheelchairvanrentals.com
- Jean Legare; www.locationlegare.com
- Disability Hire Vehicles; www.disabilityhire.com.au
- Flashcab Rentals; www.flashcabrentals.com.au
- Wheel Chair Tours Australia; www.wheeltours.com.au
- Wheelaway Van Rentals; www.wheelaway.com.au
- Galaxy Autos; www.galaxyautos.co.nz
- Wheelchair Travel; www.wheelchair-travel.co.uk
- Libertrans; www.libertans.com
- Ptitcar; www.ptitcar.com
- Lobbes; www.lobbes.com
- Paravan; www.Paravan.com
- Wheeling Around the Algarve; www.player.pt
- Mieauto; www.mietauto.ch
- City Segway Tours; www.citysegwaytours.com
- Handicapped Travel Club; www.handicappedtravelclub.com

400

- ADA Nationwide Roadside Assistance: 800-720-3132; www.americandriversalliance.com
- Flying J Truck Stops; www.flyingj.com

We Will Ride
- Greyhound Customers with Disabilities Travel Assistance: 800-752-4841
- Megabus: 877-462-6342; www.megabus.com
- BoltBus: www.boltbus.com

All Aboard
- Amtrak: 800-872-7245; www.amtrak.com
- VIA Rail: 888-842-7245; www.viarail.ca
- BritRail; www.britrail.com;National Rail Enquiries: +44-20-727-5240; www.nationalrail.co.uk
- Eurostar: +44-1233-617-575; www.eurostar.co.uk
- Eurail; www.eurail.com
- Rail Australia: +61-8-8213-4592; www.railaustralia.com.au
- Grand Canyon Railway: 800-843-8724; www.thetrain.com
- Rocky Mountaineer Railtours: 877-460-3200; www.rockymountaineer.com

Finding the Right Room
- Spin Life: www.spinlife.com
- Take Along Lifts: 877-667-6515; www.takealonglifts.com

- Nuprodx: 415-472-1699; www.nuprodx.com
- B&B Online; www.bbonline.com
- Accessible Properties; www.accessibleproperties.net
- Great Grips: 800-346-5662;www.greatgrips.com
- Port-A-Bars: 800-542-5076; www.grabitonline.com

Taking the Kids
- Tripcheck; www.tripcheck.com
- Cares Harness: 800-299-6249; www.kidsflysafe.com
- Baby B'Air: 800-417-5228; www.babybair.com
- National Park Service; www.nps.gov

Sailing Away
- U.S. Access Board; www.Access-Board.gov
- Cruise Critic;www.cruisecritic.com
- Wheelchair Cruising; www.wheelchaircruising.com
- Scootaround: 888-441-7575; www.scootaround.com
- Care Vacations: 877-478-7827;www.cruiseshipassist.com
- Special Needs at Sea: 800-513-4515; www.specialneedsatsea.com
- River Barge Excursions: 888-462-2743; www.riverbarge.com

- Stockport Canal Boat Trust: +44-161-430-8082; www.newhorizons. org.uk
- Lyneal Trust: +44-1743-252728; www.lyneal-trust.org.uk
- Saoirse ar an Uisce: +353-45-529410; www.kildare.ie/FreedomOnTheWater
- Peter Deilmann EuropAmerica Cruises: 800-348-8287; www.deilmann-cruises.com
- Le Boat: 800-734-5491; www.leboat.com
- Dialysis Finder; www.dialysisfinder.com
- Global Dialysis; www.globaldialysis.com

ALL ASHORE

- Mount Roberts Tramway: 907-463-3412
- Juneau Trolley: 907-586-7433; www.juneautrolley.com
- ERA Aviation: 800-843-1947; www.flightseeingtours.com
- Orca Enterprises: 907-789-6801; www.orcaenterprises.com
- White Pass and Yukon Route Railroad: 800-343-7373; www.wpyr.com
- Klondike Gold Dredge: 907-983-3175; www.klondikegolddredge.com
- Great Alaskan Lumberjack Show: 907-225-9050; www.lumberjacksports.com
- Polynesian Adventure Tours: 808-833-3000; www.polyad.com
- Sunshine Helicopters: 808-270-3999; www.sunshinehelicopters.com

- Lahaina Divers: 808-667-7496; www.lahainadivers.com
- Ron Bass Kayaking: 808-572-6299; www.maui.net/~kayaking/access
- Majestic Holidays: 242-322-2606; www.majesticholidays.com
- Expert Tours: 242-351-4004
- Experience Belize Tours: +501-225-2981; www.experiencebelizetours.com
- Access Bermuda: 441-295-9106; www.access.bm
- Shore Trips: 414-964-2100; www.shoretrips.com
- Elite Limousine: +345-949-5963
- Max Taxi Tours and Transfers: +345-917-0133
- Vaya con Silla de Ruedas: +506-2454-2810; www.gowithwheelchairs.com
- Tio Taxi Tours: +599-9-560-5491; www.tiotaxi.com
- Hibiscus Tours: 767-445-8195
- Noel Wilson: +876-870-6545
- Lincoln Campbell: +876-779-9211
- A-Z Jamaica Planners: +876-994-1960; www.a-zjamaicaplanners.com
- Countryside Tours: 787-593-9014; www.countrysidetourspr.com
- Wheelchair Transportation and Tours: 800-868-8028

- Kantours: +869-465-3054; www.kantours .com
- Louis Jeffers: +599-524-9204
- Accessible Adventures: 340-344-8302; www.accessvi.com
- St. Thomas Dial A Ride: 340-776-1277
- Accessible Cancun: +52-998-883-1978; www.cancunaccesible.com
- Cozumel Taxis: +52-987-872-0236
- Gabriela Altamirano Sosa y Silva: +52-1-646-128-7206
- Victor Chavez: +52-669-102-1448
- Accessible Mexico: +52-322-225-0989; www.accessiblemexico.com
- Transportes Brianchi: +52-322-222-8384
- Accessible Barcelona: +34-93-428-52-27; www.AccessibleBarcelona.com
- Disabled Accessible Travel: +34-605-918-769; www.disabledaccessibletravel.com
- Harbirk's Bustrafik: +45-44-44-32-66; www.harbirk.dk
- SO.CO.TA Taxi: +39-055-410133; www.socota.it
- Nexttravel: +358-94342-590; www.nexttravel.fi
- Accessible Portugal: +351-217-203-130; www.accessibleportugal.com
- Eddie Manning Limo: +44-7970-761-505; www.limo.co.uk

- Citysightseeing Tours: +47-9710-4742; www.citysightseeing.net
- Seascape Tours: +46-8-441-3963; www.seascapetours.se
- Liberty Tours; www.libertytour.ru
- DenRus Tours: +561-459-5534; www.denrus.ru

WHEN THINGS GO WRONG

U.S. Department of Transportation Aviation Consumer Protection Division, C-75-D
1200 New Jersey Ave. SE, Washington, D.C. 20590
http://airconsumer.ost.dot.gov

Federal Aviation Administration
Room 1030 800 Independence Avenue SW, Washington, D.C. 20591

U.S. Department of Justice Civil Rights Division
950 Pennsylvania Avenue NW, Disability Rights Section—NYAV,
Washington, D.C. 20530

FTA Office of Civil Rights
East Building—5th Floor TCR, 1200 New Jersey Ave. SE,
Washington, D.C. 20590
888–446-4511; www.fta.dot.gov

U.S. Department of the Interior Office of Equal Opportunity
1849 C Street NW, Room 1324, Washington, D.C. 20240–0002
www.doi.gov

National Center on Accessibility: 812-856-4422; www.ncaonline.org

U.S. Access Board Compliance and Enforcement
1331 F St. NW, Suite 1000, Washington, D.C. 20004–1111
800–872-2253; www.access-board.gov

Paralyzed Veterans of America: www.pva.org
Federal Citizen Information Center: 888-878-3256
ADA Technical Assistance: 800–514-0301; www.ada.gov/publicat.htm

Beyond the USA
- CTA Airline Access Regulations: www.cta-otc.gc.ca/access/regs/air_e.html
- Access To Travel; www.accesstotravel.gc.ca
- Access Canada; www.albertahotels.ab.ca
- European Network of Accessible Tourism; www.accessibletourism.org
- Equality and Human Rights Commission: +44-845-604-5510;

- National Federation of Shopmobility: +44-845-644-2-446;
- RADAR: +44-20-7250-3222; www.radar.org.uk
- J Williams & Son; +353-1-475-6307
- Access in London: www.accessproject-phsp.org/london
- Disabled Travel Advice: www.disabledtraveladvice.co.uk
- Australian Human Rights Commission: www.hreoc.gov.au
- NICAN: +61-2-6241-1220; www.nican.com.au
- City of Melbourne Access Map: +61-3-9658-9658; www.accessmelbourne.vic.gov.au
- Spinal Cord Injuries Australia: +61-2-9661-8855; www.scia.org.au
- Access Israel; www.aisrael.org
- Handi-Ramp; www.handi-ramp.com
- Magellans: 800–962-4943; www.magellans.com
- Medic Alert: 888–633-4298; www.medicalert.org
- Disabled Peoples' International; www.dpi.org

Accessible Recreation
- Wilderness on Wheels: 303-403-1110; www.wildernessonwheels.org
- Rails to Trails Conservancy: 202-331-9696; www.railtrails.org

- Trail Link Database; www.traillink.com
- California Coastal Conservancy: 510-286-1015; www.scc.ca.gov
- National Recreation Reservation Service: 877-444-6777; www.recreation.gov
- Oregon Yurts; 800-452-5687
- Safari West: 707-579-2551; www.safariwest.com
- Accessible San Diego: 619-325-7550
- *En Caliente:* 866-727-7986; www.bajaenterprises.com
- Bay Area Association of Disabled Sailors: 415-281-0212; www.baads.org
- Jubilee Sailing Trust: +44-23-8044-9108; www.jst.org.uk
- Ro Ro Sailing Project DSA): +44-1329-317279; www.disabledsailing.org
- The Sailing Web; www.footeprint.com/sailingweb
- Handicapped Scuba Association: 949-498-4540; www.hsascuba.com
- Dolphin Research Center: 305-289-1121 ext. 232—Special Needs Coordinator; www.dolphins.org
- Day on the Beach: 831-459-7210; www.dayonthebeach.org
- Disabled Sports USA; www.dsusa.org

Budget Travel
- Microtel: 888-771-7171; www.microtelinn.com

- Motel 6: 800-466-8356; www.motel6.com
- Premiere Travel Inns: +44-1582-567890; www.premierinn.com
- Hosteling International; www.hihostels.com
- YMCA; www.YMCA.net;www.YMCA.int
- Stockholm CIL Vacation Home Swap Bulletin Board; www.indendentliving.org/vacex/index.html
- America the Beautiful Access Pass; www.nps.gov/fees_passes.htm
- Chicago Greeter: 312-744-8000; www.chicagogreeter.com
- The Big Apple Greeter: 212-669-8159; www.bigapplegreeter.org
- Chamber of Commerce Database; www.chamberofcommerce.com

410

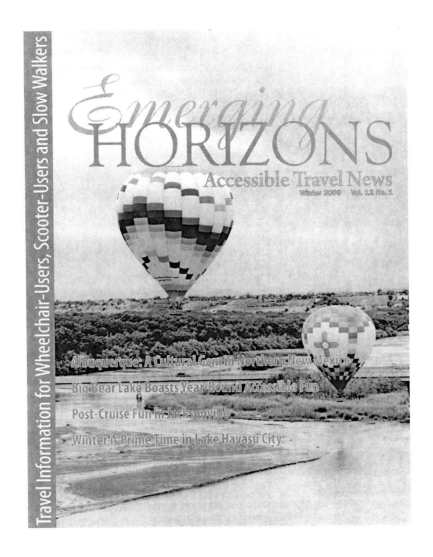

Emerging Horizons is a consumer-oriented magazine about accessible travel. Edited by Candy Harrington, it contains no advertising – just lots of information and resources. Visit www.EmergingHorizons.com for subscription information.

Back Cover Material

CANDY B. HARRINGTON

Barrier-Free Travel

A NUTS AND BOLTS GUIDE FOR WHEELERS
AND SLOW WALKERS

THIRD EDITION

"Encyclopedic in both its scope and its usefulness, *Barrier-Free Travel* is an indispensable resource for travelers with disabilities."

—Pauline Frommer, author of **Pauline Frommer's Travel Guides**

"The bible for barrier-free travel. The invaluable information in this book will ensure travelers with mobility limitations spend their time creating meaningful memories—not worrying about how they'll get there."

—Chris Elliot, *National Geographic Traveler,* Blogger/syndicated columnist/TV host

"In breadth of content the book surpasses anything else available to the traveler or travel professional."

—**Scott Rains,** *The Rolling Rains Report*

"No other book delves into the needs of mobility impaired travelers, from special oxygen requirements to challenges in hotel rooms. An essential reference."

—*Midwest Book Review*

Now in its third edition, the critically acclaimed *Barrier-Free Travel* is essential reading for every traveler with mobility limitations. With over 100 new photographs and updated travel rules and regulations, affecting access in and outside of the United States, this book gives you the tools and resources to navigate both the expected and the unexpected.

Barrier-Free Travel covers everything from the logistics of air travel and how to protect your wheelchair in flight, to how to find an accessible hotel room. Extensive chapters on cruises and accessible shore excursions—with contact information for specifically equipped foreign tour operators—are also included.

Because of the chaos and uncertainty involved in travel, people who require access accommodations rely on this indispensable guide for the best advice. *Barrier-Free Travel* provides the confidence you need to go where you want to go.

Candy B. Harrington is known as the guru of accessible travel covering the topic exclusively for 15 years. She founded *Emerging Horizons,* an accessible travel magazine and is the author of *There is Room at the Inn: Inns and B&Bs for Wheelers and Slow Walkers* and *101 Accessible Vacations: Travel Ideas for Wheelers and Slow Walkers.* In addition, Ms. Harrington pens travel columns for *Special Living, Travel World International, Stroke Smart, Inside MS,* and *Trips and Getaways.*

436

Books For ALL Kinds of Readers

At ReadHowYouWant we understand that one size does not fit all types of readers. Our innovative, patent pending technology allows us to design new formats to make reading easier and more enjoyable for you. This helps improve your speed of reading and your comprehension. Our EasyRead printed books have been optimized to improve word recognition, ease eye tracking by adjusting word and line spacing as well as minimizing hyphenation. Our EasyRead SuperLarge editions have been developed to make reading easier and more accessible for vision-impaired readers. We offer Braille and DAISY formats of our books and all popular E-Book formats.

We are continually introducing new formats based upon research and reader preferences. Visit our web-site to see all of our formats and learn how you can Personalize our books for yourself or as gifts. Sign up to Become A RHYW Registered Reader.

www.readhowyouwant.com